MW01154686

Werewolves, Witches, and Wandering Spirits

Habent sua fata libelli

Werewolves, Witches, and Wandering Spirits

Traditional Belief & Folklore in Early Modern Europe

Edited by KATHRYN A. EDWARDS

SIXTEENTH CENTURY ESSAYS & STUDIES
VOLUME 62

Copyright © 2002 by Truman State University Press

100 East Normal Street, Kirksville, Missouri 63501-4221 USA

http://tsup.truman.edu

Library of Congress Cataloging-in-Publication Data

Werewolves, witches, and wandering spirits : traditional belief and folklore in early modern Europe / edited by Kathryn A. Edwards.

    p. cm. — (Sixteenth century essays & studies ; v. 62)

    Includes bibliographical references and index.

    ISBN 1-931112-09-6 (casebound : alk. paper) — ISBN 1-931112-08-8 (pbk. : alk. paper)

    1. Folklore—Europe. 2. Folk literature—Europe—History and criticism. 3. Supernatural. 4. Witchcraft—Europe. 5. Demonology—Europe. I. Edwards, Kathryn A. 1964– II. Series.

GR135 .W47 2002
398'.094—dc21   2002018859

Cover art: "The Werewolf" by Lucas Cranach the Elder (1472–1553). Snark / Art Resource, N.Y.

Cover design by Winston Vanderhoof

Printed by Thomson-Shore, Dexter, Michigan

Set in Adobe Minion, P22 Victorian Gothic, and P22 Victorian Swash

∞The paper in this publication meets or exceeds the minimum requirements of the American National Standard—Permanence of Paper for Printed Library Materials, ANSI Z39.48 (1984).

Contents

INTRODUCTION

Expanding the Analysis of Traditional Belief

Kathryn A. Edwards

INCORPORATING THE ANOMALOUS

When Huguette Roy was visited by a ghost for two months in 1628, the event was believed to be so extraordinary that a local clergyman left a detailed chronicle of the haunting. A mixture of Counter-Reformation piety, demono-logical theory, and folkloric assumptions guided his "history," which he wrote from his own observation of the event as well as from information provided by the myriad lay and ecclesiastical observers, by the haunted woman, and by the spirit itself. Unlike many similar visionaries, however, Huguette was never tried for witchcraft nor was she put through detailed and dramatic exorcisms, events that engender the documents by which such cases are most commonly known. For this reason, the vast synthetic literature on early modern witch-craft can seem tangential to understanding Huguette's haunting. A central problem for research on stories like Huguette's thus becomes where to find information about similar cases in early modern Europe.[1]

This problem does not arise because of a lack of early modern reports about visions, spirits, and other "supernatural" or "paranormal" phenomena, to use perhaps anachronistic modern terminology. Embedded in the records of Inquisitorial and other courts, as well as in diverse other sources, are records about mysterious ladies in white, werewolves, poltergeists, and other less classifiable occurrences.[2] Millennial prophets see visions, and souls stride purposefully through castles. Integrating folkloric and theological elements in

---

1. Kathryn A. Edwards, *Visitations: The Haunting of an Early Modern Town* (forthcoming).

2. See the discussion of these beliefs in Jean-Claude Schmitt, *Ghosts in the Middle Ages: The Living and the Dead in Medieval Society*, trans. Teresa Lavender Fagan (Chicago: University of Chicago Press, 1998).

early modern spirituality, such beliefs persist and even develop in post-Reformation Europe despite attempts by religious authorities from every confession to "discipline" the minds and bodies of believers. Analyses of these cases contribute to the discussions raised about traditional religion and social discipline in early modern Europe, although their focus may seem to be on peripheral aspects.[3] In this sense, each of the articles in this collection contributes to this expansion and deepening of studies on traditional belief by developing aspects of it that are less frequently studied in more synthetic monographs.

The relationship between traditional belief and social discipline is just one of the themes that has been developed recently in social and cultural analyses of early modern Europe. Over the last several decades religious history has gradually grown to include reinterpretations of popular practices and perceptions—such as pilgrimage, miracles, sacramentals, and the cult of the Virgin—alongside more traditional works that examine theology and institutions. Many of the articles in this collection provide a brief survey of these developments as they pertain to the article's topic. Building on historical anthropology and the insights and methods of pioneering monographs, scholars working in these areas have vastly broadened the ways that early modern belief and spirituality are now approached.[4] To provide just one example, the centrality of religious ritual and the enduring nature of ritual practice have been convincingly argued during the 1990s by Susan Karant-Nunn, Edward Muir, and Eamon Duffy, among others; their conclusions question the scope and chronology of the Reformation's spread and its claims to success.[5]

By its emphasis on traditional belief, such work is inherently folkloric even when its methodology may differ from that practiced by folklorists, thus the

---

3. I here use the phrase proposed by Eamon Duffy, *The Stripping of the Altars: Traditional Religion in England, c. 1400–c. 1580* (New Haven: Yale University Press, 1992). See his introduction for a discussion of the linguistic pitfalls inherent in the analysis of these beliefs.

4. For examples see John Bossy, *Christianity in the West* (New York: Oxford University Press, 1985); Robert Scribner, *For the Sake of Simple Folk: Popular Propaganda for the German Reformation* (New York: Cambridge University Press, 1981); William A. Christian, *Apparitions in Late Medieval and Renaissance Spain* (Princeton: Princeton University Press, 1981); and idem, *Local Religion in Sixteenth-Century Spain* (Princeton: Princeton University Press, 1980). Among the more theoretical works frequently cited are E. E. Evans-Pritchard, *Witchcraft, Oracles, and Magic among the Azande* (Oxford: Clarendon, 1937); Victor Turner, *The Ritual Process: Structure and Anti-Structure* (Chicago: Aldine, 1969); and Michel de Certeau, *The Mystic Fable*, trans. Michael B. Smith (Chicago: University of Chicago Press, 1992). Many other examples may be found in the footnotes of this collection.

5. Susan C. Karant-Nunn, *The Reformation of Ritual: An Interpretation of Early Modern Germany* (New York: Routledge, 1997); Edward Muir, *Ritual in Early Modern Europe* (New York: Cambridge University Press, 1997); and Duffy, *Stripping of the Altars*.

second half of this book's title. Essential to modern studies of traditional religion in early modern Europe are questions of transmission and interpretation. Rather than being passive recipients of a falsely dichotomous learned culture, the "people"—an admittedly broad and problematic term—have been repeatedly shown to be active creators of meaning. While their creations could vary enormously depending on culture, gender, class, and individual quirks, to name but a few qualifiers, certain concerns, perspectives, and frameworks have been found to recur in sixteenth- and seventeenth-century Europe. The Eucharist retains an almost magical power, whether it be transubstantiated, consubstantiated, or symbolic; supernatural or preternatural forces abound in this world, although they can take dozens of forms including those of demons, angels, trolls, wandering souls, or flying serpents. Although such beliefs may be interpreted differently, they remain a pervasive part of early modern culture for the literate, illiterate, and the larger community in between. Moreover, not all of these beliefs were as inherently threatening as witchcraft, whether it be viewed as the practice of *maleficia* or as a diabolical conspiracy. For this reason, as well as many others dependent on the individual instance itself, such folkloric religious beliefs, their perpetuation, and the reactions to them provide valuable nuances to interpretations of early modern sensibilities.

It is inescapable that in the last two decades one of the most intensely studied aspects of folklore and traditional belief in early modern Europe has been witchcraft, and the essays in this collection echo the concerns of those works to some extent. Witchcraft studies in particular have enjoyed increased scholarly interest since the 1980s, and a number of significant books have been recently published.[6] Although these works have different emphases and cover varied geographical areas, they share certain characteristics. Among the

---

6. See *Witchcraft and Magic in Europe*, 6. vols., ed. Bengt Ankarloo and Stuart Clark (Philadelphia: University of Pennsylvania Press, 1999–); Jonathan Barry, Marianne Hester, and Gareth Roberts, eds., *Witchcraft in Early Modern Europe: Studies in Culture and Belief* (New York: Cambridge University Press, 1996); Wolfgang Behringer, *Witchcraft Persecutions in Bavaria: Popular Magic, Religious Zealotry, and Reason of State in Early Modern Europe*, trans. J. C. Grayson and David Lederer (New York: Cambridge University Press, 1997); Robin Briggs, *Witches and Neighbors: The Social and Cultural Context of European Witchcraft* (New York: Viking, 1996); Stuart Clark, *Thinking with Demons: The Idea of Witchcraft in Early Modern Europe* (New York: Oxford University Press, 1997); Carlo Ginzburg, *Ecstasies: Deciphering the Witches' Sabbath* (1976; repr. New York: Pantheon, 1992); Bengt Ankarloo et al., *Magie et Sorcellerie en Europe du Moyen Age à nos jours* (Paris: A. Colin, 1994); Lyndal Roper, *Oedipus and the Devil: Witchcraft, Religion and Sexuality in Early Modern Europe* (New York: Routledge, 1994); and Gerhild Scholz Williams, *Defining Dominion: The Discourses of Magic and Witchcraft in Early Modern France and Germany* (Ann Arbor: University of Michigan Press, 1995).

most significant is the attempt to rehistoricize witchcraft and popular perceptions, a goal which has largely succeeded within the academic community but
which remains far from achieved among the broader population. Of special
interest to many of these scholars, and of particular relevance to this study, has
been the social and psychological milieu in which such beliefs functioned and
which allowed their perpetuation and even paranoid explosions. Through
detailed reconstruction of individual cases, scholars have stressed the distinctive circumstances surrounding each witchcraft accusation and the need to
understand these events within their local setting. Supported by research
groups throughout Europe, the picture of the witch-hunts which has thus
emerged is far more complex than that presented several decades ago.[7] In particular, witch trials are perceived less as aberrations on the march to modernity
and more as threads in the tapestry of early modern social relations and belief.

In the recent growth of witchcraft studies, two themes have dominated.
The first approach examines the place of *maleficia* in witchcraft accusations
and *maleficia*'s social and spiritual implications. The second focuses on
demonological theories, especially those concerning conspiracy and domination, and notes the differences, at least in emphasis, between jurists seeped
in demonological lore, witnesses, and the accused. One of the challenges fac-
ing either type of analysis is to provide some sort of synthesis out of the disparate beliefs and practices which could constitute witchcraft in early
modern Europe among Protestants and Catholics, and among Christians
and non-Christians. In the process, more unusual aspects of these cases and
other such stories found in similar documentation—like helpful ghosts, can-
nibalistic lycanthropes, and rapturous visionaries—tend to be marginalized.

This collection is designed to provide an opportunity for the analysis and
publication of such cases. Its contributors argue such matters as Heinrich
Bullinger's beliefs about the devil; El Encubierto's interpretations of heaven
on earth; or Jepthah Joseph Juspa's descriptions of Jewish ritual magic that
speak to fundamental concerns of Protestant reformers, participants in Las
Germanías, and early modern Jews; but they do so following paths that are
less familiar to modern scholars. Through the analyses of these themes and
others which stress atypical and folkloric elements of traditional belief, this
book contributes to the growing historiography on piety and popular culture
in early modern Europe. Although there are unusual aspects to the stories and

---

7. Arbeitskreis Interdisziplinäre Hexenforschung (AKIH) in Germany is one, as is the Centre de
recherche sur la littérature et les discours du savoir (LiDiSa) codirected by Nicole Jacques-Lefèvre.

themes analyzed here, the concerns and occurrences developed in these articles were more common than they are frequently perceived to be. Finally, like other recent work, this collection aspires to motivate scholars and other readers to reexamine the categories through which early modern beliefs and perspectives are commonly approached.

In the pursuit of these goals, a variety of perspectives and methodologies as well as different geographic regions are represented here. Given the number of witch-hunts in France, Switzerland, and the Holy Roman Empire during the sixteenth and seventeenth centuries, the intensity with which scholars have studied the documentation about these trials, and the accidents of historical survival, most of the articles focus on these areas. Every attempt has been made, however, to incorporate studies about other parts of Europe and to show how similar themes are played out between confessions as well as in both Christian and non-Christian settings. Despite these differences, every contributor shares a concern with the development, internalization, and articulation of popular belief in early modern Europe. Many have worked extensively with inquisitorial and other trial records, and most have been engaged in debates over the extent and significance of the early modern witch prosecutions, particularly the need to move such work from the margins of social and intellectual history.

OVERARCHING THEMES

The articles in this collection repeatedly stress how apparently unusual themes and stories shed light on broader concerns in the history of early modern Europe in addition to the value that they have in their own right. For this reason, rather than provide an abstract of each article, the remainder of this introduction will briefly survey these concerns and discuss their development in selected articles. This survey is far from synthetic; it is intended to highlight the themes that unite this collection and to suggest the ways such case studies and more synthetic treatments may complement each other. It is designed to provoke questions and even challenges.

Binaries in belief and practice have been one of interpretive frameworks commonly applied to social and cultural histories of medieval and early modern Europe. They have also been among the most contested.[8] As philosophical, epistemological, and theological classificatory schema, the binaries developed

8. For examples of such debates, see Lynn Abrams and Elizabeth Harvey, *Gender Relations in German History: Power, Agency and Experience from the Sixteenth to the Twentieth Century* (Durham, N.C.: Duke University Press, 1996), 45; R. Howard Bloch, *Medieval Misogyny and the Invention of Western*

in ancient Greek and Roman thought were transmitted throughout Europe in various forms during the Middle Ages. The degree to which they interacted with binaries in Germanic thought—or even the existence and form of such binaries—is a matter for debate. Yet an emphasis on binary polarization is frequently treated as a particularly modern phenomenon, one which was more precisely and persistently articulated beginning in the sixteenth and seventeenth centuries. The Reformation especially has been described as doing away with the "'third world' of the medieval cosmos" (that is, the realm of spiritually liminal figures) and stressing the supernatural as part of a binary opposition between divine and demonic forces, despite the equal insistence by contemporaries that Satan could only act with God's permission.[9] The articles by Robin Briggs, Bruce Gordon, and David Lederer argue that these binaries carried powerful resonances in early modern Europe. As presented by Gordon, Heinrich Bullinger and Jakob Ruef are disturbed by a devil who can threaten the ministry of God's word in sixteenth-century Zurich, a demon who they fear may be a better pastor than they themselves. Lederer sees the treatment of and perceptions about ghosts in early modern Bavaria as part of a growing division between expressions of supernatural relations; for example, Bavaria's noble elites favored a specific type of ghost. Briggs stresses that binaries shape eschatological and ontological perceptions at various levels in early modern Lorraine. Not only are the divine and ordinary worlds perceived as dichotomies, but the beliefs about shapeshifting and apparitions can be interpreted as reflecting "an object-related and narcissistic world-view" that gives tacit support to binaries.[10]

Despite these arguments in support of binary perceptions, all of the articles in this collection attempt to refine the practice of ideological exchange underlying binaries and argue for the hermeneutical circulation of ideas. Ideas are constantly in process; in the case of beliefs brought to trial, ideas move

---

Romantic Love (Chicago: University of Chicago Press, 1991), 43–46; Lorraine Daston, "The Nature of Nature in Early Modern Europe," Configurations 6, no. 2 (1998): 149–72; William Eamon, Science and the Secrets of Nature: Books of Secrets in Medieval and Early Modern Culture (Princeton: Princeton University Press, 1994); and T. J. Jackson Lears, "The Concept of Cultural Hegemony: Problems and Possibilities," American Historical Review 90 (1985): 567–93.

9. Deborah Willis, Malevolent Nurture: Witch-Hunting and Maternal Power in Early Modern England (Ithaca: Cornell University Press, 1995), 91 ff. Also see Jean-Marie Fritz, Le discours du fou au Moyen Age: XIIe–XIIIe siècles: Étude comparée des discours littéraire, médical, juridique et théologique de la folie (Paris: PUF, 1992), 188–89; and Daston, "Nature of Nature," 154 ff.

10. As cited by Robin Briggs, page 22 below.

from accuser to accused to the public through the reading of testimony, itself an action that occurs at various levels. The connections just described are among the simpler and more linear ones developed in these cases, as they omit the judges, differing attitudes held by participants, and the negotiations which occur during the entire process. More than the exchange of ideas between two poles, idea formation is a dialogue between the accused, the accusers, the jurists, the witness, and the audience. Depositions by the accused and witnesses form confessions which, in turn, form popular perceptions when recited at executions. Traditional belief in early modern Europe reflects both the syncretic and eclectic elements in Christian and, as developed by Dean Bell, Jewish religious beliefs and practices. Such questions become particularly intense in sixteenth- and seventeenth-century Europe when, during the Reformations and the process of confessionalization, a series of beliefs and practices are "grafted" onto traditional roots, to use a term borrowed here by Sarah Ferber, and attempts are made to prune these same roots.[11] These elements can also be seen in modern psychoanalytical approaches to the early modern witch trials and to so-called folk beliefs more generally. Applying this hermeneutic more broadly, Erik Midelfort argues here that Freud should be seen as a modern demonologist and, as such, his practices reflect folk beliefs. In this sense, while perceptions may be phrased in binary terms, or even believed to be dichotomies, in practice the exchanges and conceptions in early modern Europe reflected a greater plurality and flexibility, a tendency shared by some more modern interpretations and interpreters.

A more concrete example should clarify the relationship between binaries and the circulation of ideas as developed in this book. While such circulations appear in all of this collection's articles, they are fundamental to Dean Bell's piece on Jewish magic and community in early modern Worms. Bell argues that magical practices and expressions are communal events and reflect communal values. Magic is thus as a collective creation, conceptualized and enacted by a society. For the Jews of early modern Worms, Bell stresses, the way magic was practiced and perceived mattered because it expressed Jewish identity in the distinctions that were drawn between Christian and Jewish magic. In this way the practitioner of magic, whether occult or utilitarian, is not automatically the Other, an outsider to the community that gains or enhances its sense of self through opposition to that outsider. Rather, in an interpretation reminiscent of Julia Kristeva's perspectives on otherness,

---

11. R. Po-chia Hsia, *The World of Catholic Renewal, 1540–1770* (New York: Cambridge University Press, 1998), 210, as cited by Sarah Ferber, page 55 below.

Bell asserts that the Jewish magician of early modern Worms was both a part of that community and, to some extent, its creation.[12]

Carlo Ginzburg has analyzed the circulation and production of traditional religion in early modern Europe on an even broader communal scale, as a religion that reflects the continuation of a pre-Christian, Indo-European shamanistic belief system and its principles.[13] While Ginzburg is probably the best-known recent example among English-speaking audiences, other works of history or historical anthropology with similar themes can be found in the citations of the articles gathered here. Studies on animism and animal transformation repeatedly note that beliefs about human transformation have existed, and continue to exist, in many cultures throughout the world.[14] Attempts have been made to trace these attitudes to a common human perceptional framework and to the earliest known shamanistic practices. Given the important role of skins and unguents in affecting physical transformations, these themes have also been developed frequently in both shamanism and more archetypal werewolf trials. Werewolf beliefs in early modern Europe, as developed here by Briggs, Sarah Ferber, and Nicole Jacques-Lefèvre, become aspects of a human collectivity that transcends temporal, physical, and even conscious boundaries. The animals of early modern European witch trials thus become far less domesticated than the cats and frogs common to witch iconography.

In particular, werewolves and other animalistic transformations have allowed an oppositional perspective or behavior to be expressed in many cultures and at many times. The altered state permits the articulation of an individual's distinctiveness and simultaneously retains the connection to a greater collectivity. Although early modern demonologists such as Henri Boguet and Nicolas Rémy do not explicitly make such a connection, it is implied throughout their works.[15] As developed here by Jacques-Lefèvre, the

12. Julia Kristeva, *Strangers to Ourselves*, trans. Leon S. Roudiez (New York: Columbia University Press, 1991), and eadem, *Nations without Nationalism*, trans. Leon S. Roudiez (New York: Columbia University Press, 1993).

13. See especially Ginzburg, *Ecstasies*.

14. Such works and their underlying ideologies have been thoroughly debated in a special issue of *Current Anthropology* 40 (1999) on "the culture concept," where Nurit Bird-David's article, "Animism Revisited: Personhood, Environment, and the Relational Epistemology," was at the center of the discussion, S1–S115.

15. Henry Boguet, *Discours exécrable des sorciers* (Rouen, 1603); *An Examen of Witches*, trans. E. Allen Ashwin, ed. Montague Summers (1929; repr. New York: Barnes & Noble, 1971); Nicolas Rémy, *Demonolatry*, trans. E. A. Ashwin, ed. Montague Summers (1930; repr., London: Frederic Muller, 1970).

werewolf in particular symbolizes instability and mutability, and the were-wolf's continued humanity only heightens this symbolism. Werewolves act contrary to what is human. Moreover, they act contrary to what is expected from their domestic counterparts. The dog—loyal, useful, productive—is portrayed as the mortal enemy of its opposite, the werewolf. As both human and animal—the one ideally communal and sociable, the other solitary and fierce—the werewolf embodies the tensions within humanity itself.[16]

The werewolf is just one example of the supernatural, preternatural, and at times unnatural presences which early modern Europeans believed shared their world and which appear in every article in this collection. Hostile pres-ences, not only in animal form, are frequently located in the same places as these animals; in fact, popular and authoritative perceptions could link the appearance of spiritual visitors and were-animals physically and symbolically. Early modern Europe was populated with spiritual beings whose existence could not be understood through reference to, or who only marginally belonged to, either Protestant or Catholic doctrines but whose existence was certain. As such, the common belief in these entities reflects the perpetuation of the community between the living and the dead, so cogently developed by John Bossy for pre-Reformation Europe, into post-Reformation settings. Despite Christian theology, which calls for the immediate removal of the soul from the earthly realm after death, popular belief perceived of the relationship between the living and the dead as far more complex. In this superenchanted world, ghosts and spirits, werewolves and witches, demons and dwarves all played a role. Humankind's ability to understand and interact with such forces assumed salvific importance.

For these reasons, defining these presences, assigning them attributes, and classifying them in some way becomes both essential and almost impos-sible. Reformers like Bullinger and demonologists like Claude Prieur tended to blur distinct typologies in the spirit and supernatural world, such as ghosts and the souls of suicides. Given the fear that such phenomena could actually be demonic by-products or demons themselves, such ambiguity is

16. For other recent works on medieval and early modern Europe that treat lycanthropy accord-ing to the approaches mentioned here, see Caroline Walker Bynum, "Metamorphosis, or Gerald and the Werewolf," *Speculum* 73 (1998): 987–1013; Claude Lecouteux, *Fées, sorcières et loups-garous au Moyen Age: Histoire du double* (Paris: Imago, 1992); Elmar M. Lorey, *Henrich der Werwolf: Eine Geschichte aus der Zeit der Hexenprozesse mit Dokumenten und Analysen* (Frankfurt am Main: Anabas Verlag, 1998); Gaël Milin, *Les chiens de Dieu: La représentation du loup-garou en Occident, XIe–XXe siè-cles* (Brest: Centre de recherche bretonne et celtique, Université de Bretagne occidentale, 1993); Caro-line Oates, "The Trial of a Teenage Werewolf, Bordeaux, 1603," *Criminal Justice History* 9 (1988).

understandable. While a demonic compulsion to deform God's order was assumed in early modern thought, the means and methods demons preferred to use were less certain. Ferber explores such ambiguities through her analysis of death and possession. The possessed and their witnesses firmly believe in a holistic community of the living and the dead that includes various entities which circulate between both realms and, in so doing, almost seem to form a third. Although unalive in a human sense, the beings that exist in this third realm have vital force, which allows them to animate the body of those they possess. Repressed and, therefore, dead to some extent, the possessed soul then becomes a temporary member of the third realm and able to bridge all three. The possession is thus a type of divination; the possessed, a spiritualist. In the process, however, the possessed's spiritual status is thrown into even greater doubt; as a potential receptacle for either the blessed or the damned, the possessed problematizes the connections between life and afterlife. The possessor could, after all, just as easily be a demon. In fact, its willingness to overturn the divinely ordained role of human souls suggests that it is most likely a demon.

To separate the self from the possessor and to distinguish between human and animal demands a certain degree of self-consciousness on both an individual and a communal level. Thus, the exploration of early modern means of constructing and articulating identities is a theme underlying many of the articles in this collection. In addition to the work previously mentioned, the articles by Sara Nalle and Anne Jacobson Schutte explore millennialism and witchcraft from the perspective of identity formation, subjectivity, and agency. Nalle stresses the folkloric roots of the messianic leader El Encubierto, developing the way that participants in Las Germanías saw him as reflecting their own folkloric expectations; while El Encubierto's claims for himself were quite modest, those who revolted saw him as a physical manifestation of their aspirations and the essence of their revolt. El Encubierto himself is both the embodiment of and an aspect of their folkloric identity.

As analyzed by Schutte, Asmodea's identity as a nun-witch particularly addresses the themes of subjectivity and agency that drive so many recent literary, sociological, and anthropological works.[17] Asmodea is simultaneously

17. Pierre Bourdieu, *Outline of a Theory of Practice* (New York: Cambridge University Press, 1977); Simon Critchley, *Ethics, Politics, Subjectivity: Essays on Derrida, Levinas and Contemporary French Thought* (London: Verso, 1999); Judith Kegan Gardiner, ed., *Provoking Agents: Gender and Agency in Theory and Practice* (Urbana: University of Illinois Press, 1995); Sherry B. Ortner, "Resistance and the Problem of Ethnographic Refusal," *Comparative Studies in Society and History* 37:1 (1995): 173–93; Charles Taylor, *Human Agency and Language* (New York: Cambridge University Press, 1985); and Michel Zink,

an individual, who is conscious of her distinctiveness, and a member of a community, who shares in the values and self-perceptions of the various societies which compose it. Through her self-fashioning as both a witch and a nun, Asmodea attempts to influence her own destiny and to craft her own identity, both social and personal. Witchcraft becomes a means to create herself as a subject and to form a world in which she can be the active and influential member that she may not have been otherwise. Asmodea's inquisitors, however, were reluctant to accept her identity as a witch. Schutte suggests that their attitude should be recognized as repressive rather than enlightened or progressive, the most common interpretations of the decline in witch prosecutions. The inquisitors' reluctance to prosecute Asmodea curbs her autonomy as effectively as if they believed that she was married to the devil.

In the cases of Asmodea, El Encubierto, and the others analyzed here, physicality is a recurring theme, not only in questions of bodily transformation but in the physical setting of a story, the sensible manifestations of spiritual activity, and the ways supernatural phenomena are appreciated and comprehended. Physicality is both the most obvious quality of God's creation, nature, and the most ready tool which God's greatest creation, humanity, has at its disposal. While human nature and physical nature may seem surprisingly mutable to sixteenth- and seventeenth-century Europeans, awareness and exploitation of this mutability implies some sense of a natural standard created and sustained by God. Lorraine Daston cogently summarizes the conditions and roles of natural standards and the nature of nature as they evolve in late medieval and early modern Europe:

> From the thirteenth century on, when the boundaries between supernatural, preternatural, artificial, and unnatural were fixed with at least philosophical clarity in Christian Europe, there existed considerable variations both in local practices and in theological, medical, philosophical, and legal discourses about where to draw the line between the non-natural and the natural in any given case. But the ideal types nonetheless served as reference points in contexts ranging from grafting techniques among gardeners...to ecclesiastical procedures for canonizing saints.... It was only in the sixteenth century that the reference points were themselves subjected to explicitly and massive revision, with ensuing transformations of norms and practices.[18]

The Invention of Literary Subjectivity (Baltimore: Johns Hopkins University Press, 1999).

18. Daston, "Nature of Nature," 157 ff.

The articles in this collection repeatedly examine such transformations of norms and the attempts to establish new or modified ones in their place. In the contribution by Jacques-Lefèvre on demonological theories about the formation and reality of werewolves, assumptions about nature play a central role. At issue were fundamental eschatological and ontological questions. What distinguished the nature of humans from that of the beasts? To what extent could God's creations—nature and all its variety—be corrupted or mutate? If nature reflects God's law and thus provides a standard through which humans might approach God, how could nature and possible perversions of it, such as werewolves, be understood? Finally, a concern of both theologians and practitioners of natural magic: To what extent did the form of a natural object reflect its substance?[19]

The answers to these questions focus on truth: what or who determines it; what standards exist for its proof; is there one truth or are there a multiplicity of truths? As the articles in this collection suggest, while the perception of and standards behind truth could vary enormously in early modern Europe, agreement on the source of all truth—God—remained constant. Yet these variations in perception and assessment suggest profound shifts in worldviews, shifts which may distinguish sixteenth-century Europeans from their eighteenth-century counterparts. Ulrike Krampl argues that the changes in terminology found in late-seventeenth-century and early-eighteenth-century Parisian witchcraft trials reflect fundamental epistemological changes, particularly in the methods by which truth was determined. For example, the transformation of *sorciers* (witches/magicians) into *séducteurs* highlights their political, social, and moral danger; they seduce those who are receptive to belief (the *crédule*) into politically subversive social equality. By uniting powerful lords and lowly commoners in the pursuit of magical benefits—moreover, by making those lords dependent on the commoners for magic—they undermine proper secular and spiritual government. Like the devil himself, they seduce and tempt. Like the devil himself, their goal must be to overthrow the gates of Heaven, or at least those of Versailles.

METHODOLOGICAL DEBATES

While the preceding section touches on questions of interpretation, the articles in this collection should also be read in light of the debates over the

---

19. Eamon, *Science and the Secrets of Nature*, esp. chaps. 6–8, where he defines "natural magic" and its role in the development and definition of science in early modern Europe. See the development of such topics by demonologists in Clark, *Thinking with Demons*, pt. 2, esp. chaps. 11 and 14.

appropriate methodologies to apply to historically based studies of traditional belief and folklore. While several contributions suggest the integration of mythology or Jungian archetypes, others challenge them. Psychological, psychoanalytical, even medical interpretations have been applied and reapplied to all of the topics studied here by both contemporary observers and modern analysts. To highlight this aspect of traditional belief and folklore, this collection ends with articles whose emphasis is explicitly on such interpretations in sixteenth- and early-seventeenth-century theology and demonology and in early-twentieth-century psychoanalysis.

Traditionally many of the events and ideas examined here would have been classified as some form of witchcraft, when they were even classifiable at all. As such, they were subject to the dichotomy between medieval and modern perspectives that still mistakenly exists in some studies about witchcraft. Like witchcraft, these beliefs and practices were not the products of a deluded, deprived Middle Ages. Jacques-Lefèvre notes repeatedly that the belief in witches, and in her particular study werewolves, has most commonly and mistakenly been attributed to the Middle Ages and to peasants, but that the beliefs were in fact developed most thoroughly and explicitly during the Renaissance by intellectuals. Belief in witches, ghosts, and other supernatural or preternatural forces persisted in Europe at all social levels well into the eighteenth century. In seventeenth-century Bavaria appearances of ghosts that took conventional and unconventional forms were on the rise, and in eighteenth-century Paris a series of trials of "false witches" occurred during the beginning of the so-called Enlightenment, after the time when trials and penalties for witchcraft are perceived as being on the decline and some courts even declared that witches did not exist.[20] Despite modern rationalism, such beliefs remain strong in the early twenty-first century.

Yet the characteristics of these witches, practitioners' magic, and supernatural manifestations appear to be changing. In the case of the Parisian trials, Krampl notes that the accused were not witches in the older, traditional sense of practitioners of *maleficia*; they were people who performed or promised services for others by using occult methods. While the functional aspects of magical practices, apparitions, and witches had been part of sixteenth- and

---

20. The problems with seeing belief in witchcraft and magic as essentially premodern and, therefore by implication, unenlightened have been developed well by Richard Porter, "Witchcraft and Magic in Enlightenment, Romantic, and Liberal Thought," in *The Eighteenth and Nineteenth Century*, ed. Bengt Ankarloo and Stuart Clark, Witchcraft and Magic in Europe series (Philadelphia: University of Pennsylvania Press, 1999), 191–283, esp. 191–236.

early-seventeenth-century traditional belief, it seems that functionality was developing into their dominant, or at least most valuable, characteristic. Ghosts become primarily treasure hunters and emissaries of justice. Magicians assure love and promotion at court. Supernatural transactions are described in mercantile terms. Such shifts complicate questions of truth and belief. Why do people in early modern Europe believe in such manifestations or perpetuate magical practices? The reasons for such support become as diverse as the reasons human beings have for seeking assistance from any power perceived to be superior.

That social and intellectual elites continued to support such beliefs and practices into the eighteenth century continued to trouble authorities on a variety of levels. Both Catholic and Protestant reformers attempted to impose a more rigid and structured social and political order during the sixteenth and seventeenth centuries, the process known by historians as social discipline. Contemporaries saw many of the cases presented here as highly politicized and, in some cases, felt the need to impose order on the apparently less ordered supernatural realm. Lederer argues that such a politicization occurred in the understanding of ghosts and the treatment of mediums in sixteenth- and seventeenth-century Bavaria, while, for Ferber, the transformation of the cult of the dead in light of political and religious debates was also reflected in attitudes towards and treatments of possession. Possession thus represents power from beyond the grave. Bullinger combats Satan's pastoral strengths, while lycanthropes are condemned by seventeenth-century demonologists for contributing to a degenerate political and religious system. People at all levels participate in this politicization, including the followers of El Encubierto during Las Germanías in early-sixteenth-century Spain.

Early modern interpretations of such phenomena also emphasized their physiological and psychological roots, particularly in relation to melancholy. Building on Galenic principles, early modern medical theory developed an elaborate physiological and psychological taxonomy. Human psychology was believed to be based on a balance of four humors, each of which reflected and enhanced an aspect of the human personality. According to this theory, an excess of black bile caused melancholy. Those who believed themselves to be demons or werewolves were perceived to be excessively melancholic and psychologically unbalanced. Demonologists such as Johannes Weyer, a medical doctor, developed this diagnosis to challenge the very foundations of witch trials, arguing that those who believed themselves to be witches or werewolves were actually delusional and, therefore, more in need of pity and assistance than punishment and purgation. Figures like Henri Boguet and

Claude Prieur were, however, more representative of the era. They believed witches did exist in fact but considered witches and others who believed they had unorthodox spiritual and magical connections to be deluded and melancholic. In this area, Renaissance theorists built on classical models. One frequently cited source in such discussions was Aetius's *On Melancholy,* written in the late fifth century. There he describes a disease called lycanthropia or "wolves fury" that incorporates many of the characteristics associated with werewolfism in early modern Europe albeit without the actual, physical transformation; the afflicted disturbs graves, eats bones, suffers from thirst, has a hollow, haggard appearance, and even howls.[21]

Some modern interpreters of phenomena such as lycanthropy have continued to apply medical diagnoses. Lycanthropy is linked to porphyria, a rare congenital disorder that is characterized by extreme light sensitivity, clay-colored teeth, and "ulcers which destroy cartilage and bone, cause the deformation of the nose, ears, and fingers. Mental aberrations, such as hysteria, manic-depressive psychosis, and delirium" may also accompany porphyria. With such symptoms, connections can be made between werewolf and vampire cases.[22] Following similar methods, witches are seen as experiencing ergot-induced hallucinations, from moldy rye or an overdose of magic mushrooms.[23]

Despite the persistent application of medical analysis to the study of witchcraft and other early modern beliefs, the most frequently used modern approach is that of psychoanalysis. Briggs introduces this collection by examining psychological constructs behind witch beliefs in early modern Lorraine. He does not claim that these beliefs were particularly unique; in fact, there were stock characteristics in the language of witchcraft. Yet these characteristics point to broader, psychological themes, particularly the libidinous aspects of transformations and the repetition of "classic narcissistic delusions."[24]

In this collection's final article, Midelfort returns to the role of psychoanalysis in studies of such phenomena. He stresses the complexities and ambiguities in modern analyses of demonism and questions the dispassionate

---

21. Charlotte F. Otten, ed., *A Lycanthropy Reader: Werewolves in Western Culture* (Syracuse, N.Y.: Syracuse University Press, 1986), 24–25.

22. H. Sidky, *Witchcraft, Lycanthropy, Drugs, and Disease: An Anthropological Study of the European Witch-Hunts* (New York: Peter Lang, 1997), 239; Otten, *Lycanthropy Reader,* 202ff.

23. Sidky, *Witchcraft, Lycanthropy,* 155–214; Robert Eisler, *Man into Wolf: An Anthropological Interpretation of Sadism, Masochism, and Lycanthropy* (London: Routledge & Paul, 1951).

24. Briggs, see page 23 below. Briggs develops a psychoanalytical approach to witchcraft in *Witches and Neighbors,* chap. 10.

role of psychoanalysis in such interpretations. Midelfort points to the influence of demonism on psychoanalytical theory and challenges any presentation of psychoanalysis, and thus psychohistory, as unitary. He stresses the wide variety of psychoanalytical theories, but rather than summarize the ways that psychoanalysis can be applied to the study of witchcraft and other aspects of traditional belief, Midelfort reverses perspectives and asks how the late nineteenth-century understanding of witchcraft and demonology influenced the budding art and science of psychoanalysis. Here demons and possession impact Freud's theories of hysteria and obsession, to name but two areas. In this sense, Midelfort argues, psychoanalysis and witchcraft have been linked since the origin of psychoanalysis.

Personality and perversion, standards and judgment, control and freedom are thus themes that bridge early modern and modern interpretations of witchcraft and traditional belief more generally. The contributors to this collection grapple with these themes. They animate early modern peasants and theologians, werewolves and wandering spirits. Most of all, they do so with great diversity, a diversity which this collection has tried to capture.

DANGEROUS SPIRITS

Shapeshifting, Apparitions, and Fantasy in Lorraine Witchcraft Trials

Robin Briggs

Witchcraft trials are notoriously concerned with beliefs, because the crime itself only makes sense in terms of social and psychological constructs.[1] Witnesses generally spoke of real events, but the crucial step was interpreting this testimony as supposedly valid evidence. The routine accusations relied on a temporal and logical sequence, from quarrels and threats to misfortunes, sometimes followed by an intercession that brought healing. Such charges were further validated by that slippery, yet vital element of reputation, itself the product of long-term communal processes of gossip and negotiation. At first sight the result was a remarkably efficient system of communal scapegoating, which left the accused virtually defenseless once a determined coalition had taken shape amongst their neighbors. Yet this circularity was also a weakness: it attracted criticism even at the village level and caused great disquiet among the legal and clerical elites. Several of the most powerful critiques of persecution concentrated on the danger that the innocent would be condemned along with the guilty. This danger was a powerful factor in determining the attitudes of such prominent skeptics as the Parisian *parlementaires* or the Spanish and Italian inquisitors. These worries were increased because no competent lawyer could regard the typical testimonies as proof. There was a gap which required the routine use of torture to extract confessions, despite all the well-known objections to this practice, which were perfectly familiar to early modern commentators. The more sophisticated demands that confessions should meet certain internal tests, notably by including details which only the real criminal could know, simply could not be met in these cases.

---

1. For the analysis of these psychological aspects in particular I am deeply indebted to my wife, Daphne Briggs, whose help has been invaluable.

Behind the apparent assurance of many persecutors, at all levels, there must have lurked a deep sense of disquiet. Even for the most committed there were nagging questions about their secret enemies: just how many undetected witches were there and how far might their power stretch? The persistent Manichean character of popular belief was arguably reinforced by the marked tendency to binary polarization among the elites, to deepen the threatening image of a diabolical antiworld, whose members were committed to subverting the Christian commonwealth. The orthodox countermove here was to stress that the devil operated within strict limits set by God; he could only produce illusions, not true supernatural effects, and was essentially impotent against those who equipped themselves with either true faith or approved protective rituals.[2] This too was an important feature of popular as well as elite attitudes, which emerges with surprising clarity from the evidence of the trials themselves. Yet, however many reservations of this type there may have been, the idea of dark external forces which could be directed against a fragile humanity and its institutions retained great intuitive power. Like many myths and exemplary tales, the notion of witchcraft drew much of its force from ambiguities, even from inner tensions. Forbidden and evil power was apparently available to anyone who wanted it badly enough, albeit at a terrible price—not only the loss of one's soul to eternal damnation, but subjection to a cruel master during one's lifetime. Those would-be magicians who invoked spirits from within a protective circle, often reinforced by charms, were making a splendidly naive attempt to escape the logic of the system, which further emphasized its true nature.[3] Theologians who employed the concept of the tacit pact to stigmatize all forms of magic and occultism found it easy to brush these flimsy pretenses aside, then went on to argue that all those who consulted the cunning folk also put their souls at risk, a claim which was never likely to win general acceptance even among the elites.

The popular vision of the great complex of hidden or magical forces surrounding the everyday world was evidently far more ambiguous than austere theologians formulated. Although such powers were indeed inherently dangerous,

---

2. The whole subject of demonology has been explored in unprecedented depth by Stuart Clark, *Thinking with Demons: The Idea of Witchcraft in Early Modern Europe* (New York: Oxford University Press, 1997), which places great emphasis on the type of polarized binary thought relevant to my central argument.

3. For some Lorraine cases of this kind see Robin Briggs, "Circling the Devil: Witch-Doctors and Magical Healers in Early Modern Lorraine," in *Languages of Witchcraft: Narrative, Ideology and Meaning in Early Modern Culture*, ed. Stuart Clark (New York: Macmillan, 2001), 161–78.

astute or lucky practitioners were thought to be able to avail themselves of these forces for good purposes, while in many emergencies they represented the only hope of relief. At the same time "the wonders of the invisible world," with its mysterious denizens, fascinated the early modern imagination, and provided (in principle at least) unlimited openings for fantasy and invention. This symbolic richness fed back into witchcraft beliefs at multiple levels. It also meshed with a related passion to discern signs and portents, which formed another bridge between formal religious doctrine and its popular counterparts. We might not implausibly describe this as a superenchanted world, one so full of messages and meanings that its inhabitants might well feel both bewildered and terrified, supposedly beset by invisible forces, whether benign or malign. If the arsenal of ritualized forms of protection available from the church offered much comfort, it also bolstered belief in the dangers, and it was vulnerable to petty errors no one could be sure to avoid. Such ideas have been invoked to explain the appeal of the radically simplified faith of the Second Reformation, alongside the violent reactions it provoked from others, at a time when the Second Coming was thought to be imminent.[4] One way to test these theories is to investigate witchcraft cases, looking for evidence of excited imaginings, fantasies, and obsessions in a sphere which offered exceptional possibilities for them to occur.

Signs were also important in the context of the problems of proof invoked above. The difficulties in identifying witches safely led naturally to various attempts to find more reliable tests. The most widespread test was probably pricking for the devil's mark, an insensible point on the body supposedly made at the moment of seduction. The English version was the search (often by a group of midwives) for the additional teats at which the animal familiars or imps were alleged to suck for nourishment, an image associated with the broader theme of the witch as bad mother. Popular witch-finders sometimes claimed they could detect subtle markings in the eye, while the tradition of the ordeal continued with the swimming test, again a popular rather than an official method of confirming suspicions. The failure to shed tears when in a state of distress was frequently noted in Lorraine court records, although it never seems to have acquired any real status as a proof. Witnesses often tried to establish that illnesses were abnormal or unnatural, in order to strengthen the diagnosis of bewitchment, by talking of strange

---

4. For a compelling statement of this case see Denis Crouzet, *Les Guerriers de Dieu: La violence au temps des troubles de religion, vers 1525–vers 1610*, 2 vols. (Seyssel: Champ Vallon, 1990).

noises, suspicious comings and goings, and the appearance of abnormal hostile creatures. These attempts to add verisimilitude shade into the outright curiosity found in numerous demonological works, whose authors can seem as keen to entertain or titillate as to argue a coherent case. Nicolas Rémy, *procureur-général* of the duchy of Lorraine, is one case in point, for his *Demonolatry* of 1595 is a remarkably discursive work, more a description of what witches did than a sustained plea for their eradication (he may reasonably have thought that the latter was well taken care of in the duchy, with its high rates of persecution).

Full trial records survive for approximately 375 individuals tried as witches in Lorraine between 1580 and 1630, with less complete documentation increasing this sample to about 400 accused. The extensive use of torture produced a conviction rate of 79 percent across this sample. In most cases the witness depositions can be set against confessions, which were also grounded in popular beliefs about witchcraft, then fed back into those beliefs when they were read out at executions (as seems to have been the standard practice). Just as most Lorraine accounts of the sabbat stuck to very humdrum descriptions, so it must be said that this archive is not especially rich in truly lurid details of werewolves, apparitions, and other supernatural or paranatural phenomena. After excluding a few cases that contain little more than vague hints, there are around 110 which provide significant material for analysis, some of them under two or three headings. Wolves appear in thirty-six of these, although not always with any implication that they were werewolves; cats in thirty-four; and dogs in sixteen. There are thirteen instances of what might be regarded as visitations by spirits or angels, most of them occurring in prison. In ten cases mysterious persons make attacks or threatening appearances, while six cases mention hares, five cases mention toads, and five cases refer to creatures mainly characterized as strange. Two stories include ghosts; there are two each of bears, pigs, and birds, then a bull, a fox, and a goat. These figures are necessarily approximate, because it is not always easy to decide how a particular episode should be classified, or whether a vague mention is to be included at all. Most of these stories are relatively minor items in the dossier, which attracted only marginal interest from the judges, and do not necessarily figure in the final confessions made by the accused. Nevertheless, the fact that they appear in almost 30 percent of cases, and perhaps 5 percent of meaningful testimonies, does suggest that they were an important component of Lorraine witchcraft beliefs; at the symbolic level they might even be thought to have been an integral one.

One obvious comparison must be with the animal familiars which played such a large part in English witchcraft narratives. There are some clear structural differences, which can be fairly readily explained on functional grounds, on the principle of substitution. When the Lorraine devil took animal form to communicate with witches or to help them carry out their evil work, this was an explicit and temporary form of shapeshifting. The witches neither kept the creatures in their houses nor gave them nourishment from special teats. Such notions would not have fitted very well with the standard narrative of seduction, in which the devil took human form and sealed his triumph over his female conquests by raping them. Even at the sabbat the devils rarely took animal form, confirming the view that the fantasy world of Lorraine witchcraft was decidedly anthropocentric, at least where the fundamental master-slave relationship was concerned. In many cases the logic behind the shapeshifting was simply to conceal the true nature of the transaction, whether it was the killing of animals or the coercion of the witch into new crimes. On other occasions these transformations allowed apparently safe and well-defended spaces to be penetrated, as when cats squeezed through window shutters to attack defenseless sleepers. It would have stretched even the flimsy logic of local demonology too far if these functions had been attributed to the more exotic types of familiar, though imaginary creatures in the style of Griezel Greedigut or Vinegar Tom. The absence of the vast range of more ordinary fauna—birds, mice, ferrets, moles, and the rest found in the English trials—reinforces the point that the Lorraine animals bore no resemblance to pets, while the concentration on wolves, cats, and dogs reflects the elementary fact that these creatures were frequently seen in situations which could be interpreted as witchcraft.[5] Because trials in the duchy collected written evidence, then allowed the accused to hear it read to them when they were confronted with the individual witnesses, most confessions were primarily responses to the specific charges made, which also formed the basis for questioning by the judges. Inevitably the character of the material was very much influenced by the procedures which generated it. In Lorraine the procedure mostly worked in favor of a realistic everyday style, in which routine misfortunes were given a diabolical explanation of a distinctly economical type.

5. Vinegar Tom and Griezel Greedigut were among the numerous familiars of Elizabeth Clarke of Manningtree, tried in 1645 during the Matthew Hopkins crusade. For details see C. L'Estrange Ewen, *Witchcraft and Demonianism* (1933, repr., London: Muller, 1970), 264–65. The index to this volume lists an astonishing range of creatures under the heading "familiar."

Another contrast to Lorraine witch trials is with the rich werewolf stories from the neighboring Franche-Comté.[6] The werewolf theme is merely
hinted at in most of the Lorraine trials where attacks by wolves on animals
are mentioned. In the 1614 trial of Claudon Marchal of le Vivier, Epnon
Burquey alleged that Claudon had been angry after Epnon's husband had
underbid Claudon for the post of village herdsman; soon afterwards Epnon's
husband lost a cow attacked by wolves in the middle of his herd, when no
other animal was touched. Claudatte Claudon told how three years earlier
her son, Curien, had a quarrel with one of Claudon Marchal's sons; then the
same day a foal belonging to them was strangled in the middle of the herd by
a wolf which refused to let go even when burning sticks were put against its
throat. When Claudon was tortured he made a series of confessions which
neatly mirrored the specific accusations against him, simply admitting that
he had given consent for his master Napnel to kill these animals in the form
of a wolf.[7]

Noel George testified against Idoult Charpentier of Saint Blaise in 1603
that two years earlier he was cutting hay with Jean Reullement when they
heard Jean's son, who was guarding the animals, cry out. When they reached
him he said two wolves had attacked the animals and he had recognized the
head of one of them as that of Idoult. This striking detail made no further
appearance in the case, even when a full confession was extracted. One partial
explanation may be that Idoult continued to deny killing some of George's
children.[8] In 1591 an unnamed witness said that about five years earlier, after
a dispute arising from some damage done by their animals, Colas Mengin of
Saint Rémy said the witness and her family would repent. Shortly afterwards a
wolf killed one of their calves, and on account of Colas's previous evil reputation she suspected him of causing this. Some five weeks before the trial, on
her way to market, she saw two men running and thought one was Colas.
Then she thought she saw him change into a wolf and jump a hedge before
seeing him in his normal shape again, beginning to plow. Here too, there was
nothing in Mengin's confessions (which were decidedly partial and which he
more than once tried to withdraw) about this incident.[9]

6. See Caroline F. Oates, "Trials of Werewolves in the Franche-Comté in the Early Modern
Period" (Ph.D. thesis, Warburg Institute, 1993).

7. Archives départementales de Meurthe-et-Moselle, Nancy (hereafter ADMM), B8712 no. 6.

8. ADMM, B8691 no. 18.

9. ADMM, B8667 no. 7.

An unusually complex story emerged in the trial of Claudon Hardier of Hesse in 1608. Hardier was another herdsman who had lost his position. Although he claimed that he had given it up willingly, because the recent death of his wife would have made it difficult for him to do the job, several remarks attributed to him suggest that he was resentful and let this show. His successor, Stepf Georges, recounted an incident six years earlier when Claudon had expressed anger at the appearance of some sheep owned by a group of merchants. He allegedly said, "That is the devil of a flock of sheep; I would like to be a witch for eight days, I would make a wolf who would really get his paws on them." When Stepf was being appointed earlier that year, Claudon had said "whoever had the job would find he had plenty on his hands," and this had proved correct, because the herd:

> was sometimes plagued by a wolf, whose attacks did not seem to fit an animal of that kind, insomuch as instead of leaping upon some animal to feed on it, it only twisted and turned around them and scratched them. This had happened in recent days to two or three heifers, which had scratches on their left cheek the day after they were attacked; then these produced swellings that closed their eyes, after which they died in a few days.

Claudon had undertaken to treat one of these heifers, and when Stepf complained of the wolf, which he said was not a true wolf, he replied "that it was the devil, and the witness did not know the method for healing such scratches; one had to make the sign of the cross over the animal and rub the affected part with mithridate." This surprised Stepf, who only knew of the use of mithridate (a counterpoison, named after the king from antiquity) as an antidote when an animal had eaten something poisonous, not as an ointment. Another witness claimed that the dogs ran away from this unnatural wolf. Under interrogation Claudon admitted some of his compromising remarks (although not those about making a wolf) and recited four magical prayers which formed part of his treatment for sick animals. When he later confessed under torture he told of seeing two of his fellow witches transformed into wolves, while he denied that he had done this himself. This case brings out very well how a herdsman with rather elaborate pretensions to healing animals risked acquiring a dangerously ambiguous reputation, when good and evil power were effectively thought to overlap.[10]

---

10. The trial documents, now lost, are printed in extenso in C.-E. Dumont, *Justice criminelle des duchés de Lorraine et de Bar*, 2 vols. (Nancy, 1848), i–xxvii, 11.

In addition to the cases discussed so far, there are at least three others in which specific accusations of werewolf activity were made, and four more in which these accusations were followed by confessions to actually taking wolf form. Dieudonnée Jalley of Mazelay, tried in 1618, was accused by both Rémy Valdeliepvre and his wife Marie—a couple Dieudonnée and her husband sometimes hired as day laborers—of having turned herself into a wolf. The husband believed this was how she had taken some of his animals, while the wife told of how a great wolf ran through the village trying to prevent her reaching her home. An attack by a wolf on Marie's own small son was also cited, partly because she and her husband allegedly said it was a witch rather than a wolf, while there was another story about a wolf they had been unable to drive away from their house. In her confessions, although she denied any transformation, Dieudonnée said this last wolf had been her master coming to incite her to further evil.[11] Ten years earlier Marion Flandrey of Le Faing de Sainte Marguerite was alleged to have been the wolf that killed three sheep belonging to a man with whom she had quarreled; she denied all charges and withstood the torture.[12] Jennon Grand Didier of La Rochatte, tried in 1630, attracted stories involving a white cat and a great black dog as well as wolves; one of the latter killed an ass after the suspect said "may the evil wolf strangle and kill them" during a quarrel with its owner, and the dogs refused to chase it. Jennon was convicted, but her confession has not survived.[13]

The trial of Mengette Cachette in 1602 mobilized fifty witnesses against a suspect whose mother had already fled after being tried herself. There was clearly a great deal of rumor and hostility directed against Mengette by the other villagers of Flin, so it is hardly surprising that shapeshifting featured among the lengthy depositions. There was a circumstantial story that she had been the unseen wolf that killed a horse fifteen years earlier. More recently, Claudon Hursieu and his wife thought Mengette had taken wolf form to make their son ill and to kill a horse; in her confessions Mengette denied the first charge, "but admitted she had strangled his horse, being in the form of a werewolf after her master, Persin, had greased her whole body and pinched her forehead, but she reckoned it was her master who had done the harm and that he made her believe that it was her doing." Mengette's cousin, Zabel

---

11. ADMM, B8721 no. 1.
12. Archives départementales des Vosges, Epinal (hereafter ADVosges), G708 no. 1.
13. ADVosges, G710.

Hanry, had deposed against Mengette's mother, then fallen ill. During Zabel's convalescence a cat tried to get on her bed with loud cries, attacked her and her son, aged three; Zabel called on her mother to get a holy image given her by some preachers, but she could not find it. When Zabel finally found the image the cat left like a wind, knocking over everything in their stable, so Zabel was sure that if Mengette was a witch she had taken this cat-form. Jean Purel claimed that when he had been ill fourteen years earlier, three women, including Mengette and her mother, had appeared in his room at night and tried to strangle him. While Mengette was technically a self-confessed were-wolf, it must be said that this charge had no special prominence in the case against her, based as it was on a classic mixture of stories about quarrels, threats, and losses. Mengette's own admission implied a fairly sophisticated awareness of the blurred area between reality and illusion, as did her com-ment (echoed by her husband at his own trial the next year) "that after her death they would see very well if misfortunes ceased in Flin."[14]

Two more cases including werewolf admissions were both tried in 1614, although they originated in villages which were about eight miles apart, and there is no sign of any direct link. Jean Callerey of Pajaille was another suspect encumbered by a family reputation, since both his parents had been executed. There was just one relevant charge, that a fine cow had been mysteriously strangled by a wolf in the herd. Jean confessed that the strangulation had been the work of his master, to whom he had given his consent. He also admitted that a year earlier his master, Houbelat, had approached him and an accom-plice, "ordering them to take the form of wolves, which they did by means of a certain grease which Houbelat applied to them and a skin like a wolfskin with big teeth which he put over them." In this guise they killed a cow and took part of it to the sabbat; this was an offense not mentioned in the testimonies.[15] Claudatte Dabo of Grattain was accused by the convicted witch Jehennon le Renard from her previous village of Robache, who said that she had taken the form of a wolf the previous year and helped devour a child, then taken the heart away to eat it with her companions. Claudatte confessed to these acts, without adding any other details, but did say that she had also taken the form of a wolf to attack the sheep at Grattain, only to be driven off by the shepherd-ess.[16] It would appear from another trial that the purpose of eating a child's

14. ADMM, B6723 no. 1.
15. ADMM, B8712 no. 1.
16. ADMM, B8712 no. 2.

heart was to obtain some kind of immunity during the judicial process.[17] This story was getting much nearer to the classic version of the werewolf as a threat to humans, even if it was still told in a very unadorned way.

Perhaps the most elaborate and circumstantial charges were those made against Mengeon Claude Perrin of Brehimont, tried at the end of 1600. The testimonies, with their accounts of fights and allegations that he had enclosed common land, suggest that Mengeon (aged about sixty) was an aggressive and rather unpopular character. Another substantial peasant, Colas Claude Girard, told of a quarrel about trespass in a field nine years earlier, after which Mengeon threatened him, wishing he might be buried in the field. The same day as his children were guarding animals a wolf appeared and tried to attack the children. Colas rushed up in his cart to help them; then the wolf fled but only to a certain distance, and as he looked at it he thought it was Mengeon transformed into a wolf. The fourteen-year-old girl Jennon Perrin said that two years earlier she had reported seeing Mengeon taking pears from a tree which belonged to her father and others. A few days later she went to a garden to fetch a pig which had strayed when Mengeon met her, called her "slut and liar," saying that this time he would have her, then put his hand to the ground and transformed himself into the guise of a wolf to chase her on four legs, still saying he would have her. She was quick enough to get into her house, then looked back to see he had vanished, although he had been within five or six paces of her. Jennon was terrified for the next two days, thinking that she saw Mengeon chasing her in his wolf form. There was an additional story about Mengeon threatening two girls, and when they ran away a hare passed in front of them several times. The hare then vanished, and they saw Mengeon in front of them with a spade on his shoulders. At this the girls were so frightened that they took another way and went back to the village to tell their story. The accused admitted turning himself into the form of a wolf with grease given to him by his master in order to carry out his attacks on the children. In so doing he confirmed the marked preference of all participants in Lorraine trials for pseudomechanical or realistic explanations, seen at their most extreme in Jean Callerey's use of a wolf-skin complete with teeth.[18]

The same theme can be seen in some of the more elaborate stories about transformations into cats. Two women who were tried around Christmas

17. This is the case of Claudatte Parmentier of Sainte Marguerite, tried in 1598; see Robin Briggs, *Witches and Neighbours: The Social and Cultural Context of European Witchcraft* (London: HarperCollins, 1996), 358.
18. ADMM, B8687 no. 10.

1599 in the village of Sauceray were involved in the concoction of one such tale. It began with one of their neighbors, Demenge Thieriat, whose original deposition (partly lost through damage to the document) seems to have been about the theft of some timbers by the sons of the first accused, Marion Arnoulx. During the confrontations Demenge added a completely new and much more vivid account of how three years earlier he had woken at night to find there were people in the room. He grabbed hold of a woman's clothes only for them to be torn out of his grip, then heard a voice he recognized as Marion's say, "We will never have this devil here." Demenge also heard another voice, that of Barbeline Mareschal, but when his wife lit a candle they found the room empty and the door shut. He also claimed that his attackers had put a grain of barley or wheat in his mouth, which he could not spit out, so he had to swallow, after which he immediately fell seriously ill for more than a month. When Marion made her confessions she was prompted by the judges to reply to this specific charge; she said that Barbeline (whom she had already identified as an accomplice) had instigated the attack because she hated Demenge. They had approached his house around midnight, where:

> they met the devil Persin their master, whom they told what they were envious of doing, and when they arrived right outside Thieriat's house the said Master Persin undressed them completely naked, then rubbed them with a certain grease he had. They were suddenly trans-formed into the guise of cats, in which form they entered Thieriat's bedchamber by the window, having a lot of difficulty getting through between the wooden slats in it. When they were in the chamber Persin brought them their clothes and restored them to their normal form, after which the accused went to the front of Thieriat's bed and the said Barbeline to the rear, where Barbeline put a grain of wheat, which they had poisoned with their powders, into Thieriat's mouth in order to make him ill for a certain time. At that point Thieriat woke up and started to cry Alarm, calling his wife; then throwing his arm out in front of the bed, he caught hold of the skirt of the accused, but she tugged it so hard that she made him lose hold. It was at that point that Barbeline said the words, "We will never have this devil here," and at the same moment Persin transformed them into cats again, so they left the same way as they had entered; Persin told them they had done nothing to Thieriat, and was very angry about this.[19]

19. ADMM, B8684 no. 2.

These confessions were duly read out in public after Marion's conviction. While it is recorded that she was confronted with Barbeline, no transcript of this encounter survives. Demenge Thieriat repeated his testimony virtually word-for-word once the second suspect was on trial. Since damage affects a different section of the document, it becomes clear that only days before the attack at night he had evicted Barbeline Mareschal from a house she rented from him. In due course Barbeline made a confession which is almost indistinguishable from Marion's. The only small differences are that she said it was Persin who gave them the grain of wheat, which he had already poisoned, while she makes no mention of the clothes being brought into the chamber by their master. The judges, who had accepted Marion's story without any apparent demur, now expressed unexpected skepticism, asking:

> if it was not in dreams or illusions that she had thus entered the said bedchamber in the guise of a cat, or if she had done so really and in truth, because we cannot possibly believe that the devil has this power, to be capable of transforming a human body into the form or guise of a smaller animal like a cat, nor that she could have passed through a small window which she could not possibly have got through being in her true nature as she is presently.
>
> She replied it was the truth that she had entered the bedchamber in the form of a cat as she had told us, after being greased by the said Persin, but she could not give us any further explanation of how that could have happened.

In this imaginative tale the shapeshifting element was wholly supplied by the accused, after the witness had told of an attack by women, whose only unnatural feat had been to disappear from a closed room. It is clear that Barbeline simply took over Marion's story, which she had at least two opportunities to hear. If she forgot the detail about Persin ensuring they could resume their clothes in the bedchamber and attributed the poisoned grain to him, these were hardly the kind of details to which the court paid attention. Why the general issue of transformation into a small animal was only raised the second time around remains puzzling, but given the presumptions of the whole account the most implausible claim is perhaps that the whole elaborate process of stripping and greasing necessary to become cats a second time could have been completed while Thieriat's wife was fetching a light. No doubt Persin was supposed to be devilishly quick with his hands—or claws.[20]

20. ADMM, B8684 no. 5.

Within little more than a year, in May 1601, there was a remarkably similar case only a few miles away, involving two suspects from La Rochatte, a suburb of Saint Dié. There must be some likelihood that news of the trials at Etival had spread at least this far. Jacotte Simon deposed against Mengeatte Lienard, then three weeks later against Penthecoste Miette. After telling a story about remarks by Mengeatte, which suggested that she knew more than she should about what happened at the sabbat, Jacotte said that during a long illness some eighteen months earlier two cats came into her room before dawn and tried to strangle her, but were driven off when her husband came in. One had been changed into a woman she recognized, but the other remained a cat. Since she had often quarreled with the accused she suspected that Mengeatte had been this second cat. During her confessions Mengeatte told the story of how she and her accomplice, Penthecoste, had been angry with Jacotte, who was always calling them witches, and wanted to try to strangle Jacotte or to cause her some other great harm. Persin sent an unnamed devil to assist them, who gave them gray cat skins, but they found they had no power over the victim who must have protected herself well with the sign of the cross. When Jacotte's husband came with an ax they fled. Since Jacotte had also accused Penthecoste of being at the sabbat with her, the two women were confronted when the cat story was one of those told. Jacotte recited her tale again in her evidence, with a few additional details, describing how during the previous Lent her husband had got up before dawn to practice his trade as an oil-maker, and when alone in bed she felt something press down on her so that she could not even move her arms to make the sign of the cross. She recommended herself to God and made the sign of the cross with her tongue, calling to her husband for help. Jacotte then managed to lift her head a little and saw the accused at the foot of her bed, but there was no reply when Jacotte spoke to her. Jacotte's husband then came in with a light and saw two "marvelously big and hideous" cats, the one black and the other gray, which left the room with a great noise. Penthecoste duly confessed to this joint attack, explaining that Persin put a cat-skin over each of their heads as they returned from the *veillée* to disguise them.[21]

A quite different story was told by another witness, Loudevic Thoussainct, who said that two years earlier Penthecoste's husband had been breaking stones on the mountainside for the *receveur* and the *prévôt*, but Loudevic offered a better price and was given a contract for six hundred cartloads. Penthecoste was

---

21. ADMM, B8687 nos. 4 and 6.

angry and said "may he be unlucky with his dealings, and may he break his neck while breaking his stones, because without him her husband would have made a nice amount of money." A few days later when Loudevic was working on the mountain a great hideous cat went to eat his bread, and when he threw his hammer at it the cat jumped at his throat. He made the sign of the cross, took an ax, and said, "ho, wicked witch, you have not got me yet," at which the cat jumped back twenty feet and disappeared. As Loudevic was looking where it had gone a great stone came rushing down the valley, and he only just escaped it, but fell over and hurt his leg. Since that time he believed that Penthecoste had been trying to kill him by witchcraft. Nothing was said about this dramatic episode in the confessions.

Jennon Zabey of Leintrey was another witch about whom a vivid cat story was told, who steadfastly denied everything even under torture and was released in 1608. Mesenne Vannier had claimed that six years earlier, on her way to harvesting, she had heard Jennon talking behind a hedge, after which Mesenne was surrounded by a whirlwind and became ill for three weeks. At about ten on a clear morning, as she lay in bed, three cats appeared and talked, their voices identifying them as Jennon, the widow of Rudepoil, and the wife of Claudon Marchal. They discussed whether they should cause Mesenne's death; finally they said no, because she was young and recently married (she would have been about nineteen at the time).[22] In this case Mesenne may have been experiencing some kind of hallucination while in a fever, but she may also have been giving expression to her feelings that she was too young to die, attaching these feelings to some well-known local suspects.

There are several other cases of individual's being terrified by strange hostile presences when in bed, without any suggestion that these took animal form. These cases too were prominent in the group of trials which took place at Etival in 1611. Marguitte Laurent of Brehimont was accused of carrying out such attacks by the brothers Demengeon and Colas Girard; the latter told a particularly elaborate story. Eight years earlier Colas had been involved in a court case with Marguitte and her husband after allegedly calling them witches. The Girards had been angry when they failed to prove their case and had to pay costs. During this case Colas's teenage son called out to him one night that there was someone on his bed who was trying to suffocate him, and had put a thumb in his mouth so he could neither speak nor breathe. Then the same thing happened to three of his daughters, before finally Colas himself

22. ADMM, B3335 no. 1.

"felt two persons climb on his bed, who seized him by the throat and tried to strangle him, but he had just enough strength to cry for help, at which his servants rushed in with a candle. There was nothing to be seen, save that the bed he had been sleeping in looked as if a dozen people had been disturbing it." He naturally attributed this to witchcraft by Marguitte; in her confession she claimed it had been the work of her master, Jolybois, with her consent, but he had been unable to harm the intended victims because they had recommended themselves to God and made the sign of the cross.[23]

A suspect from the same group, Jennon Ydoulx of Nompatelize, attracted similar stories. Jean Regnauldin had earned her enmity by deposing against Jennon on a previous occasion, so she uttered threats against him, wishing that he might have the bar of a door across his stomach. That night,

> something like a person climbed on his bed and grasped him by the throat with such force and violence that he thought he was about to be strangled, then was held in that state for a good time unable to move or defend himself; finally having taken courage and recommended himself to God he used his two arms to throw off the thing which was holding him by force to the end of the bed, where it struck an adjoining chest with a great blow. At the same moment he heard his cock and hens start to make a noise as if the creature was trying to strangle them.

Jean predictably claimed that this was Jennon with the assistance of her master, as she subsequently admitted to have been the case.[24]

The experience of being attacked in one's own bed was obviously a particularly threatening one, with its implication that not even shutters and locked doors offered any security. The modern explanation would be sleep paralysis, a state which affects many people at least intermittently, and which seems to involve some disconnection between brain and body when on the fringe of sleep. The sense of an evil presence, coupled with an inability to move, is then liable to be explained by the most plausible elements in the local cultural repertoire. There may well have been some overlap with the dream-like experiences that made a significant contribution to the confessions of the witches themselves, notably in their accounts of the sabbat. There was a local belief in a spirit called a "Sottrel," which made unwelcome visits at night. Sottrel appeared in the 1600 trial of Dieudonnée Henry of La Croix. She claimed

23. ADMM, B8708 no. 3.
24. ADMM, B8707 no. 8.

that while she had been in prison a woman in white had appeared to her and told her she would soon leave this place and see her children. Dieudonnée had also seen small angels flying around her. When asked if she had been visited by other spirits, Dieudonnée said that twenty years earlier when she was in service *le sottrel* had visited her; it was very heavy and lay on her so that she could hardly breathe. The creature had sometimes visited her when her husband was away, and again when she was in prison. She denied the suggestion that it had intercourse with her, since such spirits were well known to seek this, but admitted it had sometimes kissed her.[25]

Judges were generally quick to convert any visitations by supposed guardian angels or other spirits into something much less attractive. In 1592 Laurence Tolbay of Sainte Marguerite rashly mentioned an encounter with a good angel, who had told her that if she would believe in him he would not abandon her, then was subjected to remorseless questioning on the subject by the judges. She said that the angel was dressed like a woman, was about four feet tall, and spoke honestly in a clear voice, promising to give her bread when she was in need. The judges replied that this must have been an evil spirit, to which Laurence responded she was sure it had been good, and if not an angel, it had been the soul of her father or another dead man come to comfort her. She also rejected the idea that the spirit had given her some powder, only to concede when threatened with torture that she had received some black powder. Her first account was that the angel had given no explanation for the powder, which she threw away; then she rather pathetically said it was to make soup for poor people, before finally admitting on the rack that her encounter had been with Persin.[26]

Laurence identified Jehenne Stablo of Haillieule as one of her accomplices. During Jehenne's first interrogation in 1592 she was asked if she had met any spirit, presumably because she had already made some admissions about this. She told a story about going to a local shrine to make an offering for her sick husband, where she met a big man all in white, who she thought was God. He had a shining face and asked her how she lived in her household. Jehenne then described another meeting with the apparition she called her "good angel," whom she told that she was praying for the recovery of her sick animals, at which he commended her devotion and vanished. She too was finally induced to agree that it had been Persin, although even then she made

---

25. ADMM, B8684 no. 10.
26. ADMM, B8667 no. 9.

the curious claim that she had tried the powder herself in a soup, but it had done nothing so she threw it away.[27]

Another accused who had a supernatural encounter was Dieudonné Jean Thierion of Brehimont, tried in 1614. One witness, Demenge Gerard, said that some three months after the execution of Dieudonné's father (convicted as a witch in 1600), Gerard had invited Dieudonné to thresh in his barn. On this occasion Dieudonné had told the witness a story about knockings on his door in the night, which made him seek advice from the abbot of Etival; afterwards, when he opened the door he found it was his dead father. Dieudonné said that the apparition had been in the garden around twilight. His father told Dieudonné he was in pain because he had moved a fence between his garden and that of Jean Claudon Thirion to get possession of a pear tree, then asked him to replace it so that "he would make him his bed in Paradise" before disappearing.[28] This was of course a classic ghost story, with the unquiet spirit unable to rest until a wrong done in its lifetime was put right by its descendants.

When suspicious animals appeared, people who thought they were hostile might behave like Loudevic Toussainct and adopt an aggressive stance. In the 1611 case of Esnel Bourrotte of l'Hoste du Bois one witness, Claudatte Mareschal, said that seven or eight years earlier her sister, Alizon, had quarreled with Esnel and called her a witch. As the sisters went home they were followed by a large cat which, they told one another, must be the accused. Finally Alizon said to the cat, "Old witch, what are you doing here; you have come to hear and spy on what we are saying; my father will have you burned next week." At this the cat vanished, but Alizon then had a long illness, which they thought Esnel had given her while in the form of the cat. In her confessions Esnel said it had been Persin who scared the girls in this way; she used the same explanation for a charge about three wolves which had carried off some pigs in the woods.[29]

When Nicolas Adam of Dompierre was on trial in 1620, Bastien Hanna alleged that the previous summer he had seen Nicolas (from whom he had been trying to collect a debt) and another man in the fields, then found a hare running near his cart. This made him think that Nicolas might have transformed himself into the hare, so that the creature had appeared either to arrange or to foretell some harm. He then called out to the hare, "Nicolas Adam, I know you

27. ADMM, B8667 no. 1.
28. ADMM, B8712 no. 5.
29. ADMM, B8707 no. 9.

well; if any misfortune comes to me or to my horses I will make it known and accuse you as soon as I am back home." The fact that the startled animal promptly disappeared was reported as if it might be significant.[30]

François Lhermite of Saint Dié, tried in 1630, confessed to a strange encounter on his way to the woods, when "he met a black bear, which told him he should always be a good man, and that he should never do any harm," then rather puzzlingly said this was the only time he had been tempted.[31] In 1601 Jannon Pierat had allegedly talked of seeing a great black beast when on a pilgrimage, which she explained by saying that she had been taking two cheeses to someone through the woods when she saw the animal, which she thought was a bear, sometimes in the water and sometimes on land. She had crossed herself, and the animal did her no harm; she did not speak to it, and when on her return she told her neighbor Jean George about it he started laughing and said it was the bear.[32]

There were various other stories about animals who were marked by some oddity. In 1610 Chrestien Brabant told of a strange episode the previous year when Franceatte Charier of la Neuveville les Raon knocked on Chrestien's door at night, accompanied by what he thought was a black pig, which turned out to be a white one when Chrestien got close; then it ran off. In Franceatte's confessions she said that Chrestien's wife had told her there would be work for her that day, but he turned her away. Later Franceatte went to his door with her master in the form of a black pig, with the intention that he should do harm to Chrestien's animals, especially the pigs, but she became frightened "that she would be discovered and they would accuse her of this," so she told her master to leave, at which he gave a jump and vanished.[33] Another pig appeared in testimony against Catherine la Rondelatte of Essegney in 1607–1608, when Jannon Adam told of the death seven years earlier of Isabel Famel, an orphan lodging in their house. Isabel had bought a chest from Catherine, but it had not been satisfactory, and Isabel had not paid while waiting either to return it or to negotiate a reduction in the price. Isabel had been apprehensive about what might happen as a result, and one evening saw a strange black pig rolling on the ice of a stream, at which she was so frightened that she lost her wits and could not even receive the sacraments before her death.[34]

30. ADMM, B3804 no. 1.
31. ADVosges, G710.
32. ADMM, B3755.
33. ADMM, B8704 no. 1.
34. ADMM, B4094 no. 1.

In the 1612 case of Claudon Bregeat of Sallonnes, the witness Jennotte Rodeans told a story about a dispute over an apprenticeship for Claudon's son. After the dispute a mysterious woman kept appearing in Jennotte's husband's workshop; no one could catch her, then the husband fell ill. The suspect seemed to have cured him; then they had another dispute. Shortly after this Jennotte's husband was on his way to the church in the early morning when he was attacked by a wolf, which threw him to the ground. Two days later they saw a strange black animal in their garden, which could not be driven away when they threw stones at it, and when her husband went out that evening to his vines he became ill, with his legs so weak that Jennotte had to help him home with a stick. He then took to his bed and died, saying that Claudon was the cause of his illness.[35]

Fleuratte Maurice of Docelles said during her first interrogation in 1615 that a year before, as she was on her way to the woods early in the morning, a strange animal like a hare had crossed her path. During a repeat performance it spoke to her and asked her if she wanted to believe in it. A month before her arrest it had reappeared in her stable, this time looking like a black cat so far as she could see in the dark. She said, "You come back too often, wicked beast," to which he replied by asking why he should not come, and she told him "to be off and never return." Those present assumed she was speaking of Satan, and when she was asked if the animal spoke with a broad accent, she said it was broad enough.[36]

Such stories certainly resemble the English pattern of Satan as the animal familiar, although few as closely as that of Jean Lallemant of Saint Lienard, who was tried twice, in 1590, then in 1600. On the first occasion the witnesses seem to have been questioned in accord with charges prepared by a neighbor who had brought the case, which would explain why witness Jean Voignier was asked if he had seen Lallemant with a number of toads in a room, which he fed and whistled to, a suggestion he rejected. Ten years later there was a similar claim that one of his servants had talked about toads around their fire. Lallemant prevented the servant from killing the toads, saying "it was these which kept him fed." This time Lallemant confessed, saying that his master had told him to keep them. He had kept two under his bed for a year, feeding them until they became very big; then Persin took them. Lallemant was sure this was to commit some major crime, and later Persin brought him some

---

35. ADMM, B2192 no. 2.
36. ADMM, B3789 no. 1.

grease he said came from them, telling Lallemant to use it to kill a person he hated—but he did not want to, so he threw it away in the fields.[37]

Incriminating stories also came from children, as in the 1620 case against Margueritte le Charpentier of la Bourgonce, whose son, Cesar, had allegedly claimed that a black dog carried them up their chimney and to a fine room where they ate as much meat as they wanted. Cesar had also prevented other children at school from catching a bird which came to the window, saying it was his master and that of his mother. On his way back from school Cesar told two other children that he and his mother ate from the same plate with a little black dog, which then took them to a place where they danced and "performed marvels." Cesar said the dog went so fast they would have gone through a person without being noticed. Cesar threatened other children either with giving them some powder or getting his black dog to bite them. There were more stories in the same vein, and although Margueritte tried to blame the other children for making Cesar talk in this way, she soon gave way when told of confessions he had made directly; simply she tried to insist that she had prevented her son from entering her master's service.[38]

A second child who helped bring about his mother's conviction was Jean Colombain of l'Estraye in 1624. Another boy told of a quarrel with Jean when they were guarding some animals a month earlier. Jean threatened to kill the boy and make his teeth fall out. A year earlier Jean had told him and other boys "that he went to the sabbat with his mother, and that his father went to fetch money among some rocks in a meadow called Menaprey, riding a little black horse, which had big ears, no hair, and which it was hard to stay on, adding that his mother said he must tell no one about this." On another occasion when they were with the animals, Jean became angry with the boys and said, "Tantedient, my father, will soon have some of your animals." A big wolf then appeared and carried off a goat, while Jean's father was working nearby at the time.[39]

Children's capacity to fantasize and use such material in highly unwise ways is also evident in some of the most elaborate Lorraine accounts of the sabbat and in stories about various other forms of magical activity. In truth the number of cases of this type seems rather low, so it may well be that most people had a shrewd sense of the dangers and only took such evidence seriously when there was strong corroboration from other sources.

37. ADVosges, G707 no. 1, and ADMM, B8684 no. 7.
38. ADMM, B8726 no. 1.
39. ADMM, B2583 no. 4.

What can we conclude about this rich yet often baffling set of stories? Do they suggest that the people of Lorraine inhabited a terrifying superenchanted world, full of mysterious beings which constantly threatened their well-being? That would surely be going too far, because these testimonies are fairly thinly scattered amongst a vast body of material. On the other hand, the way they were accepted by all parties, including the judges, makes it clear that the existence of diabolical and magical powers was commonplace. This is borne out by the sections in Nicolas Rémy's *Demonolatry* where such matters are discussed, usually with examples from the trials he drew on (for which the manuscript evidence has not survived). He referred to apparitions of the devil, witches in prison, demons which took animal form, and witches who entered houses as cats, mice, or even locusts. Where he became less certain was in a long and confused chapter on these transformations, notably into wolves; where he started by suggesting these must be diabolical illusions, then seemed to say that the devil's preternatural powers stretched even to turning humans into animals.[40] This was going some way beyond the standard view, but many of the accounts in the trials evaded this difficulty by making the devil commit such actions on behalf of his minions or indeed, had him using threats or violence to extract their reluctant consent. These responses implied that the devil could only operate with their assistance, raising yet another problem to which there was no truly satisfying logical answer. This may be one of the more general lessons historians should learn, because there is no good reason to expect a high level of logic or consistency from belief systems. Sixteenth-century villagers did not normally go round in a state of superstitious terror, because their natural inclination was to view their environment in a thoroughly commonsensical way. That attitude coexisted with a substratum of beliefs about magic and diabolism, which could readily surface in the right circumstances to become the common stuff of tales about witchcraft. It must be admitted that these fantasies were curiously stereotyped and culturally bounded—which is indeed in line with the experience of modern professionals dealing with similar phenomena. As a language or code for describing human relations, witchcraft created even its most dangerous spirits from a small range of stock characteristics; the reader of these accounts is often fascinated yet rarely surprised. That predictability was stressed by both believers and skeptics among the elites to produce diametrically opposed conclusions. For the first

---

40. Nicolas Rémy, *Demonolatry,* trans. E. Allen Ashwin, ed. Montague Summers (1930; repr. London: Frederic Muller, 1970), 27–28, 69–72, 104, 108–14.

group it was powerful confirmatory evidence; for the second it demonstrated the feebleness and circularity of the whole style of reasoning involved.

For those firmly committed to the view that witchcraft should be located in the mind, these fantasies offer a rather different opportunity to investigate their psychological content. This investigation reveals a remarkable overlap between the categories of witchcraft belief and those of psychoanalysis, one which does not merely add new layers of meaning, but helps to explain why the dichotomy between the everyday and the diabolical worlds proved both so potent and so convincing. Essentially these are aspects of the contrast between the object-related and the narcissistic universes. The object-related world may be (rather crudely) characterized as that built up through developing human relationships from babyhood onward; it involves a healthy progressive separation from parents, coupled with respect for the value systems associated with them, and an acceptance of outside reality. What people also carry with them, though rarely to a crippling degree, is a narcissistic and magical world of the imagination, one of utter solitude and total belief in the power of one's own wishes. In its most destructive forms this is a place of loneliness and hatred, with a perverse fascination for bodily functions, one in which relationships are based on control instead of love. Narcissism seeks to secure invulnerability yet leads those with personality disorders of this type into doing things despite themselves. To behave in this way is very like making a compact with the devil, because it implies gaining doubtful benefits at great cost while seeking power because that is all one feels able to control. Fantasies rooted in this perverse world also invariably contain a gang leader, whose despotic behavior is thoroughly satanic. Although most people have little or no memory of the childhood states in which such fantasies were accessible to their conscious minds, there is still a hidden stratum which may break through at times when they are frightened or confronted with material related to the unconscious.

Numerous aspects of the stories and confessions related above can be interpreted in these terms. The sexual implications of cats slipping into bedchambers are manifest at several levels, for example. They invoke childhood fantasies about parental relationships, which may be positive, but frequently involve fighting and killing, the kind of diabolical universe in which both parents and cats do terrible things at night. The routine equation between the house and the body makes entry through a small window an act of penetration in the sexual sense, while being stripped and greased by the devil has clear overtones of masturbation and perversity. The way the power attributed to witches and their master blurs boundaries can be seen in Barbeline Mareschal's reply to the judges, when she said she could not explain how she had been transformed; how indeed could she account for crossing the boundaries between two different kinds of reality, outer and inner? The symbolic association between the wolf and predatory sexuality runs through much of European folklore, one of the most explicit cases where animality carries a special charge of the forbidden and libidinal. Less obvious is the way biting is a standard expression of power for the narcissistic personality so can be represented by a range of carnivores. The toads, brown and slimy, can be equated with excreta as poison. They also have their keeper nursing evil, encouraging it to grow, keeping it hidden under the bed, then finally using it—this amounts to a stereotypical infantile fantasy. The sad story of Laurence Tolbay (whose early replies demonstrated a solid grasp on the object-related world) shows how a suspect could be bullied into making a transfer from one realm of fantasy to another, for her angel was patently a good object, even possibly linked to her parents, which she was ultimately forced to call diabolical. The children's stories emphasize their capacity to surround bodily-based fantasies with rich narrative detail, in a manner impossible to normal adults. Jean Colombain's tales about his father's riding a diabolical horse to visit a hoard of treasure evoke the type of antiparent which narcissistic states create in the mind, wholly understandable in this eleven-year-old boy isolated from his peers and his family by a speech impediment.

These readings are highly relevant to our understanding of both witchcraft beliefs and the actual process of the trials, because they help explain how such apparently fantastic tales could provide powerful reinforcement for their underlying structures. The parallel between the diabolical antiworld and the narcissistic one is exceptionally strong, leading to the conclusion that they are in fact versions of the same thing, rooted in the same psychological materials. There was no need for shapeshifting to appear in any individual trial; what would be astonishing, in light of what has been said, would be to find it absent from any local body of witchcraft beliefs, when it has such close associations with the underlying theory and is effectively identical with much of the imagery of diabolism. Shapeshifting is indeed found across Europe, in many local variants, to confirm this link. The witchcraft suspects and their judges shared a substratum of infantile fantasy; this was particularly dangerous because it was buried in the unconscious yet could be activated when real-life issues were swamped with unconscious primitive process. This did not have to be anything as exotic as shapeshifting, because the central element in virtually all trials is the association between ill will and actual harm, itself one of the classic narcissistic delusions. When they responded to the promptings of their judges the witches were in a state of extreme isolation and distress, precisely the condition which drives individuals into the omnipotent retreat of narcissism and sadomasochism, so the presence of infantile material in their confessions was almost overdetermined. Judges and other observers, committed as they were to a vision of the world as polarized between good and evil, instinctively recognized these admissions as emanating from the dark side they had repressed. This was the most insidious and dangerous aspect of the superenchanted world, terrible proof that fantasy can be a truly potent force advancing the evil it might be supposed merely to symbolize.

L IVING WITH THE DEAD

Ghosts in Early Modern Bavaria

David Lederer

I do not wish to offend you, Mr. Eder, but for your information please, there are often ghosts in noble families, but there are never Kobolds; Kobolds are not appropriate to aristocratic traditions.
Ellis Kaut, *Meister Eder und sein Pumuckl:*
Das Schlossgespenst

A re there any such things as ghosts? The answer is a qualified yes; in fact several presently cohabit in my office. The *New Webster Dictionary of the English Language* verifies their existence in many different forms as:

> the soul or spirit of a dead person; a disembodied spirit, esp. one imagined to haunt the living; a specter or apparition; a mere shadow or semblance, as, the *ghost* of a chance; a spiritual being; *TV,* a duplicate image, usu. faint and slightly displaced from the main image, due to wave reflection; opt. a bright spot or secondary image, as from a defect in lenses.

Rhetorically speaking then, the important question is how one defines ghosts instead of whether they "truly" exist. *Encyclopedia Britannica* on CD-ROM (2000) poses the issue as one of dualistic beliefs: "Belief in ghosts is based on the ancient notion that a human spirit is separable from the body...," with links to spirit possession and, indirectly, to exorcism. The ethnologically sensitive *Encyclopedia of Religion,* edited by Mircea Eliade, substantiates apparitions of a nearly ubiquitous and timeless variety, making *ghost* close to an anthropological constant. The present examination likewise assumes a philosophy of ghosts less ontological than epistemological. Moreover, the sure knowledge that Webster's and Britannica's ghosts keep abreast of the latest developments in telecommunications (now haunting us through our television screens and computer monitors) obviates a need to locate them in a specific place at a specific time.

The venerable *Oxford English Dictionary* introduces us to the etymological evolution of the refined English *ghost* from its Germanic ancestors, who were simply instruments of blind terror and rage.[1] If that makes Samuel Johnson's eighteenth-century *Dictionary* redundant, then perhaps J. Andreas Schmeller's *Bavarian Dictionary* is more relevant to our present inquiry. His nineteenth-century etymology cites examples from early modern Bavarian texts to suggest a notable relationship between ghosts *(Gespenster)* and the devil, a definition that will come back to haunt us.[2] As we shall see, other Bavarian folklorists and antiquaries, motivated primarily by local and regional interests, were keen to record ghost stories and legends as quaint examples of folk beliefs. Many towns and villages in the region boast a haunted castle, an abandoned chapel, or buried treasure, as seen in the popular collections of legends by Alexander Schöppner, Willibald Schmidt, and Franz Maria Ferchl (the influential cofounder of the Historical Society of Upper Bavaria).[3] Similar collections supply tourists with countless tales to titillate their morbid curiosity at the expense of their childlike ancestors. No matter which reference work one consults, one thing is clear; ghosts mean different things to different people at different times, and historians can derive great solace from the hermeneutics of the problem.

A rhetorical digression alone does not necessarily qualify ghosts as objects for historical study. Ghosts were a deadly serious matter in early modern Europe, integral to supernatural beliefs and, therefore, a fundamental component of a rational cosmology. The example of ghosts in early modern Bavaria indicates just how dangerously politicized the supernatural had become in the sixteenth and seventeenth centuries. Concourse with ghosts and spirits literally cost many their lives. That danger intensified when supernatural beliefs coupled with so-called modernizing tendencies: in classic Weberian terms, the spread of reason of state, the rise of nascent territorial states, the tensions of

---

1. *Oxford English Dictionary,* s.v. Ghost…Common WGer.: OE. *gást* (also *gǽst*) str. masc. = OFris. *gást,* OS. *gêst* (Du. *geest*), OHG. (MHG., mod.Ger.) *geist:* OTeut. type **gaisto-z.* Although the word is known only in the WGer. langs. (in all of which it is found with substantially identical meaning), it appears to be of pre-Teut. formation. The sense of the pre-Teut. **ghoizdo-z,* if the ordinary view of its etymological relations be correct, should be "fury, anger"....

2. *Bayerisches Wörterbuch* (1872–77; facs.1985), s.v. Gespenster.

3. Franz Maria Ferchl, *Fuß-Reisen durch Oberbayern: Ohne Ausschließung der übrigen bayer'schen Länder* (Munich, 1843); *Sagenbuch der Bayerischen Lande: Aus dem Munde des Volkes, der Chronik und der Dichter,* ed. Alexander Schöppner (Munich, 1866); Willibald Schmidt, *Sagen aus dem Isarwinkel* (Bad Tölz, 1936).

confessionalization, and the introduction of uniform and efficient bureaucratic and judicial procedures. Analogous research on early modern Spain has been very successful in revealing the functional aspects of social behavior generally derided as irrational superstition since the Enlightenment.[4] Microhistories like Richard Kagan's thoughtful analysis of Lucrecia de León's dreams about Philip II are especially compelling, since they drive home the political potential available to even the most common individual through supernatural channels of empowerment.[5] The suggestion that these "birth pangs of the modern world"[6] resulted from a clash of two irreconcilable belief systems— one atavistic and communal, the other a product of a modern world system— misses the point. In fact, quite the contrary is the case. Traditional and novel attitudes mixed all too easily, concocting a heady cocktail of fear and repression and facilitated the worst stupor of witchcraft hysteria in European history. Wolfgang Behringer has masterfully charted the contemporaneous interplay of religious zealotry, reason of state, and popular magic in a regional study of witchcraft persecutions. He offers a blow-by-blow commentary on witch beliefs and court factionalism in seventeenth-century Bavaria.[7]

In Bavaria, attempts to eliminate superstition and limit charismatic freedom played themselves out in a triangular relationship between the representatives of institutional religion, representatives of central authority, and local communities, with individual interlocutors assuming a pivotal negotiatory role. The tensile stress on that relationship (often simplified as a bipolar struggle between popular and elite or official and unofficial cultures) is a recurring theme among historians. Much ink has been spilled over the superimposition of artificial dichotomies, and the history of ghosts in early modern Bavaria demonstrates just how difficult the boundaries of popular culture are to define. If we think of popular culture as the banality of shared symbols easily recognizable to all members of a particular group,[8] then the ghost was as much

4. William A. Christian, *Local Religion in Sixteenth-Century Spain* (Princeton: Princeton University Press, 1981); and idem, *Apparitions in Late Medieval and Renaissance Spain* (Princeton: Princeton University Press, 1981). These twin studies provided a major impetus to study the functional implications of so-called irrational modes of behavior.

5. Richard L. Kagan, *Lucrecia's Dreams: Politics and Prophecy in Sixteenth-Century Spain* (Berkeley: University of California Press, 1990).

6. Brian P. Levack, *The Witch-Hunt in Early Modern Europe* (London: Longman, 1987), 140.

7. Wolfgang Behringer, *Witchcraft Persecutions in Bavaria: Popular Magic, Religious Zealotry, and Reason of State in Early Modern Europe*, trans. J. C. Grayson and David Lederer (New York: Cambridge University Press, 1997), esp. 212–310.

8. Clearly it is not necessary to take this conceptualization to its logical extreme as suggested by Peter Burke, *Popular Culture in Early Modern Europe* (London: T. Smith, 1978), 23.

a part of pop culture in early modern Bavaria as Andy Warhol's *Campbell's Soup Can* was in America only a few decades ago. Nearly everyone in early modern Bavaria shared common beliefs about ghosts, even if there is also evidence of mounting social polarization between popular tradition and elite innovation, a cleft which increased slowly but surely over the ensuing centuries. Therefore, it is important to contextualize evidence since it is often ambivalent and, at times, seemingly contradictory.[9]

For example, medieval theologians since Aquinas systematically treated superstitions with cautious respect, because diabolical magic was considered efficacious and harmful, and it implied apostasy.[10] In 1585/86, the papal bull *Coeli et Terrae* condemned all forms of incantations and superstitious ceremonies, such as the practice of necromancy (that is, divination through congress with dead spirits) and treasure finding, as covenants with the "Father of Lies."[11] As subjects of the empire's staunchest Catholic territory, ordinary Bavarians were heavily subjected to orthodox teachings on spirits in the wake of the Tridentine reforms. The Catholic Church had an even longer doctrinal tradition concerning the supernatural, and recent Evangelical and Reformed opinion deviated from that tradition in subtle but important ways.[12] Nonetheless, Catholic demonological theory continued to evolve and change after the Reformation, achieving a novel level of complexity in the late sixteenth century as theologians worked feverishly to standardize doctrine. This is especially true of the militant Jesuits, who closely associated themselves with the archangel Michael, that warrior leader of the heavenly host in the fight against Satan.[13] While Protestants generally categorized all spirits as evil, Catholic

9. This important point is also made by Nancy Caciola, "Spirits Seeking Bodies: Death, Possession and Communal Memory in the Middle Ages," in *The Place of the Dead: Death and Remembrance in Late Medieval and Early Modern Europe,* ed. Bruce Gordon and Peter Marshall (New York: Cambridge University Press, 2000), 68.

10. Mary R. O'Neill, "Superstition," in *Encyclopedia of Religion,* ed. Mircea Eliade and Charles J. Adams (New York: Macmillan, 1933, 1987), 14:163–66.

11. Part of the text of the bull is translated in P. G. Maxwell-Stuart, ed. and trans., *The Occult in Early Modern Europe: A Documentary History* (London: Macmillan, 1999), 59–60; for a synoptic table of papal legislation against superstition and the occult, see Emile Brouette, "The Sixteenth Century and Satanism," in *Satan,* ed. Bruno de Jésus Marie, trans. Malachy Carroll (London: Sheed & Ward, 1951), 310–48, esp. 346–47.

12. On changes after the Reformation in England, see Keith Thomas, *Religion and the Decline of Magic: Studies in Popular Beliefs in Sixteenth and Seventeenth Century England* (New York: Oxford University Press, 1971), 587–614.

13. See the magnificent synthesis of Stuart Clark, *Thinking with Demons: The Idea of Witchcraft in Early Modern Europe* (New York: Oxford University Press, 1997); a good synopsis is available in *A*

demonologists like the jurist Martin Del Rio differentiated between good and evil spirits.[14] Accordingly, Del Rio condemned the veneration of evil spirits as vile superstition according to one contemporary definition (that is, dangerous and efficacious magic).[15]

The Rhineland Jesuit Peter Thyraeus agreed, adding that there were three specific types of evil spirits troublesome to the living. The first were incorporeal manifestations of the devil.[16] The other two types were of human origin (that is, ghosts), generally the souls of persons condemned to hell or temporarily consigned to purgatory—unbaptized infants, for example. Theological opinion about ghosts reached the masses through the printed word, preaching, and witnessing during the wave of spectacular exorcisms that overtook Europe at the end of the sixteenth century.[17] In Bavaria, this process went hand in hand with the Tridentine confessionalization of the duchy, largely supervised by the secular authorities in collaboration with the Society of Jesus.[18] New

---

History of Magic and Experimental Science, 8 vols., ed. Lynn Thorndike (New York: Columbia Unversity Press, 1941), 556–59. The Jesuits in Munich founded Saint Michael's college and church in Munich, completed in 1597. In a sacred geography of the duchy by a Tirolian Jesuit, Mattheus Rader, *Bavaria Sancta et Pia* (1628), supplementary volume to *Bavaria Sancta*, 3 vols. (Munich, 1615–27), the title page depicts Saint Michael offering up the Duchy of Bavaria to the Virgin Mary. Andrea Pozzo, S.J., architect of the Jesuit church (later elevated to university chapel) in Vienna, had the fall of Lucifer at the hands of Saint Michael depicted in a prominent ceiling fresco to commemorate Catholic victories over Protestants at the Battle of White Mountain and the Turks at the gates of Vienna—as well as the ideological victory of the Jesuits over the other faculties at the university.

14. Martin Del Rio, *Disquisitiones Magicarum Libri Sex* (Antwerp, 1599–1600), bk. 4, chap. 3, Q. 6. Recently translated by P. G. Maxwell-Stuart, *Martin Del Rio: Investigations into Magic* (Manchester: Manchester University Press, 2000). Since St. Augustine, Catholic theologians discouraged popular beliefs in ghostly apparitions outside of dreams. Nevertheless, Catholic doctrine remains ambivalent, and the widespread medieval belief in the return of souls from purgatory as ghosts was difficult to discourage and, at times, even promoted by the clergy: see Jean-Claude Schmitt, *Ghosts in the Middle Ages: The Living and the Dead in Medieval Society,* trans. Teresa Lavender Fagan (Chicago: University of Chicago Press, 1998), esp. 11–34.

15. Del Rio, *Disquisitiones Magicarum Libri Sex*, bk. 6, chap. 1, Q. 2.

16. Peter Thyraeus, *Loca infesta: hoc est, De infestis, ob molestantes daemoniorvm et defvnctorvm hominvm spiritvs, locis, liber vnvs ...* (Cologne, 1598), 16; on spirits from purgatory, see 19.

17. On the rising numbers of exorcisms at this time, see H. C. Erik Midelfort, *A History of Madness in Sixteenth-Century Germany* (Stanford: Stanford University Press, 1999), esp. 49–78; David Lederer, *A Bavarian Beacon: Spiritual Physic and the Birth of the Asylum* (forthcoming).

18. For a good overview of the confessionalization of Bavaria, see Walter Ziegler, "Bayern," in *Die Territorien des Reichs im Zeitalter der Reformation und Konfessionalisierung: Land und Konfession, 1500–1650. 1. Der Südosten*, ed. Anton Schindling and Walter Ziegler (Münster: Aschendorff, 1989), 56–71.

doctrines condemned lingering popular beliefs, not as irrational and useless nonsense, but as dangerous malevolence which, if left unchecked, held grave consequences for the entire commonwealth. Therefore, the campaign against superstition tacitly admitted the real power of many undesirable but widely held beliefs.

As anthropologists know, ghosts are stock expressions of preternatural beliefs with their roots in social mores. Until quite recently, however, early modern historians have been cautious about forays into the realm of the dead and dealings with ghosts. French medievalists assumed an early lead in the field.[19] In 1986, Claude Lecouteux, a Germanist, produced a seminal history of ghosts from 500 to 1500.[20] Although biased toward literary sources, his was much more than a folkloric collection of sagas and legends. By assuming a decidedly diachronic method, Lecouteux remained focused on cultural change. He showed how changing relations in society, the family, religion, and the cult of the dead all affected and were affected by perceptions of ghosts. Jean-Claude Schmitt (whose reputation for historical and archeological spadework was secured by *The Holy Greyhound*) has taken another historical journey into the afterlife in his recent study of medieval ghosts. His "social history of the imaginary" employs literary criticism and structural anthropology to stress the very real social implications of fantastic belief structures.[21] Based largely upon the structural analysis of texts, Schmitt's genre study is slightly less developmental than Lecouteux's, concentrating instead on living interlocutors and the heuristic function of ghosts as harbingers of virtuous or (more often) infamous behavior and teachers of social and cultural morality.

Encouraged by the initial successes of Carlo Ginzburg, early modernists have proven more willing to comment on ecstatic shamanism as a remnant of archaic belief structures in Christian Europe. Recent research validated beyond any shadow of a doubt an ongoing relationship between living communities and the dead in southeast Germany and Italy.[22] Éva Pócs demonstrated the

19. Ronald C. Finucane, *Appearances of the Dead: A Cultural History of Ghosts* (London: Junction Books, 1982), notwithstanding.

20. Claude Lecouteux, *Fantômes et revenants au moyen âge* (Paris: Diffusion Payot, 1986).

21. Schmitt, *Ghosts in the Middle Ages*, 10.

22. Carlo Ginzburg, *The Night Battles: Witchcraft and Agrarian Cults in the Sixteenth and Seventeenth Centuries* (Baltimore: Johns Hopkins University Press, 1983), trans. of idem, *I Benandanti: Stregonevia e culti agrari tra Cinquecento e Seicento* (Turin: Einaudi, 1966), is the classic starting point for that line of inquiry. He has since broadened his initial thesis from the Friuli in idem, *Ecstasies: Deciphering the Witches' Sabbath* (1976; repr., New York: Pantheon, 1992), buttressing claims of an archaic

easy communications between the living and the dead achieved through sha-manistic intermediaries in early modern Hungary. They took part, it was believed, in gatherings of the dead as doubles or soul images (the so-called *mora* and werewolves).[23] Pócs has also shown how other persons might be forced to participate in ghostly form at gatherings of the dead when witches possessed them. If she is correct, then spirit possession and travel to alternative worlds figured prominently in the popular consciousness surrounding appari-tions of ghosts. Pócs suggests that much of the activity involving the communal or impersonal dead occurred during "death periods": at the beginning of the year, in midwinter, at the celebration of the winter solstice, and at the Celtic New Year (November 1). The period from Christmas to Epiphany as well as the ember days was more popular for the appearance of demonic soul troops (for example, the "communal visitors" or phantoms of the night) and night bat-tles.[24] Alternately, the individual or "personal dead" returned sporadically and remained with the living for an indeterminate amount of time. The latter form is significant for our present discussion, since elite culture in Bavaria came to favor an individualized, personalized ghost—a modern ghost, if one prefers—and incidentally the type more familiar to twentieth-century observers.

Cases of shamanism, apparitions, and spirit possession from sixteenth-century Bavaria graphically illustrate the confrontation between novel theo-logical orthodoxy and popular beliefs. Two cases in particular have achieved prominence, one in its own day, the other far more recently. The first involved the reported activities of Satan at the household of the Fugger

---

pan-European culture of communal pantheism put forth in idem, *The Cheese and the Worms: The Cosmos of a Sixteenth-Century Miller,* trans. John Tedeschi and Anne Tedeschi (Baltimore: Johns Hop-kins University Press, 1980). Ginzburg's thesis is addressed more critically in the ethnographic thick-description of Wolfgang Behringer, *Shaman of Oberstdorf: Chonrad Stoeckhlin and the Phantoms of the Night,* trans. H. C. Erik Midelfort (Charlottesville: University of Virginia Press, 1998). Ginzburg finds a more receptive audience in a recent historical/folkloric study of village communications with the "otherworld" in Hungary by Eva Pócs, *Between the Living and the Dead: A Perspective on Witches and Seers in the Early Modern Age,* trans. Szilvia Rédey and Michael Webb (Budapest: Central European University Press, 1999; dist. Yale University Press). Most recently, the reciprocal structure of the rela-tionship between the living and the dead in German-speaking lands in the late Middle Ages has been analyzed by Mireille Othenin-Girard, "'Helfer' und 'Gespenster': Die Toten und der Tauschhandel mit den Lebenden," in *Kulturelle Reformation: Sinnformationen im Umbruch, 1400–1600,* ed. Bernhard Jussen and Craig Koslofsky (Göttingen: Vandenhoeck & Ruprecht, 1999).

23. Pócs, *Between the Living and the Dead.*

24. Pócs, *Between the Living and the Dead,* 30; Behringer, *Shaman of Oberstdorf,* 22, identifies the four sets of ember fast days as times generally associated with the appearance of spirits in folk beliefs.

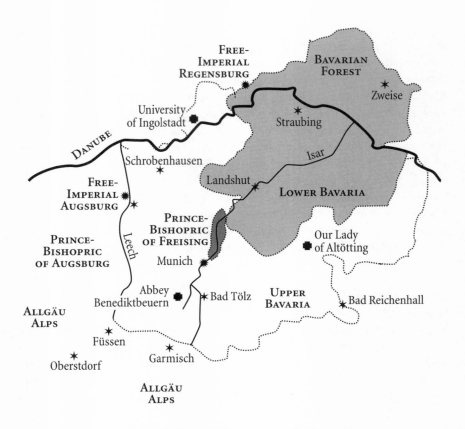

FIG.1. EARLY MODERN BAVARIA

bankers in Augsburg in the 1560s (see fig. 1). Peter Canisius, S.J., had been installed as cathedral preacher by the emperor, the local bishop (Cardinal Otto Truchseß von Waldburg), and the Fuggers. Canisius delivered fiery sermons on rising levels of diabolical activity and involved the Society of Jesus in exorcisms at the Fuggers' home. Ursula Fugger was visited by a spirit in 1568, who told her that the protracted possession of her lady-in-waiting would be cured by a pilgrimage to Loreto and Rome.[25] However, it soon

25. Philip M. Soergel, *Wondrous in His Saints: Counter-Reformation Propaganda in Bavaria* (Berkeley: University of California Press, 1993), 120–27.

became clear to Bishop Otto that the Fuggers' views represented an "old and damnable heresy," for Johann Fugger believed that the possessed woman was not a victim of the devil, but a vessel for a repentant soul from purgatory to permit its own corporeal torment, exorcism, and redemption as an expression of God's power over death.[26] In other words, Johann Fugger, a highly respected member of the mighty Augsburg banking dynasty, held the same views as any Hungarian peasant might: dead souls were "free to roam the earth and to torture human beings in search of good works and godly intervention."[27] Otto expressed his dismay over these beliefs in correspondence to Duke Albert V of Bavaria, and he did everything possible to convince the Fuggers of the serious errors inherent in these false opinions. Although Johann Fugger's name was not expressly mentioned, his deviance evoked a published critique of popular attitudes toward purgatory in a famous account of a 1570 exorcism involving another Fugger servant that Canisius conducted personally.[28]

Less than ten years later, a similar incident occurred in the mountains of the Allgäu south of Augsburg involving a less prominent person. On 20 February 1578, while on his way to cut lumber in a forest, the horse wrangler Chronrad Stoeckhlin met and conversed with the ghost of his recently deceased friend Jacob Walch. In this second case, however, the spiritual interlocutor represented neither the Society of Jesus, a prominent banking family, nor the bishop of Augsburg. The spirit (who inspired no horror) announced to Stoeckhlin that he had been charged to "walk about the earth for three years and then suffer four years of pain and torture in the fires of purgatory."[29] The ghost of Walch had returned to fulfill a vow he and his friend

26. Soergel, *Wondrous in His Saints*; Franz Zoepfl, *Geschichte des Bistums Augsburg und seiner Bischöfe im Reformationsjahrhundert* (Munich: Schnell & Steiner, 1969), 2:404. Despite Bishop Otto's claim, there is no evidence that official Catholic doctrine specifically condemned such beliefs as heretical. Again, however, Counter-Reformation theologians and demonologists, such as Peter Thyraeus, tended to categorize ghosts from purgatory as evil superstitions, while in the popular consciousness these ghosts were benign and even offered the opportunity to benefit through good works on the ghost's behalf.

27. Pócs, *Between the Living and the Dead*, 62–63.

28. Soergel, *Wondrous in His Saints*, 122–23; Martin Eisengrein, *Unser liebe Fraw zu alten Oetting* (Ingolstadt, 1570). Eisengrein's account of Canisius' exorcism at Altötting in 1570 was immensely popular and went into more than a dozen editions. It became a model for Jesuit exorcisms throughout Europe; see David Lederer, "Exorzieren ohne Lizenz…: Befugnis, Skepsis, und Glauben im frühneuzeitlichen Bayern," in *Dämonishe Besessenheit: Zur Interpretation eines kulturhistorischen Phänomens*, ed. Hans de Waardt, Sönke Lorenz et al. (forthcoming).

29. Behringer, *Shaman of Oberstdorf*, 12.

Stoeckhlin had taken and warned Stoeckhlin about the possible torments of the afterlife if he did not repent his waywardness and drinking. The horse wrangler's report of a returning spirit, who sought to shorten his time in purgatory through good works on earth (that is, the exhortation to penance) was very much in tune with the ideas of the Fuggers regarding their possessed servant. Stoeckhlin was also visited by a personal angel who bore no resemblance to a Christian guardian angel. This angel became his soul-guide and took him from the Allgäu on out-of-body ecstatic flights to join with other nocturnal phantoms—ideas more akin to the Hungarian peasantry's beliefs than official doctrine. Of course, ghosts returning from the hereafter to warn the living were part of Catholic tradition and even appear in the sermons of Canisius himself.[30] However, in the battle against evil superstitions and heretical errors (which some clergy shared as well[31]), reformers took a harsh stance on apparitions. Stoeckhlin and many others in the village of Oberstdorf were executed for diabolical intercourse and witchcraft—a much different fate than the one which befell the mighty Johann Fugger.

The authorities throughout the entire region expressed growing concern about apparitions of evil spirits and ghosts at this time and took special measures to prohibit their invocation for maleficent purposes. In 1595, during the interrogation of the accused magician Christoph Gostner from the Puster Valley, the authorities questioned him as to whether he had ever invoked or banned evil spirits, an accusation he strongly denied.[32] Unfortunately, two books (one with his name penned in) describing methods for the invocation of angels and for driving evil spirits from houses were found with other incriminating evidence among his personal possessions. In a commentary on penal law published in Ingolstadt in 1551, the jurist Andreas Perneder recommended death by immolation for persons invoking evil spirits with maleficent intent.[33] Perneder's penal code still excluded "white magic," but the *Great Bavarian Mandate against Superstition and Sorcery* of 1611/12 (the most comprehensive piece of legislation against magic in early modern Europe) widened the band of criminal offenses to include all forms of magic, illegal blessings, soothsaying, and congress with evil spirits—that is, banning, invoking, or exorcising—

30. Behringer, *Shaman of Oberstdorf,* 14.

31. Mary R. O'Neil, "*Sacerdote ovvero strione*: Ecclesiastical and Superstitious Remedies in 16th Century Italy," in *Understanding Popular Culture: Europe from the Middle Ages to the Nineteenth Century,* ed. Steven L. Kaplan (New York: Mouton, 1984), esp. 53 ff.

32. Reprinted in a collection of documents, Wolfgang Behringer, *Hexen und Hexenprozesse in Deutschland,* 3d ed. (Munich: Deutscher Taschenbuch Verlag, 1995), 39–47.

33. Behringer, *Hexen und Hexenprozesse,* 127.

without ecclesiastical authorization.[34] Its high degree of specificity reveals the extent to which the central authorities in Munich were familiar with actual superstitious practices as well as demonological theory. For example, the mandate condemned the superstition of attributing special healing powers to persons born with the caul, which they continued to carry about their neck—a custom also common in Friuli.[35] Aegidius Albertinus, secretary to the Munich Court Council and a prolific moralist, cautiously differentiated between guardian angels, who accompanied Christians from birth, and the invocation of spirits, an activity he denounced as part of the "angelic" (that is, black) arts:

> The aforementioned angelic arts also teach about particularly shocking invocations, whereby foolish persons believe the heavenly spirits will obey them and do their will, becoming their servants and not their masters, leaders and guardians. In a like fashion, godly wisdom does ordain that each person has their own special guardian and protective Angel, who accompanies them from birth....[36]

The severity of official condemnation was matched by extraordinary vigilance. However, if reports of ghostly apparitions multiplied in the first half of the seventeenth century as a consequence, they still might deviate from orthodox demonology. For example, some apparitions took animal form (lycanthropes). These were not "ghosts" in the strictest sense, but were a related phenomenon. In 1612 (the same year as the publication of the mandate on superstition), officials reported that wolves from the dense Bavarian forest had been attacking small children in the county of Zwiesel in the northeastern province of Straubing; several children had been strangled, others severely bitten.[37] The members of the Court Council in Munich (the highest legal authority in the land after the duke himself) commented that wolves did not naturally wander so far from the forest during the summer in search of game, and when they did they generally attacked cattle and sheep. Therefore, they suspected that a person or creature had been transformed into a werewolf

34. Behringer, *Witchcraft Persecutions*, 269; on witchcraft legislation in Bavaria, see Wolfgang Behringer, ed., *Mit dem Feuer vom Leben zum Tod: Hexengesetzgebung in Bayern* (Munich: Hugendubel, 1988); see 165–91 for the text of the mandate, "*Landgebott wider die Aberglauben, Zauberey, Hexerey und andere sträffliche Teuffelskünste.*"

35. Behringer, *Mit dem Feuer*, 176.

36. Aegidius Albertinus, *Lucifers Königreich und Seelengejaidt* (Munich, 1616); I have used a later edition, Joseph Kürschner, ed., *Deutsche National-Literatur*, 26:81–82.

37. Bayerisches Hauptstaatsarchiv Munich (hereafter BayHStA) Kurbayern Hofrat (hereafter HR) 105, fols. 147r–148r.

by a necromancer or sorcerer, perhaps from among the local herdsmen. The Court Council ordered all local inhabitants to be on the lookout for the beast and placed a bounty of 50 florins in cash on its head, dead or alive. The appeal was printed, distributed, and posted in Zwiesel and all neighboring counties.

The devastation of the Thirty Years' War cost the lives of as many as one-third of the inhabitants of Bavaria, providing a catalyst for apparitions during the rest of the seventeenth century. Chroniclers noted how the wide-spread abandonment of fields and villages had encouraged the return of wolves to the area, whose foraging brought them into conflict with the inhabitants especially in the winter months and exacerbated the general climate of fear during the war years.[38] The electorate suffered three separate waves of famine and epidemic disease in 1623, 1627/28 (in demographic terms, the most catastrophic), and 1634, the latter outbreak being accompanied by the ravages of the Swedish occupation. The end of the last plague and the withdrawal of Swedish forces was a celebrated event, witnessed by the consecration of a gilded Marian column in the town square of Munich (*Marienplatz*). Sightings of strange animals occurred in other places as well. In 1633, in the midst of the Thirty Years' War, the watch at the church of SS. Ulrich and Afra in nearby Augsburg twice spotted a ghost appearing at night in the form of a stag, but two torch-lit excursions led by Chaplain Hans Ferber failed to turn up anything.[39] Animal apparitions were a source of fear and terror among common folk, as demonstrated by their complaints in miracle books, such as the one from the shrine of Saint Anastasia in Benediktbeuern.[40] There, one woman reported being terrorized by a black dog, another by a black cat; both animals were assumed to be the devil.[41] In 1664, a shepherd had to be bound and carried to Benediktbeuern after a headless

38. See, for example, the war chronicle of P. Maurus Friesenegger, *Tagebuch aus dem 30 Jährigen Krieg* (Munich: Süddeutscher Verlag, 1974); also Schmidt, *Sagen*, 111, for a brief portrayal of the catastrophe of the war years.

39. Staat- und Stadtsbibliothek Augsburg (hereafter SStBA) 2 Cod. S. 65, entry for 6 November 1633.

40. Benediktbeuern was the most important center for the treatment of spiritual afflictions in Bavaria; see David Lederer, "Reforming the Spirit: Society, Madness, and Suicide in Central Europe, 1517–1809" (Ph.D. diss., New York University, 1995).

41. BayHStA Benediktbeuern 121, Anastasia Miracle Book (hereafter AMB), entries for 26 May 1657 (570526) and 17 May 1660 (600517). Again, there seems to have been considerable overlap here between the beliefs of common persons and the educated. For example, Oswald Myconius reported on Karlstadt's visions of the devil in the form of a black dog just before the radical reformer's death; see Bruce Gordon, "Malevolent Ghosts and Ministering Angels: Apparitions and Pastoral Care in the Swiss Reformation," in *Place of the Dead*, ed. Gordon and Marshall, 88.

wolf standing upright attacked his flock.[42] On three separate occasions (two during carnival) in 1665, individuals suffered terrible bouts of shock after revelers masquerading as animals surprised them.[43]

Appearances of more conventional ghosts were also on the rise at this time. Early modern Europeans generally believed that the ghosts of suicides (*Wiedergänger, revenants*) returned from the dead to haunt places associated with strong emotions from the past—regret, fear, and the terror of their self-murder—or the location associated with their earthly remains, often disposed of in degrading funerary rituals.[44] The same was true of early modern Bavarians, who expressed fears both collectively and individually. There were at least a half-dozen communalist "suicide revolts" in Bavaria during the seventeenth century, aimed at removing corpses from cemeteries to erase suicide from living memory and avoid celestial wrath visited upon communities as hailstorms.[45] Bavarians harbored fears as individuals too, as exemplified by Hans Staudinger, a common laborer from Traunstein. In 1681, when an unidentified man hanged himself on the side of a road, the county judge hired Staudinger to keep watch over the corpse, which was left hanging from a tree for five days and nights until the arrival of the Munich executioner; being of dishonorable trade, only he was authorized to remove the dangling cadaver.[46] The county remunerated Staudinger, who was ordered to prevent any person or domestic animal from inadvertently coming into contact with the hanged self-killer. However, Staudinger was too frightened to stand watch alone at night, and a second laborer had to be hired to keep him company after sunset.[47]

42. BayHStA AMB 640120.

43. BayHStA AMB 650224; 650331; 650923.

44. For example, see Michael MacDonald and Terence R. Murphy, *Sleepless Souls: Suicide in Early Modern England* (Oxford: Clarendon, 1990), 44–48 and passim; Vera Lind, *Selbstmord in der Frühen Neuzeit: Diskurs, Lebenswelt und kultureller Wandel am Beispiel der Herogtümer Schleswig und Holstein* (Göttingen: Vandenhoeck & Ruprecht, 1999), 36–38.

45. David Lederer, "Aufruhr auf dem Friedhof: Pfarrer, Gemeinde und Selbstmord im frühneuzeitlichen Bayern," in *Trauer, Verzweiflung und Anfechtung: Selbstmord und Selbstmordversuche in spätmittelalterlichen und frühneuzeitlichen Gesellschaften,* ed. Gabriela Signori (Tübingen: Edition Diskord, 1994), 189–209.

46. Suicides could only be removed by members of dishonorable professions, because physical contact with the corpse (and with the executioner) was deemed damaging to personal honor. See Jutta Nowosadtko, *Scharfrichter und Abdecker: Der Alltag zweier "unehrlicher Berufe" in der Frühen Neuzeit* (Paderborn: Ferdinand Schöningh, 1994). The Munich executioner was granted a monopoly over this profitable activity by Elector Ferdinand Maria after winning a protracted suit against local knackers in the region.

47. BayHStA General Registratur (hereafter GR) Faszikel (hereafter F) 139, 110.

Milkmaids from Wolfratshausen expressed similar fears. When a poor widow killed herself there in 1695, her remains were interred in a remote pasture, deemed the only feasible location by the county court. Shortly thereafter, however, representatives of the community complained that "during the summer months, their cattle had to graze in the pasture both day and night, but their servant girls would not go out to milk the cows for fear."[48] The authorities in Munich, fearing the ever-present threat of contagion, finally intervened and had the poor widow's rotting bodily remains cremated. Of course, the burial of suicides in remote places like pastures, swamps, and woods only enhanced the reputation of those sites as godforsaken places frequented by ghosts, werewolves, and witches.

Some people expressed more than vague fears of ghosts, and there were many reported sightings. The climate of fear prevailing during the era of the Thirty Years' War is best illustrated by a series of unusual occurrences in the year 1640, when things were not right in Bavaria. First, the Ecclesiastical Council of Freising investigated reports of "unusual specters" attacking travelers in the Ebersberg forest just east of Munich. Several travelers had already "paid with their lives" and, for three consecutive nights, no one dared to take the road through the forest. The Ecclesiastical Council also ordered another investigation at a nearby parsonage, where a ghost had been involved in an unspecified "unusual incident."[49] In April of 1640, the provincial administrator (*Rentmeister*) of Landshut requested reports from officials in Haag and Markt Schwaben after numerous nighttime sightings of ghosts in the forests around the city.[50] He and the Court Council in Munich sent warnings to electoral representatives in the town of Wasserburg and to the administrator of Straubing, who reconfirmed the sightings and increased patrols along the lower Bavarian roads. At this time, the town secretary of Neustadt on the Danube, just north of Landshut, was found hanging from his belt in an inaccessible thicket. It appeared impossible for him to have hanged himself there without help, and the Court Council in Munich suspected a ghost or some other evil spirit.[51] The Court Council simultaneously investigated an extremely macabre incident involving the consort of a Swedish soldier. The woman had been recently executed for crimes in Markt Schwaben. The executioner from Haag abused the

48. BayHStA GR F 139, 110.
49. Archiv des Erzbistums München (hereafter AEM), Erscheinungen von Geister (hereafter EG), communiqués to the pastor of Kirchdorf and the chaplain of Fraichoven, 1640.
50. BayHStA HR 267, 69r–v, 255v, 339v–340r, 493v.
51. BayHStA HR 268, 66v–67v.

beheaded corpse in gruesome fashion, skinning it and removing the heart, a clear violation of the mandate on superstition that condemned the use of body parts as sorcery.[52] Actually, it was a common practice among executioners and knackers, who engaged in a profitable, albeit highly illegal trade in human organs for magical healing purposes.[53] Summoned to appear in Munich, the executioner of Haag thought better of it and fled the duchy to avoid unpleasant questions.[54]

In another incident, Hans Gröbner, brewer and citizen of Bad Reichenhall (a rich salt-mining center directly across the southeastern border from Salzburg), described an apparition to the provost. In 1683, Gröbner claimed to have been awakened by a loud noise on the night after his servant took his own life on the premises.[55] He swore under oath that the ghost of the deceased servant had made the noise to announce his presence in his master's shop. Several days prior to his suicide, the servant had confided in a neighbor, Maria Mörz, that he suffered pangs of guilt for his misconduct while serving at a monastery just two years ago. He explained that he had since vowed to join a confraternity and make offerings. He extorted a promise from her to fulfill his obligations should he be unable to do so. Now the servant's ghost had returned to exact that pledge.

Given the increased activities of ghosts, werewolves, and witches in Bavaria from the late sixteenth century and especially during the horrors of the war, it would be naive to expect that the inhabitants of Bavaria stood by passively and lived with the visitations of the dead without taking action. Unable to rely on the elector (who at one point fled the capitol with his Jesuit advisors for the safe fortifications around the university town of Ingolstadt), the people turned to traditional methods and practitioners to protect their homes and families from the rampant apparitions of ghosts which accompanied (and outlasted) the Swedish invasion. In the absence of any recognizable guarantor of justice, even members of the ruling elite resorted to procedures that bordered sharply on superstition, such as lay exorcisms of spirits. In Augsburg, one lay-

---

52. BayHStA HR 268, 66v–67v; Behringer, *Mit dem Feuer*, 172.

53. On the healing practices of executioners in Bavaria, see Nowosadtko, *Scharfrichter und Abdekker*, 162–94. For Augsburg, see Kathy Stuart, "Des Scharfrichters heilende Hand: Medizin und Ehre in der Frühen Neuzeit," in *Ehrkonzepte in der Frühen Neuzeit: Identitäten und Abgrenzungen*, ed. Sybylle Backmann et al. (Berlin: Akademie Verlag, 1998), 316–48; eadem, *Defiled Trades and Social Outcasts: Honor and Ritual Pollution in Early Modern Germany* (New York: Cambridge University Press, 1999), 149–88.

54. BayHStA HR 268, 407v–408v, 449r–450r, 488r–489v.

55. BayHStA GR F 139, 110.

person's involvement in an exorcism ended in a criminal investigation. Hans Ehrmann was charged with illegal exorcisms of ghosts performed on sick people and animals, but he denied the charge.[56] Under torture, Ehrmann was questioned about other black arts he learned while traveling with gypsies. In Bavaria, the mandate against superstition expressly condemned as sorcery the exorcism of evil spirits without ecclesiastical authorization. Standard procedure in the region required a license to exorcise issued by a bishop or an abbot. While in theory it was not impossible for either a woman or a layperson to be officially authorized to conduct exorcisms of ghosts and spirits, it was highly irregular. In 1665, for example, a woman from Füssen was denied a permit to exorcise by the Ecclesiastical Council of the bishop of Augsburg because she lacked the requisite experience.[57]

For every rule there are exceptions, and such is the case with Rosina Blökhl-Huber, wife of a common carpenter from Aresing in the Bavarian county of Schrobenhausen northeast of Augsburg. Today, Rosina is almost forgotten, but in her own time she was nicknamed "the pious" and became the stuff of legend. I first encountered Rosina in the quarterly protocols of the Munich Court Council in the Bavarian State Archives, where her arrests in 1641 and 1643 were noted. Later research found her to be the subject of a detailed report intended for the bishop of Freising, now stored in the diocesan archives. Recently, at a fund-raiser for a local boarding school housed in a sixteenth-century castle, I received a private tour of the premises from the rector, who jokingly showed me around the "ghost room." There, he casually related the story of the woman from Munich who expelled the ghost in the seventeenth century. In response to my curiosity, we consulted a local history; the exorcist turned out to be none other than the pious Rosina.[58] Rosina Huber is extraordinary not simply because she seems to have been the only authorized lay exorcist in Bavaria, nor because she was a woman possessed of great charismatic piety, but also because of her tenacity as an individual. By poaching in a domain traditionally reserved for a special elite of the male clergy, she invited begrudgery from powerful quarters. After her first arrest in 1641 for the illegal expulsion of ghosts, she appeared before the bishop of Augsburg, who ordered her transfer to the territorial jail of her secular overlord in Munich, the infamous Falcon's Tower (*Falkhenthurm*). There, Rosina suffered

56. Stadtsarchiv Augsburg Urgichtensammlung 1610a: III, 31. Many thanks to Georg Feuerer for help with this reference.

57. Archiv des Bistums Augsburg (hereafter ABA) Geistlicher Rat (hereafter GRat), 1618–69, 169.

58. Bärbel Kiener, *Schoss Reichersbeuern: Geschichte und Rundgang in Bildern: 50 Jahre Landerziehungsheim Reichersbeuern Max-Rill-Schule 1938–1988* (Reichersbeuern: n.p., 1988), 21.

no less than fifteen excruciating weeks of grueling interrogations conducted by a virtual tag team of monks (*ordens Leute*) under the most severe torture.[59]

Fortunately for Rosina, the Jesuit phalanx at court had lost a vociferous advocate of witch-hunting following the death of an intransigent war hawk, Adam Contzen, S.J., in 1635. Contzen's replacement as father confessor to the elector by the moderate Pater Vervaux, S.J., of Lorraine reflected a shift in mood at court. Still, this extraordinary historical actor deserves her own special encore. In the face of her Inquisitorial persecutors, Rosina did not throw caution to the wind—otherwise, we might now possess extensive interrogatory protocols revealing arcana about pan-European popular beliefs. Nor did she confide hidden secrets to her confessor in an attempt to curry political favor or avoid torture. Rosina was defiantly reticent. She must have been exceedingly obstinate to withstand the excruciating torture visited upon her by the professional hand of the Munich executioner and perfectly ingenious to answer probing and probably leading questions without confessing to anything unorthodox, leaving her frustrated ecclesiastical tormentors without any shred of incriminating evidence to use against her. Perplexed, they were compelled to exonerate her of all charges. Her tenacity only enhanced her reputation of charismatic piety and imbued her with an aura of virtuosity, since through her torture, literally known as "martyrdom" (*das Martyrium*), she had withstood the ultimate ordeal. Rosina was subsequently released and personally informed by the court high judge (*Hofoberrichter*) Rothafften (later the provincial administrator of Straubing) that, as far as the elector of Bavaria was concerned, she was free to go and would not be prevented from redeeming lost souls from purgatory in the future, provided she consulted with her ecclesiastical superiors beforehand. In March 1643, new charges raised by petty officials in Schrobenhausen and Friedberg met with a sharp rebuff from the Court Council in Munich, since Rosina had informed the parish priest of Friedberg of her intention to exorcise a ghost prior to conducting the ritual.[60] The judges were ordered to set Rosina free and allow her to practice unhindered.

In 1644, Baron Johann Maximilian von Preysing, cameral and court councilor to the elector, became aware that one of his rural properties was haunted. It was the unoccupied castle of Reichersbeuern, fifty kilometers south of Munich near the market town Bad Tölz. In September his local representative,

---

59. "*... in beysein allerley geistlichen ordens Persohnen: wie nit weniger in alhiesigem Falckhenturm 15 Wochen lang außgestandener gefenkhnus aufs schärfste examinert*": AEM EG, report of Johann Caspar Luzen, personal secretary to the count of Törring, 10 January 1658.

60. BayHStA HR 278, 373 r–v, which also mentions her previous arrest and exoneration.

Conrad Rueff, had hanged the powerful herb *flagellum diaboli* on the doors to the reception hall of the lower floor to keep the ghost at bay.[61] However, rumors circulating among the peasantry were causing discontent. The baron quickly took matters into his own hands, procuring Rosina's services (at that time she too resided in Munich) and dispatching her on 24 December to Reichersbeuern with a formal letter of introduction. In the letter, he told Rueff to receive her with the utmost respect. In two astonished letters of eyewitness testimony, Rueff described Rosina's arrival in Reichersbeuern that very evening in the company of a mason and an unidentified woman and detailed her subsequent exploits.[62]

The days from Christmas to Epiphany were the winter ember days, one of the times of year when the dead were known to visit the living, either "as hosts of 'cloud-leading souls' swooping in tempests, or as repentant souls (or, in their most common Christian variant, unbaptized souls)."[63] In this region, it was considered especially important to protect oneself against magic at these times by observing a number of rituals designed to drive off witches and evil spirits; the house might be smoked out (hence, this time of year was known as the *Rauchnächte*[64]), prayers were chanted, the stalls of livestock were cleansed with blessed herbs and holy water, threshing was avoided, and people were wont to sneeze in buckets. On Christmas day, after attending confession and communion, the intrepid little band entered the chapel in the courtyard of the castle for prayer at around 7:00 P.M. Now seven strong, they included three prominent locals (a landed peasant, Georg Gering; the former caretaker of the castle, Hans Reiserer; and the local sheriff). With Conrad Rueff in the lead, they proceeded into the reception hall. Just then, the ghost tossed a board across the courtyard behind them. Rosina immediately called for a cru-

61. Ferchl, *Fuß-Reisen*, 9. In my attempts to identify this herb ("*Krautlein*," Schmidt, *Sagen*, 112), Sarah Ferber has kindly pointed out that a related substance, *fuga daemonum* (Hypericon), is referred to in Pierre Crespet, *Devx Livres de la hayne de Sathan et malins esprits contre l'homme, & de l'homme contre eux* (Paris, 1590), 213r.

62. The following is based upon the text of the original letters, reproduced in Ferchl, *Fuß-Reisen*, 9–13. Their contents are confirmed by the account of Schmidt, *Sagen*, 111–15, and Christian Schonger, *Beiträge zur Geschichte der ehemaligen Hofmarken Reichersbeuern, Sachsenkam und Greiling* (s.l., 1853). Many thanks to Bärbel Kiener, local historian and teacher at the boarding school of Reichersbeuern, who based her account on Schonger and helped me locate a copy of this rare lithograph, now in the parish archive.

63. Pócs, *Between the Living and the Dead*, 30; see also Behringer, *Shaman of Oberstdorf*, 20–22, 56–60, 150–51.

64. Also known as the *Rauhnächte*; see *Handwörterbuch des deutschen Aberglaubens*, ed. Hanns Bächtold, vol. R, 529–32.

cifix, three consecrated wax candles, holy water, and several lanterns and lights. Over the next half-hour, they heard the ghost sniveling, wafting, and walking about. The noises continued until midnight. At Rosina's insistence, the party remained in the hall throughout the night, and Rueff removed the *flagellum diaboli* to enable the ghost to move about freely. However, the rest of the night passed without incident.

The party (less the former caretaker, who had gone to fetch the slothful peasant) returned the following day, again around 7:00 P.M. Rosina, Rueff, and the mason moved directly to the hall, while the other woman and the sheriff waited in the courtyard, chatting. Suddenly, two objects struck the chapel door. Rueff compared the noise to peas tapping on a window during the *Klopfnächte* (Knocking Nights).[65] After the ghost announced its presence in this fashion, the party moved into the reception hall, anxious to bring the encounter to a conclusion. The ghost began wheezing, moving about, and knocking on a table, continuing with these signs until finally, at midnight, Rosina initiated the exorcism. She explained that "every good ghost praises God his Lord," to which the ghost responded unclearly, uttering something to the effect of "Yes!" or "Me too!"[66] When asked what it wanted, the ghost replied that she was the former lady of the castle, but it had been so long since her death that no one in these parts cherished her memory. She could be redeemed if two masses were read in her honor at Our Lady in Munich, a third at the local church of Our Lady, and a fourth in the castle chapel. A measure of wine and one kr. in bread needed to be offered at each mass, and each person in attendance was to be asked for a further donation of one kr. of bread. The party agreed and decided to return the next day to verify if the ghost had indeed been redeemed. Rueff bore all expenses for the masses on behalf of the baron. Although Rosina became weak from exhaustion and could not inquire about the ghost's actual identity, Rueff suspected that she

65. This ritual would have been fresh in Rueff's mind and he immediately associated it with the ghostly apparition. The reason for this is found in the popular understanding of the *Klopfnächte*. According to this regional custom, young people went door-to-door on the last three Thursday nights during Advent, throwing peas and small stones at window panes or knocking on doors with padded hammers. They sang or simply begged for fruit, ham, and sausages. The function of the noise was to drive off evil spirits that endangered agrarian fertility. The revelers sometimes masked themselves as ghouls or devils to drive off the evil spirits, dancing in the fields to ensure a good harvest next season. Some believed the souls of the dead themselves actually knocked and could be bought off with token offerings to save the household larder. Despite Christian overtones, *Klopfnächte* were opposed by the church. See Ginzburg, *Night Battles,* as in the Friul; *Handwörterbuch,* vol. K, p. 1542–46.

66. Ferchl, *Fuß-Reisen,* 10.

was the Lady Sophia von Pienzenau (born Clossen). Pienzenau had endowed a perpetual mass in 1588, but her daughter had left for Munich and the anniversary had been forgotten.

The local inhabitants, who had initially reacted to the ghost with such horror, were supremely grateful for their deliverance from the ghost, but Rosina and her traveling companions exacted no compensation from them. All they requested for that evening was plenty to eat and drink and, apart from the usual measure of beer, a goodly portion of wine (however, as Rueff mentioned in his report to the baron, custom dictated that she should be recompensed). The next day, the chapel at the castle was packed to overflowing, and afterwards the vicar sprayed holy water throughout the entire complex. The party returned at 7:00 P.M. and by 10:00 P.M., after completing their prayers, they encountered the ghost for the last time. At this encounter, she did in fact reveal her true identity as Lady Sophia and acknowledged her redemption. During a scene lasting a quarter of an hour, she thanked them for their prayers and for reinstating the anniversary. Then she emerged from behind a large oven and, seen only by Rosina, rose up to the ceiling and vanished. In addition to the landed peasant and another village leader, the former caretaker, the sheriff, and the rest of the party, the holder of the ecclesiastical benefice in Reichersbeuern also witnessed the last meeting. Rosina and the mason were content with the honors showered upon them by the locals, while her female companion requested a license from the baron to distribute wheat beer from her home in Munich. Rueff dispatched his final report on 27 December 1644.

News of Rosina's remarkable success spread quickly. Thereafter, she received a personal invitation from the prince-bishop of Freising, Veit Adam of Gepeckh, to drive a ghost from the apothecary at his episcopal residence above the town. Rosina discovered that the apothecary's departed mother was haunting the shop. Through the mercy of God, Rosina succeeded in the operation, redeeming this soul as well. Rosina was now a toasted celebrity at court with powerful patrons. It soon became almost obligatory to have Rosina up to the house for an exorcism and although one jealous clergyman was of the opinion that the ceremonies were quite superfluous, Rosina was subsequently employed by the court chamberlain Baron Haslang, the court chamber president Baron Johann Mändl of Deitenhoven, Mayor Ridler of Munich, the city's wealthiest patrician, and a member of the Welser banking family from Solln, among others.

In the winter of 1657, Count Albrecht of Törring, the greatest landed nobleman in Bavaria, also invoked Rosina's aid. For some time, a ghost haunted his Munich town house on the corner of Schwabingergasse and Kreuzgasse, terrorizing his housekeeper, Rosina Bernecker, who suffered horrible fits of falling-sickness thereafter and was bedridden. At first, the count approached the fathers of the Society of Jesus to ban the ghost, but they categorically refused, attributing the difficulties to an evil spirit or witchcraft. The count then turned to the Capuchins and Carmelites for help. Each order sent four monks to hold watch for two consecutive nights, blessing the house from top to bottom, hanging crucifixes above all the portals, and spraying holy water about. When these sacramentals failed, they determined that a benevolent ghost must be responsible rather than an evil spirit, in blatant contradiction to the opinion of the Jesuits.

The ghost's reputation grew at large and members of high society urged the count to seek out Rosina's help. Count Albrecht of Törring wrote personally to the county judge of Schrobenhausen, who relayed the message to Rosina, and she agreed. The count also requested the permission of the pastor of Our Lady, Anthony Mändl, Dr.Th., to perform the "exorcism" in his parish, reminding him that Rosina's services had been approved by both ecclesiastical and secular authorities. Pastor Mändl sanctioned her "quasi-exorcism [sic]," personally hearing her confession and celebrating the Eucharist with Rosina on the night of 22 December in the presence of the count before she went about her work. Rosina stood vigil during the next three nights, with several clergymen in the wing of the house most frequently haunted by the ghost. On Christmas Eve between 11:00 P.M. and midnight, the ghost arrived as an unseen woman, accompanied by knocking at the doors and walls of the rooms. Without resorting to any suspicious means of communication or superstitious blessings, Rosina gently asked the ghost what she sought and how she could be helped.

The soul identified itself, with very strong sobs and sighs, as the widow Westacher, a former tenant of the house, who had died without a light at her side, before receiving absolution, and before she had fulfilled a vow to have three holy masses each said at Our Lady and the Carmelite monastery. Rosina assured her that the masses would be said on her behalf and alms would be distributed among the poor. The promise of fulfilling the intended good works placated the ghost, and she departed with audible sighs of relief. The next day, the countess of Törring paid the Capuchins and Carmelites to hold the six masses and then distributed alms from her own hands to the poor. Three nights later, the ghost appeared once again before a portrait of the black Madonna of Altötting. In the presence of the countess and four men, Rosina asked whether the ghost was satisfied. She responded, "Yes"—that all she desired and more had been done on her behalf.[67] The shadowy ghost finally disappeared with a sigh and was never seen nor heard in the house again. Both the count's private secretary and the pastor of Our Lady praised Rosina in their personal correspondence as a pious, humble, and simple woman, who had a good reputation for handling such cases with satisfactory results. The count and countess also expressed their gratitude in coin. Rosina's charismatic authority to drive out ghosts, certified by her piety and a test of virtuosity under torture, was further enhanced by the patronage of the court elite. She was an anomaly in a system dominated by the ecclesiastical hierarchy, but one who had received the seal of popular legitimacy and was therefore beyond reproach. Nonetheless, the Ecclesiastical Council of Freising kept close tabs on Rosina Huber's activities, despite the fact that they were sanctioned by the bishop himself.

The rise in ghost sightings in Bavaria at the height of the Thirty Years' War paralleled growing ecclesiastical ambivalence toward reported apparitions. Though the belief in spirits was officially sanctioned by the church, its representatives became rationalistic and increasingly reluctant to recognize extraordinary preternatural phenomena. This reluctance manifested itself in skepticism. In neighboring Austria, for example, two women who claimed to exorcise souls from purgatory met with stiff resistance from the ecclesiastical authorities of the bishop of Passau. In 1689, when the vicar of Kirchberg am Wagram extolled the abilities of a woman, Barbara Zägl, in a sermon, he was arrested and ordered by the consistory to preach another sermon, this time on the orthodox doctrine of purgatory.[68] As late as 1713, Maria Zach of Pillichsdorf, a self-proclaimed "redeemer of souls," fled internment in Vienna when the consistory sentenced her to appear publicly in the stocks after she admitted (under threat of torture) that her activities were a hoax.[69] In Bavaria, in 1643, a baker at Altomünster described to his father confessor the visit of a ghost from purgatory requesting the performance of an unfulfilled vow.[70] Only then could the spirit rest in peace. The monk repeated this confession to the Ecclesiastical Council in Freising, which found itself in an awkward position; while they could not deny the possibility of an apparition outright, the Council insisted

67. AEM EG, report of Johann Caspar Luzen, 10 January 1658.

68. Theodor Wiedemann, *Geschichte der Reformation im Lande unter der Enns* (Leipzig, 1886), 5:171–72.

69. Rudolf Hösch, *Heimatbuch der Marktgemeinde Pillichsdorf* (Pillichsdorf: n.p., 1987), 115. My thanks to Dr. Peter Schilling for referring me to his contribution to the *Heimatbuch*.

70. AEM EG, report from the father confessor of Altomünster, 4 September 1643.

that the story failed to meet certain critical criteria.[71] The Council communicated ten discrepancies to the father confessor, among them the outward appearance of the ghost and the time of the apparition. The baker claimed that the spirit appeared brightly lit and joyous during the day as well as at night. Ghosts from purgatory, the Council reminded his father confessor, were spirits of the dark, tending to sadness and usually showing themselves around midnight. The Council recommended that he reexamine the baker and iron out any inconsistencies in his description.

In a more dramatic and controversial incident, a sacristan from Lohrkirchen, Andreas Werner, publicly exorcised a ghost in front of three hundred people.[72] The Ecclesiastical Council of Freising received the report (including a catalog of some 128 questions and formulaic commendations) with skepticism, even though the ghost witnessed the power of the Catholic sacraments, the veneration of the saints, and the catechism. Werner claimed that the good ghost had been in purgatory for thirty years, because it failed to keep a vow to conduct a pilgrimage to Our Lady of Altötting, the so-called heart of Bavaria and its most popular pilgrimage site.

The story of wayward souls seeking redemption for unfilled promises was also a recurrent motif in the accounts jotted down by folklorists in the nineteenth century. They regularly associated ghosts with abandoned castles and religious structures beyond the secularization, which occurred in 1803. In one case a whole army of ghosts took revenge on pillaging Hungarian troops (*Panduren, Tolpatchen*) who entered the cemetery in Lengries during the War of the Spanish Succession in 1705.[73] Stories of treasure hunters who invoked ghosts to help them find hidden moneys from the time of the Thirty Years' War were also quite popular. One such tale, the story of a knacker from Garmisch who conjured a ghost in the abandoned alpine castle of Werdenfels in the nineteenth century, suggests the persistence of supernatural beliefs.[74] Treasure hunting through supernatural means, condemned by the Bavarian mandate on superstition, remained a capital crime until the mid-eighteenth century because it implied a tacit pact with the devil.[75] Nevertheless, its popularity rose during the last third of the seventeenth and the first half of the

---

71. AEM EG, directive to the father confessor of Altomünster, 1 October 1643.

72. AEM EG, *Geisterbeschwörung* of Andreas Werner, Cooptor of Lohrkirchen, 1665.

73. For example, Schöppner, *Sagenbuch*, 234, 247; and Schmidt, *Sagen*, 54.

74. "Die Geisterbeschwörung in Schloße Werdenfels," in *Sagenbuch der Bayerischen Lande: Aus dem Munde des Volkes, der Chronik und der Dichter*, ed. Alexander Schöppner (Munich, 1874), 211; my thanks to Stephan Deutinger of the Institute for Bavarian History for providing me with excerpts from Schöppner.

75. Behringer, *Witchcraft Persecutions*, 338 ff.

eighteenth centuries. Criminal cases were not limited to commoners, but often mentioned an educated ringleader, in one case a nobleman. During 1677, nine inquiries into treasure seeking were conducted in Bavaria, one involving fourteen men, five of whom paid with their lives.

Since treasure seeking involved the invocation of ghosts (specifically persons who buried treasure but were unable to retrieve it), it is related to our discussion, although it represents a new evolution in popular beliefs; by the eighteenth century, ghosts had been associated with the morality of a money economy. On one hand, since tales of treasure hunting are often tales of failure, ghosts represented a warning against the dangers of obtaining money through illicit means, that is, selling one's soul to the devil. On the other hand, archival holdings testify to a very real market for handbooks and manuscripts to assist would-be treasure hunters. These finder's manuals, confiscated by the authorities during trials, were often destroyed, but a good many remain in the diocesan archive of Augsburg arising out of several investigations conducted as part of the Enlightenment campaign against popular superstition by Bishop Klemens Wenzeslaus in the late eighteenth century.[76] However, even in a Catholic prince-bishopric, the enlightened view of superstition was decidedly worldly in comparison to its previous definition as efficacious magic. One investigation centered on a pair of confidence men (one an ex-Jesuit) who swindled unsuspecting peasants in the region, while another focused on the clandestine activities of a parish priest who organized a group of rural treasure hunters including several prominent locals.[77] Yet another southeast German example of a manual is found in the Herzog August Library in Wolfenbuttel. This *Little Treasure Book* is actually a collection of thirteen (how could it be otherwise?) separate formulas for finding treasure through the invocation of ghosts.[78] Many of the standard ideas about ghosts are still audible for those who listen. For example, one recipe requires several varieties of woods be burned to ash on Christmas Eve between 11:00 P.M. and midnight and details what signs will reveal possible locations where the ash powder has

76. Archiv der Diözese Augsburg (hereafter ADA), DA 15, 211 (Superstitiosa) contains several treasure seekers' handbooks, some in Latin, others in German, which were employed throughout the eighteenth century, esp. fols. 6–8 and 12, in addition to a talisman and spells for curing cows unable to give milk.
77. ADA, DA 15, 310. See also Anton Gulielminetti, "Klemens Wenzeslaus, der letzte Fürstbischof von Augsburg, und die religöse Reformbewegung," in *Archiv für die Geschichte des Hochstifts Augsburg,* ed. Alfred Schröder (Dillingen, 1909–11), 521–22.
78. Herzog August Bibliothek Wolfenbuttel, NOVI 648, *Schatz Büchel, Worinen 13 Stuckh geheime stuckh zu finden, 1748, d. 21 Novembriß.*

been spread. Another formula—which recommends confession, communion, the recital of thirty Our Fathers, thirty Hail Marys, and one Credo, and depositing 30 pfennigs in a collection box—apparently operated on the principle of spending money to make money. The illustrations in the *Little Treasure Book* offers users cryptic symbols to help control ghosts once they appear (figs. 2 and 3). One crude symbol was intended to be scratched onto a mirror. Another needed to be written onto lead plate and included the names of the four evangelists. Once the spot for digging had been located, the plate was held along with a root while the treasure seeker recited a prayer:

> Oh heavenly Father, grant me grace with my root, so that all ghosts must yield from this treasure and give me power, strength, wit, and sense through your heavenly host and through the Holy Trinity and through the intercession of all the saints of God, to receive this treasure, for the benefit of myself and all Christendom and for the consolation and peace of the poor souls, now buried, in the name of the Father [genuflection] and the Son [genuflection] and the Holy Spirit [genuflection]. Amen.[79]

Despite the Christian overtones, these were hardly the type of rituals the church was likely to condone, even after the Enlightenment. Furthermore, in several less Christian rituals, the anonymous author of the *Little Treasure Book* recommends some not-so-innocent methods of warding off ghosts: cutting a seven-year-old (age of first communion) boy's thumbnails with broken glass until it pains him, using the candle held by a seven-year-old virgin girl during first communion, or the violent slaughter of animals and the use of their blood to find the treasure. Some of these activities probably represented serious breaches of criminal codes, not to mention laws prohibiting sorcery and the illegal conjuration of spirits.

Treasure seeking moves us beyond our initial parameters but has been included here to demonstrate how the history of ghosts would continue into the nineteenth century, as well as the twentieth and the twenty-first.[80] It indicates how patterns of belief changed and evolved, in this case from the religious concerns of the late sixteenth to the mid-seventeenth centuries to economic ones from the late seventeenth to the mid-eighteenth centuries.

---

79. *Schatz Büchel.*

80. See, e.g., Diethard Sawicki, "Die Gespenster und ihr Ancien régime: Geisterglauben als 'Nachtseite' der Spätaufklärung," in *Aufklärung und Esoterik,* ed. Monika Neugebauer-Wölk (Hamburg: F. Meiner Verlag, 1999), 364–96.

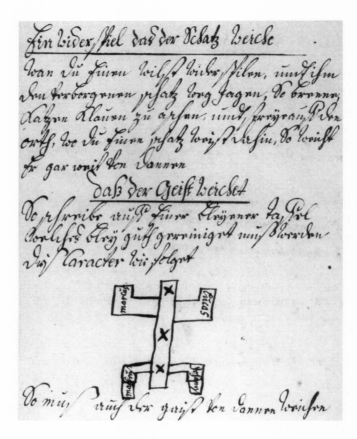

Fig. 2: From *Schatz Büchel, Worinen 13 Stuckh geheime stuckh zu finden, 1748, d. 21 Novembriß* (Herzog August Bibliothek Wolfenbuttel, NOVI 648; used by permission)

However, if the later era reinvented the ghost, it could not do so in a discursive vacuum. Pre-Christian traditions mixed with Christian ones were magnified during the era of crisis at the end of the sixteenth century and then distorted through the prism of the Thirty Years' War and the growth of a mercantilist economy in the region. Therefore, ghosts continued to reflect popular beliefs and aspirations in a specific social context, just as today's ghosts have learned to keep up with new technologies.

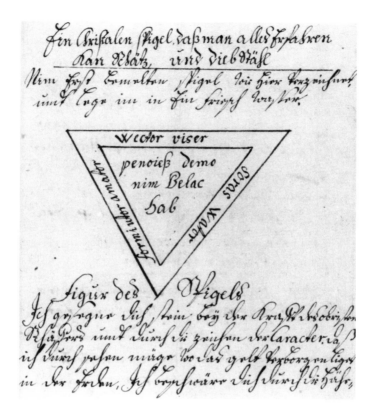

Fig. 3: From *Schatz Büchel, Worinen 13 Stuckh geheime stuckh zu finden, 1748, d. 21 Novembriß* (Herzog August Bibliothek Wolfenbuttel, NOVI 648; used by permission)

The question of popular beliefs in ghosts has formed another integral part of our investigation and has revealed just how broadly the contours of popular belief extend. Popular attitudes toward ghosts were not just a substratum shared by common people in agrarian communality, but also had their place among the nobility, the educated urban elite, and even reached into the highest levels of society to include members of the clergy. It is not so obvious where to draw the dividing line when wealthy bankers share common beliefs with the peasantry; when respected members of court society successfully employ a lay exorcist after monks had unsuccessfully orchestrated her

torture and interrogation; or when the highest political and judicial organization in Bavaria, the Court Council, posts wanted posters to bring in a werewolf "dead or alive." Perhaps the greatest difficulty is represented by the thin
line between clerical and popular *practice* (what David Gentilcore has called
"medical pluralism"[81]), which in some cases hinged solely on whose definition of orthodoxy is applied.[82] For example, Peter Canisius was a powerful
theologian, but his participation in controversial exorcisms earned him the
contempt of Jesuit superiors and colleagues and was one of the deciding factors in his transfer from Upper Germany to the backwaters of Swiss exile. The
blessing of livestock is another problem, one which might have cost Hans
Ehrmann his life in Augsburg in 1610 but which was and still is practiced by
Bavarian priests each year during the Saint Leonhard pilgrimage.[83] One thing
is certain, however: magic, or what the authorities defined as witchcraft, sorcery, and superstition, was most certainly practiced by real persons and was
much more common than has been generally accepted by most historians.
These practices were not just dreamed up by misogynous clergymen in spare
moments of sexual frustration. Even if the vast majority of the accused in
witch trials were not involved in diabolism (rare but extant devil's pacts indicate that some people surely were), many practiced beneficent "white" magic.
In that regard, Rosina Huber was a most rare and fortunate exception, having
received official sanction.

After researching ghost tales, we should now look differently at nineteenth-century folklorists, especially when their subsequent stories can be
corroborated by independent evidence, such as court records, which indicate
just how seriously this phenomenon was taken by the authorities. Context is
the vital link; witness the evolutionary changes in definitions of "superstition." This last point is once again illustrated by the shift from rational sixteenth-century explanations of ghosts as dangerous representatives of Satan
or repentant souls from purgatory who needed redeeming to economically
rational explanations of ghosts in the eighteenth century, when their primary
concern was guarding abandoned treasures and properties. This evolution
reflects novel social relationships in a regional market economy intent on

81. David Gentilcore, *Healers and Healing in Early Modern Italy* (Manchester: Manchester University Press, 1998).

82. O'Neil, "*Sacerdote ovvero strione*," 53 ff.

83. Steven D. Sargent, "Religion and Society in Late Medieval Bavaria: The Cult of St. Leonard,
1258–1500" (Ph.D. diss., University of Pennsylvania, 1982), and idem, "Miracle Books and Pilgrimage
Shrines in Late Medieval Bavaria," *Historical Reflections* 13 (1986): 455–71.

monetary exchange. Ghosts can tell us a great deal about attempted repression of popular culture by the Catholic Church or the rise of reason-of-state politics, natural law, and the triumph of the Enlightenment. Although the dreadful immanence of ghosts in the early modern period has been replaced by the legends of romantic folklorists and laid to rest in the nineteenth century, perceptions persist. Ghosts continue to haunt our children around the campfire and on television, imbuing them with values that are in some ways new, in others as ancient as the tales themselves.

REFORMED OR RECYCLED?

Possession and Exorcism in the Sacramental Life of Early Modern France

Sarah Ferber

A large vessel filled with holy water was brought. In addition, a sacred stole (as it's called), with the opening verses of St. John's Gospel hanging from it, was draped over Faunus' shoulders. In his pockets he had a waxen image of the kind blessed annually by the pope and known as an Agnus Dei. Long ago—before a Franciscan cowl became so formidable—people used to protect themselves by this armor against harmful demons.
Desiderius Erasmus, "Exorcism," 1524

Now that Human nature is not only freed from the captivity of the devil, but is even honored by the fraternity of Jesus Christ, who clothed it and elevated it with him above the highest heavens, it seems that the illustrious title [of exorcist] which gives us jurisdiction over demons is the appanage of our new dignity.
Léon d'Alexis [Pierre de Bérulle], *Traicté des Energumenes*, 1599

It is now established in the historiography of early modern Europe that in the period of the Catholic Reform and religious renewal, "popular" religious practices were either suppressed or reformed,[1] orthodoxy was grafted onto traditional practices,[2] and in general, Catholic authorities paid greater attention to separating the spheres of illicit folk magic and licit church-magical

My thanks are due to Katie McConnel for her comments and suggestions and to Charles Zika for his generous advice on argumentation and style.

1. Mary R. O'Neil, *Discerning Superstition: Popular Errors and Orthodox Response in Late Sixteenth Century Italy* (Ph.D. diss., Stanford University, 1981); eadem, "*Sacerdote ovvero strione:* Ecclesiastical and Superstitious Remedies in 16th Century Italy," in *Understanding Popular Culture: Europe from the Middle Ages to the Nineteenth Century*, ed. Steven L. Kaplan (New York: Mouton, 1984), 53–83.
2. R. Po-chia Hsia, *The World of Catholic Renewal, 1540–1770* (New York: Cambridge University Press, 1998), 201.

practices.[3] The precise definition of what was orthodox in regard to the rite of exorcism was at times closely contested among a wide range of reforming Catholics in early modern Europe.[4] As part of the Catholic cult, the value of exorcism of the possessed had been long disputed, and in this period it continued to provide the church with new dilemmas, which ran not only along class lines, but also caused deep tensions among Catholic elites. In the fifteenth and early sixteenth centuries, reform-minded Catholics, with quite diverse agendas, such as the authors of the *Malleus Maleficarum*, Erasmus, Martin De Castañega, and the Thomist humanist Pedro Ciruelo argued against what they saw as objectionable exorcism practices.[5]

In sixteenth- and seventeenth-century France, however, such a classic reformist schema was complicated twice over: in theory (as it could be at any time) by the fact that the status of the objects deployed in Catholic sacramental practices can never be fixed and is always open to mixed interpretations;[6] and, in actuality, by the religious wars and subsequent spiritual revival, when demonic possession and exorcism assumed a new place in the avant-garde of

3. Robert W. Scribner, "Ritual and Popular Religion in Catholic Germany at the Time of the Reformation," *Journal of Ecclesiastical History* 35 (1984): 47–77.

4. Carleton Cunningham, "The Devil and the Religious Controversies of Sixteenth-Century France," *Essays in History* 35 (1993): 33–47, at 43. Cf. Marc Venard, "Le démon controversiste," in *La controverse religieuse: XVIe–XIXe siècles: Actes du 1er Colloque Jean Boisset, VIème colloque du Centre d'histoire de la Réforme et du protestantisme*, 2 vols., ed. Michel Péronnet (Montpellier: Université Paul Valéry, 1980), 2:45–60.

5. *The Malleus Maleficarum of Heinrich Kramer and James Sprenger*, trans. Montague Summers (New York: Dover, 1971), 180–88; David H. Darst, "Witchcraft in Spain: The Testimony of Martin De Castañega's Treatise on Superstition and Witchcraft (1520)," *Proceedings of the American Philosophical Society* 123 (1979): 298–322, esp. 312, 317–21; *Pedro Ciruelo's A Treatise Reproving All Superstitions and Forms of Witchcraft: Very Necessary and Useful for All Good Christians Zealous for Their Salvation*, trans. Eugene A. Maio and D'Orsay W. Pearson (Rutherford: Fairleigh Dickinson University Press, 1977), 265–88.

6. This singular feature of Catholicism is referred to variously as belief in religious immanence (Ann W. Ramsey, *Liturgy, Politics, and Salvation: The Catholic League in Paris and the Nature of Catholic Reform, 1540–1630* [Rochester, N.Y.: University of Rochester Press, 1999], 3–4); "sacramental" religiosity ("2. Of the nature of, relating to, or expressed by, an outward sign or symbol," in *Shorter Oxford English Dictionary*), and, in reference to manifestations in the human body, "embodied" religiosity (Alison Weber, "Demonizing Ecstasy: Alonso de la Fuente and the *Alumbrados* of Extremadura," in *The Mystical Gesture: Essays on Medieval and Early Modern Spiritual Culture in Honor of Mary C. Giles*, ed. Robert Boenig [Burlington, Vt.: Ashgate, 2000], 143, 158). On Protestant versus Catholic positions, see Lyndal Roper, "Exorcism and the Theology of the Body," in *Oedipus and the Devil: Witchcraft, Sexuality, and Religion in Early Modern Europe* (New York: Routledge, 1994), chap. 8.

proselytism.[7] The sharply contrasting characterizations of the exorcist by Erasmus and Bérulle encapsulate this mixed status of exorcism. Erasmus's exorcist is a shabby representative of the Catholic priesthood, a simpleton who places faith in uttering words and wielding objects rather than attending to his own spiritual comportment and trusting in the power of God to act independent of material prompting. Pierre de Bérulle's exorcist is no less than the image of Christ. Yet each author would qualify as in some way representative of Catholic Reform and spiritual renewal. The aim of this essay, therefore, is to explore the ambiguous place held by cults of possession and exorcism in the reforming climate of early modern France in order to elicit some of the ways that traditional or popular religiosity became enmeshed in both the critiques and innovations of reform Catholicism. This will be done by examining two features of French possession cases.[8]

First to be considered is how the religion of the so-called vulgar was characterized in several cases of demonic possession, to suggest that while anxieties about popular superstition indeed informed the views of reform-minded

7. A similar rise in the public profile of possession and exorcism occurred across western Europe. See, for example, Stuart Clark, *Thinking with Demons: The Idea of Witchcraft in Early Modern Europe* (New York: Oxford University Press, 1997), chaps. 26–28; Roper, "Exorcism and the Theology of the Body," chap. 8; Michael MacDonald, ed., *Witchcraft and Hysteria in Elizabethan London: Edward Jorden and the Mary Glover Case* (New York: Routledge, 1991); James Sharpe, *The Bewitching of Anne Gunter: A Horrible and True Story of Deception, Witchcraft, Murder, and the King of England* (New York: Routledge, 2000); Daniel P. Walker, *Unclean Spirits: Possession and Exorcism in France and England in the Late Sixteenth and Early Seventeenth Centuries* (London: Scolar Press, 1981); O'Neil, *Discerning Superstition*; and eadem, "*Sacerdote ovvero strione*"; H. C. Erik Midelfort, "The Devil and the German People: Reflections on the Popularity of Demon Possession in Sixteenth-Century Germany," in *Religion and Culture in the Renaissance and Reformation*, ed. Steven E. Ozment (Kirksville, Mo.: Sixteenth Century Journal Publishers, 1989), 98–119; David Gentilcore, *From Bishop to Witch: The System of the Sacred in Early Modern Terra d'Otranto* (Manchester: Manchester University Press, 1992); and idem, *Healers and Healing in Early Modern Italy* (Manchester: Manchester University Press, 1998).

8. The essay aims to develop incrementally arguments already established on the centrality of demonology to learned thinking in Clark, *Thinking with Demons*; reflection on the concept of "traditional" belief, in Wolfgang Behringer, *Shaman of Oberstdorf: Chonrad Stoeckhlin and the Phantoms of the Night*, trans. H. C. Erik Midelfort (Charlottesville: University of Virginia Press, 1998); and insistence on the political and rhetorical aspects of witchcraft beliefs, in Ia Bostridge, *Witchcraft and Its Transformations, c. 1650–c.1750* (New York: Clarendon, 1997). In particular, the essay seeks to endorse and elaborate on the argument where reform sometimes entails conflict over different approaches to reform, in Robert Bireley, *The Refashioning of Catholicism, 1450–1700* (Basingstoke: Macmillan, 1999). On the question of sacramentals, evangelism, and class, see Peter Brown, *Relics and Social Status in the Age of Gregory of Tours* (Reading: University of Reading, 1977).

elites, this did not occur consistently.[9] Rather, the evidence endorses the increasingly shared view of historians who have argued for more mutable lines between elite and popular,[10] but it also reveals that invoking the idea of such categories was nonetheless a significant part of various reforming agendas. The next consideration will be the role of the cult of the dead in cases of possession and exorcism. Like exorcism, the cult of the dead has traditionally been the target of critiques from reforming elements within the church, and in this period the cult was a notable feature in several cases of possession. To consider these two cults enables us to see that the continuation of controversial sacramental aspects of Catholic culture in high-profile possession cases was not necessarily a reflection of a desire among the elites to accommodate the needs of the uneducated,[11] nor a retrograde tendency in an increasingly intellectualizing religion. Rather, the way exorcists and the possessed used these cults in early modern France shows that rituals, and the deployment of the human body and holy objects for devotional purposes, were positioned at the very heart of Catholic Reform and renewal.[12] Elites participated in these cults for their own distinct and constantly evolving reasons, and they found within them new and exciting prospects for achieving the devotional and reformist aims of Catholicism, as they understood them.

"MURMURS AMONG THE VULGAR"

Militant French Catholics first deployed exorcism early in the Wars of Religion (1562–1629) as a high-profile ritual which displayed the power of holy objects and church personnel to reconvert Huguenots and to rouse crowds to passionate defense of Catholicism. In the 1565/66 story of Nicole Obry, the sixteen-year-old daughter of a butcher from Vervins in Picardy, exorcists

---

9. See the indispensable chapter, Clark, "Superstition," in *Thinking with Demons*, chap. 32.

10. See, for example, Jonathan L. Pearl, *The Crime of Crimes: Demonology and Politics in France, 1560–1620* (Waterloo, Ont.: Wilfrid Laurier University Press, 1999), 150; Cunningham, "Devil and the Religious Controversies," 44; Allyson M. Poska, *Regulating the People: The Catholic Reformation in Seventeenth-Century Spain* (Boston: Brill, 1998), 8–10; Gentilcore, *Healers and Healing*, 203.

11. Bireley, *The Refashioning of Catholicism*, 96, has argued that evangelizing and Christianizing ordinary people "always implied adaptation to their situation." Hsia, *The World of Catholic Renewal*, 197, cites "persistent public demand" as the reason for liturgical continuity in many rural areas; he also refers to the "persistence of traditional religiosity," 226. It is also argued that "Tridentine Catholicism … had to seek accommodations with established popular cultures and cults," Michael A. Mullett, *The Catholic Reformation* (London: Routledge, 1999), 180.

12. O'Neil, *Discerning Superstition*, 293–94, identifies the church's decision to continue with its sacramental uses as the source of conflict surrounding exorcism.

deployed the Host against possessing demons in a series of dramatic exorcisms which came to be known as the "Miracle of Laon." Yet exorcism, with its focus on the uncontrolled body of the possessed (usually a woman in major French cases), its more or less fetishistic attention to the powers of particular cult objects (notably the Host but also saints' relics and other sacramental aids), and its appeal to mass audiences displayed precisely the type of beliefs and behaviors which, by the standards of Erasmian reform, were highly suspect. Indeed, Huguenot opponents argued that the exorcists were no better than magicians and, of course, rejected the view that the priesthood could perform miracles, either by consecration of the Host or through exorcism. [13] In a climate of intense fear of the Huguenots, seen as agents of the devil, the majority endorsed the Catholic view of the "Miracle," and several major books celebrated this story. These events gave public exorcism of the possessed new respectability as a vehicle of militant Catholicism.[14]

Later in the Wars, however, the so-called superstitious aspects of exorcism came under attack from Catholics in the case of the demoniac Marthe Brossier. In late February 1599, Henri IV persuaded a reluctant Parlement of Paris to register the Edict of Nantes.[15] The edict aimed to provide limited toleration to the Huguenots, as new *politique* elements within French Catholicism were pressing back the influence of the recently defunct militant Catholic Holy League. Into this volatile political climate, opponents of the edict introduced Brossier, a twenty-six-year-old woman of the *menu peuple*, from Romorantin, whose stridently anti-Huguenot public exorcisms divided Parisian Catholic intellectuals, in effect along political lines. *Politiques* ridiculed the possession and League sympathizers promoted it.[16]

Marthe Brossier, the woman ostensibly at the center of the debate, was little more than a cipher. Her subject position was negated by her identity as a

13. Walker, *Unclean Spirits*, 27.

14. For a thorough treatment of the literature of the case, see Irena Backus, *Le Miracle de Laon: Le Déraisonnable, le raisonnable, l'apocalyptique et le politique dans les récits du Miracle de Laon (1566–1578)* (Paris: J. Vrin, 1994), esp. 197–204. See also the attentive reading of Denis Crouzet, "A Woman and the Devil: Possession and Exorcism in Sixteenth-Century France," in *Changing Identities in Early Modern France*, ed. Michael Wolfe (Durham, N.C.: Duke University Press, 1997), 191–215. Also see Walker, *Unclean Spirits*, 19–28, and Moshe Sluhovsky, "A Divine Apparition or Demonic Possession? Female Agency and Church Authority in Demonic Possession in Sixteenth-Century France," *Sixteenth Century Journal* 27 (1996): 1039–55.

15. Mack P. Holt, *The French Wars of Religion, 1562–1629* (New York: Cambridge University Press, 1995), 167–68.

16. I thank Alfred Soman for this important observation.

demon and by the public function she served: to enable elites to engage in political debates without taking up arms.[17] Under exorcism, Brossier's demon railed against the Huguenots for several days toward the end of March when the bishop of Paris, Henri de Gondi, sought medical advice to establish if her possession were valid.[18] Two groups of doctors provided the bishop with conflicting reports and at this point of stalemate, royal authorities intervened. The *Lieutenant Criminel* arrested Brossier and locked her in the Châtelet. At the request of Henri IV, Michel Marescot, a court physician, wrote a pamphlet which derided Brossier's exorcists for their belief in the reality of her possession and in the power of sacramentals used to exorcise her.[19] Marescot jeered at the use of a fumigant in exorcism (an example is the recipe from the *Flagellum Daemonum* of the famous Italian Franciscan exorcist Girolamo Menghi, which contained asafetida and Saint John's wort). Marescot described a farcical attempt to use the fumigant, which had led the cathedral chapters of Orléans and Cléry to revoke permission for exorcists to exorcise Brossier in public. Brossier had been tied to a chair, Marescot writes; then "they did set fire to this Perfume, and offered those villainous and stinking vapors to her Nose," at which Brossier is said to have cried out, "Pardon me, I am choked. He is gone away." Marescot provided the recipe for the fumigant, as if this quite licit means of exorcism were self-evidently ridiculous.[20]

Marescot framed his story so as to alert the reader to the dangers of "too great credulitie [which] is the path that leadeth headlong to falsehood, fraud, follie and superstition." He portrayed the exorcisms as a threat which drew the populace to believe in false miracles.[21] To identify exorcism with superstition in this way was a standard jibe, but any ready characterization of its practitioners as ignorant was only as tenable as polemicists were able to make it. In this case, Brossier's supporters included some of the theological luminaries of

17. See the sympathetic analysis of Edmund H. Dickerman and Anita M. Walker, "'A Woman under the Influence': A Case of Alleged Possession in Sixteenth-Century France," *Sixteenth Century Journal* 22 (1991): 534–54.

18. Pierre de L'Estoile, *Journal pour la règne de Henri IV, 1, 1589–1600*, ed. Louis-Raymond Lefèvre (Paris: Gallimard, 1948), 567.

19. [Michel Marescot], *Discovrs veritable sur le faict de Marthe Brossier de Romorantin, pretendue demoniaque* (Paris, 1599). I am using here the English translation, *A true discourse, vpon the matter of Martha Brossier of Romorantin, pretended to be possessed by a deuill*, trans. Abraham Hartvvel (London, 1599), 32.

20. *A true discourse*, 31–33.

21. *A true discourse*, 2–3.

the day: André Duval, already an eminent theologian of the Paris Faculty and a supporter of the League; Benet of Canfield, the Capuchin mystic who later wrote the influential mystical text, *The Ryle of Perfection;* and Pierre de Bérulle, later the founder of the Oratorians and a cardinal, at this time a young humanist scholar and trainee priest. Notwithstanding the status of Brossier's allies, Michel Marescot identified the key threat she posed as being related to the beliefs of "weaker mindes."[22] In order to reduce her and her exorcists to purveyors of popular entertainments, he said her exorcists treated her "like an Ape or a beare."[23] He noted the participation in exorcisms of members of the elite—"Divines, Religious persons, and Phisitians" [physicians]—on the side of Brossier, but he implied the involvement of these people required some explanation; he did not know if they believed in her possession "either through credulitie, or to follow the opinion of the people, or for some other reason."[24] The *politique parlementaire* Jacques-Auguste de Thou, in his chronicle of the case, echoed Marescot's rhetorical association of belief in exorcism with a lack of learning when he referred to André Duval, in particular, as "an otherwise learned man."[25] De Thou also reflected that Brossier's imprisonment had led to "rumblings among the vulgar,"[26] whipped up by the preaching of her supporters. Interestingly, this desire to resist the vulgar was not unique to the opponents of the possession. Bérulle, who wrote a rejoinder to Marescot, also fell in step with this kind of argumentation and established his own and his colleagues' elitist credentials. Keen to distance the exorcists from any association with the superstitions of the masses, he stated emphatically that exorcists had at one point removed Brossier from the public view because the people are "not fit to determine

---

22. *A true discourse,* 3.

23. *A true discourse,* 22. On the link between exorcism and theater, see Stephen Greenblatt, "Exorcism into Art," *Representations* 12 (1985): 15–23.

24. *A true discourse,* 2.

25. Jacques-Auguste de Thou, *Historiarum sui temporis,* 5; translated into French: *Histoire de Marthe Brossier pretendve possedee tiree dv Latin de Messire Iacqves Avgvst de Thov, President au Parlement de Paris. Avec qvelqves remarqves et considerations generales sur cette Matiere, tirées pour la plus part aussi du Latin de Bartholomaeus Perdulcis celebre Medecin de la Faculté de Paris. Le tovt liure intitulé* La Pieté affligée ou Discours Historique & Theologique de la possession des Religieuses dictes de Sainte Elizabeth de Louuiers &c. (Rouen, 1652), 1–16, esp. 10.

26. *Histoire de Marthe Brossier,* 11. The exorcists of Marthe Brossier might have been glad to see riots disrupt the progress of the Edict of Nantes, and the king did indeed have more to fear from Paris crowds than did the Leaguers. This example was intended only to illustrate a point about the rhetorical identification of class and belief.

truth."[27] This move by Bérulle is clearly not evidence of an accommodationist position in regard to the vulgar; on the contrary, it shows an educated, militant Catholic defending ecclesiastical magic in spite of, rather than in the service of, the uneducated.

Similarly mixed views about the nature and value of the public emerged in relation to the first major possession case of the seventeenth century: the possessions at the Ursuline convent in Aix-en-Provence, from 1609 to 1611. This case led to the execution in April 1611 of the priest Louis Gaufridy for causing the possession of several nuns through witchcraft and also for sexual seduction.[28] One commentator at the time associated the witchcraft of Gaufridy with his eloquence, which had "falsely deluded" the "Marcellian Vulgar" by whom he was "exceedingly reverenced, and very much respected."[29] Elsewhere, Sébastien Michaelis, the noted Dominican reformer and the man who lobbied the Parlement of Aix to execute Gaufridy, referred favorably to the "great troupes" of onlookers who came to witness the exorcisms, including "the poore of adioyning villages."[30] Thus crowds are characterized in the same case and from the same perspective, indifferently, as both a caution for their weakness and as a source of support, apparently righteously drawn towards the truth.

In 1612, Michaelis was again involved in a case of possession, this time in a Brigidine convent at Lille in the French-speaking Low Countries.[31] Jean le

27. Léon d'Alexis [Pierre de Bérulle], *Traicté des Energumenes, Suiuy d'vn discours sur la possession de Marthe Brossier: Contre les Calomnies d'vn Medecin de Paris* (Troyes, 1599), 47–48.

28. He was convicted of "kidnapping, seduction, impiety, magic, witchcraft, and other abominations": *Arrest de la Covr de Parlement de Prouence, portant condamnation contre Messire Louis Gaufridi, originaire du lieu de Beau-vezer lès Colmaret, Prestre beneficié en l'Eglise des Accoules de la ville de Marseille: Conuaincu de Magic, & autres crimes abominables du dernier Auril, mil six cens onze* (Aix-en-Provence, 1611), 3.

29. *The Life and Death of Lewis Gaufredy: A Priest of the Church of the Accoules in Marseilles in France... whose horrible life being made manifest, hee was Arraigned and Condemned by the Court of the Parliament of Aix in Prouence, to be burnt aliue, which was performed the last day of Aprill, 1611.... Translated and faithfully collected out of two French Copies* (London, 1612), unnumbered fourth page.

30. Sébastien Michaelis, *The Admirable Historie of the Possession and Conversion of a Penitent woman: Sedvced by a magician that made her to become a witch.... Wherevnto is annexed a Pnevmology, or Discourse of Spirits*, trans. W. B. (London, 1613), 30, 31. Translated from idem, *Histoire admirable de la possession et conversion d'vne penitente, Seduite par vn magicien, la faisant Sorciere & Princesse des Sorciers au pays de Prouence, conduite à la S. Baume pour y estre exorcizee l'an M. DC. X. au mois de Nouembre, soubs l'authorité du R. P. F. Sebastien Michaelis... Ensemble la Pneumalogie ou Discours du susdit P. Michaelis* (Paris, 1613).

31. Alain Lottin, *Lille: Citadelle de la Contre-Réforme? (1598–1668)* (Dunkerque: Westhoek Editions, 1984), 171.

Normant, a noble layman and passionate devotee of the exorcisms of Michaelis, published a voluminous and detailed account of the case.[32] Its reception among the elite was somewhat mixed. The Paris Faculty of Theology took strong exception to its publication "in the vulgar idiom" (French) of "descriptions of obscenities and prodigious abominations and impieties of witches" which, it observed, were "deadly for the curious, the weak-minded and the wicked."[33] Yet only a few months earlier, in October 1622, two members of the same faculty, Soto and Le Gendre, had signed an approbation for the book, and it was printed early in 1623 in both Latin and French.[34] It is not possible to determine whether the approbation was for the Latin edition only or for both editions. The accompanying royal privilege issued on 8 October 1622 refers specifically to both, suggesting the theologians' approbation may well have applied to both languages. This difference between two sets of theologians from the same faculty would suggest the existence of a hairline fracture in the principal corporation in France to declare upon questions of orthodoxy.[35]

These examples show that those who were depicted as weak-minded or vulgar were seen as most likely to be seduced by appearances and emotions, by the lure of rabble-rousing or charismatic preachers (in the Brossier and Gaufridy cases), or by lurid descriptions of witchcraft. For the members of the elite who expressed such views, "vulgar" was as much a byword for what not to be, or to whom not to appeal, as it was a pointer to any demographic reality.[36] Statements presented as the product of unambiguous theological

32. Jean le Normant, *Histoire veritable et memorable de ce qvi c'est passé sovs l'exorcisme de trois filles possedées és païs de Flandre: En la descouuerte & confession de Marie de Sains, soy disant Princesse de la Magie; & Simone Dourlet Complice, & autres*, vol. 2: *De la vocation des magiciens et magiciennes par le ministre des demons*, 2 vols. (Paris, 1623).

33. *Censvra facvltatis Theologiae Parisiensis Libri Latino & Gallico Idiomate conscripti, cuius Titulus est. Vera ac Memorabilis Historia de tribus Energumenis in partibus Belgij, &c. Cum tribus Appendicibus: 1. De Mirabilibus huius Operis 2. De conformitate ipsius ad Scripturas, &c. 3. De potestate Ecclesiastica super Daemones &c. Edita in lucem diligentia Ioannis le Normant, &c, Paris* [1623], BN MSS fds Dupuy 641 (fols. 167r–170r), fol. 169v. My thanks are due to Constant Mews for kindly translating this document.

34. Le Normant, *Histoire veritable* (unpaginated, first two pages after 346 in first volume).

35. The second response was probably prompted by the fact that Le Normant was an upstart layman who declared on matters of theology.

36. Such ambivalence is also evident in Italy, where the great promoter of exorcism, Girolamo Menghi, sniffed at those whom he referred to as the "elevated intellects," who did not believe in the value of exorcism; see O'Neil, "*Sacerdote ovvero strione*," 54. A late inclusion on this topic is Nancy Caciola, "Spirits Seeking Bodies: Death, Possession and Communal Memory in the Middle Ages," in *The Place of the Dead: Death and Remembrance in Late Medieval and Early Modern Europe*, eds. Bruce

truths may only have been the justifications of sophisticated authors, asserting an ideological agenda by identifying a social group with particular beliefs
or practices. This is not to suggest that those who allowed rites which were
elsewhere the subject of censure were acting out of pragmatism or bad faith.
Indeed, it was something of a tradition for exorcism to find its place in
Catholicism suspended between the frontline of reform and conversion (as a
marvelous means of proselytism) and the underworld of suspect magical
remedies, with their appeal to the allegedly short-term, materialist, and selfish
mentality of the uneducated. The precarious status of exorcism is inherent in
traditional doctrines which allow for the manifestation of holiness in the
physical realm but in which the prerogative of interpretation lies to a large
extent within the workings of hierarchy.[37] In early modern France, moreover,
the priorities and indeed the nature of religious hierarchies were changing at a
rapid rate in light of the wars and in relation to the spiritual revival which followed them. In a climate of profound fear of the devil's incursions, many
members of the Catholic elite saw it as their duty to confront the threat
directly. For many, possession and exorcism were means to the re-Catholici-
zation of France. In this context, aspects of the cult of the dead—a cult which
was just as theologically ambiguous—played an important part in underpin-
ning the innovations in cases of possession and exorcism.

POSSESSION AND THE REALM OF THE DEAD
Relations with the world of the dead were, like exorcism, part of the "soft"
interpretative edge of reformed Catholicism: defended as orthodox, they were
still the subject of only qualified endorsement because of their association with
superstition. The Council of Trent reinforced the importance of the cult of the
dead in relation to traditional church beliefs in purgatory, allowing for the continued use, for example, of masses and prayers for the dead. It cautioned, however, against practices which "tend to a certain kind of curiosity or superstition"
which were thus to be prohibited as "scandals and stumblingblocks [sic] to the
faithful."[38] These problem areas likely included belief in appearances of the

---

Gordon and Peter Marshall (New York: Cambridge University Press, 2000), 66–86.

37. The utility of traditional "objective" criteria for discernment, such as the division between
knowledge based on necessity and that discovered through curiosity, and caution in the face of perceived excess was nonetheless often subject to ambiguous political situations where equally powerful
protagonists held opposing views. Clark, *Thinking with Demons*, 475–77.

38. *Canons and Decrees of the Council of Trent: Original Text with English Translations*, trans.
Henry Joseph Schroeder (St. Louis, Mo.; London: B. Herder, 1941), 214. The kingdom of France did

dead, possession of the living by the souls of the dead, and divination about souls in purgatory. Gabriella Zarri has argued that in spite of the Catholic Church's adhering to its traditional beliefs about communication between the living and the dead, greater skepticism within its ranks in the sixteenth century nonetheless led to a growing demarcation between the world of the living and that of the dead. One of the ways this came about was through the "demonization" of the cult of the dead.[39] For France, the story of the young Nicole Obry is notable for the way in which it demonized one "popular" aspect of the cult of the dead—belief in the capacity of the dead in purgatory to possess the bodies of the living in their quest for deliverance—and redeployed it to serve the aims of confessional polemic.

Obry initially claimed that her discomfort was caused by the restless soul of her deceased grandfather. She said that she had seen his tormented spirit at his grave and that he had then entered her body. The spirit, speaking both inwardly to Obry and also through her mouth, urged her and her family to have masses said, to give alms, and to go on pilgrimages on his behalf. A Dominican suspected the presence of the devil and proceeded to exorcise Obry.[40] Under his tutelage, Obry went on to become a symbol of Catholic ritual aggression towards the Huguenots. In demonizing Obry's traditional view of her possession (and also possibly a traditional means of expressing grief), a new use was found for this belief within the exigencies of anti-Huguenot polemic. Faith in this manifestation in the living of the "personal purgatory" of the dead appears to have been widely contested by reform-minded demonologists, keen to extirpate what they saw as superstitious attributions of possession but who thereby left that much more room for an attribution to the devil to be validated. Pedro Ciruelo had declared, "The spirit that speaks in a possessed person is not a soul of some dead man; rather, it is most certainly the deceiving devil." Jean Bodin reported a 1458 case in which a man claimed he spoke with the voice of a dead woman, but, Bodin reports, the spirit fled when

---

not officially adopt the Council's reforms, but its "mood" pervaded French practice nonetheless; Hsia, *World of Catholic Renewal*, 69.

39. Gabriella Zarri, "Purgatorio 'particolare' e ritorno dei morti tra riforma e controriforma: L'area italiana," *Quaderni Storici* 17 (1982): 466–97, at 488–89. See also Jean-Claude Schmitt, *Ghosts in the Middle Ages: The Living and the Dead in Medieval Society*, trans. Teresa Lavender Fagan (Chicago: University of Chicago Press, 1998), 116–21.

40. Jehan Boulaese, *L'abbregee histoire dv grand miracle par nostre Sauueur & Seigneur Iesvs-Christ en la saincte Hostie du Sacrement de l'Autel, faict à Laon 1566* (Paris, 1573), fol. 4 r–v.

asked to say a *Miserere*, thereby revealing itself to have been demonic.[41] Martin
Del Rio wrote that when the devil pretends to be the soul of a deceased person,
the claim is always false.[42] Referring to the Obry case specifically, the Parisian
Celestine Pierre Crespet refuted Obry's belief and wrote that it was "against the
nature of souls, for they can never enter the bodies of the living" and added "so
it came to be known that in the end this was a devil and not a soul or an
angel."[43] Thus, even while this traditional or popular notion grew out of the
Catholic theology of purgatory and belief in meritorious action to help the
dead, it was nonetheless subject to revision and redeployment in the Obry
case, if not for the family's purposes.[44] Many other cases of possession nonetheless retained the idea that the dead could contact the living to elicit the sympathy and aid of the living, to make known their state in the afterlife, or even to
cause torment through witchcraft.

The capacity of the dead to appear to the living, for example, had the qualified endorsement of most demonologists. Ciruelo said, "Occasionally, God
permits a soul from the next life to appear to the living," and Guazzo, following
Augustine, wrote, "We must understand that such apparitions are not the ordinary rule, but occur in accordance with the special and singular permission of
God."[45] Crespet cautioned that "often Satan borrows the form of the deceased
in order to deceive men."[46] This belief played a part in the infamous case of
possession at the Ursuline convent in Loudun during the 1630s. Here the possession of the nuns was initially attributed to sightings of the returning spirit of

41. *Pedro Ciruelo's A Treatise Reproving all Superstitions*, 279; Jean Bodin, *De la démonomanie des sorciers* (Paris, 1580), fol. 157v.

42. Martin Del Rio, "Anacephalaeosis," in *Disqvisitionvm magicarvm* (Louvain, 1599–1600), 334.

43. *Devx Livres de la hayne de Sathan et malins esprits contre l'homme, & de l'homme contre eux* (Paris, 1590), fol. 208r.

44. On the question of the demonization of folklore, see, for example, Midelfort, "The Devil and the German People," 102; Charles Zika, "Appropriating Folklore in Sixteenth-Century Witchcraft Lit-erature: The *Nebelkappe* of Paula Frisius," in *Problems in the Historical Anthropology of Early Modern Europe*, ed. R. Po-chia Hsia and Robert W. Scribner, (Wiesbaden: Harrassowitz, 1997), 175–218.

45. *Pedro Ciruelo's A Treatise Reproving all Superstitions*, 279; Francesco Maria Guazzo, *Compen-dium Maleficarum: The Montague Summers Edition*, trans. E. A. Ashwin (1929; repr., New York: Dover, 1988), 60. On this point in Augustine, see Schmitt, *Ghosts in the Middle Ages*, 21.

46. *De la Hayne de Sathan*, fol. 199r. The Paris Capucin Noel Taillepied in his *Psichologie ov traité de l'apparition des esprits* (Paris, 1588) rejected the "new" skeptical views but argued for the need to distinguish good from bad apparitions: Ronald C. Finucane, *Appearances of the Dead: A Cultural His-tory of Ghosts* (London: Junction Books, 1982), 100–1. On Hungarian traditions, see Éva Pócs, *Between the Living and the Dead: A Perspective on Witches and Seers in the Early Modern Age*, trans. Szilvia Rédey and Michael Webb (Budapest: Central European University Press, 1999; dist. Yale Uni-versity Press), esp. 122–29.

the convent's recently deceased spiritual director, Father Moussaut. In September 1632, movements at night disturbed the convent. Nuns saw the shadowy figures of men moving through the house, one of which they initially believed to be the specter of Moussaut.[47] Interest in Father Moussaut's appearances waned quickly, however, as the living priest, Urbain Grandier, became increasingly the focus of the interrogations done to the nuns' demons. The nuns began to appear possessed, and they said under exorcism that Urbain Grandier had caused their possession through his desire to seduce them.[48] One senses that the often-cited politicization of this case led this possession to slip from being about a haunted convent, and perhaps unresolved grief, to being about priestly morality and threats to the nuns' virginity.

Another feature of exorcism in this period showed exorcists drawing on the devil's capacity to have knowledge of distant and occult events, including knowledge of the world of the dead and the state of souls in purgatory. Several possessed women were believed to have gained access to this knowledge through the gift of demonic clairvoyance. The French Augustinian Sanson Birette condemned as an "intolerable abuse" divination through the possessed "on the misfortunes of illnesses, of death, of accidents, of losses, of animals and of occult crimes, in order to have revelation about them" and described it as an "error of the vulgar."[49] Yet such behavior in the possessed closely resembled the percipience of saintly ecstatics, and this similarity seems to account for the degree of acceptance it found in this period. A new emphasis on the saintlike suffering of the possessed tended to blur lines between diabolic possession—which had often been seen as the consequence of sin—and divine ecstasy.[50] Encapsulating this trend, the Franciscan Jean Benedicti wrote in 1611, "Often good people carry their purgatory in their bodies," referring in this instance not to the possession of the living by the dead, but simply to

---

47. Robert Rapley, *A Case of Witchcraft: The Trial of Urban Grandier* (Montreal: McGill–Queens University Press, 1998), 75–82; Michel de Certeau, *La possession de Loudun* (1970) (Paris: Gallimard, 1980), 24. Quite a different kind of ghost—one who did the housework—came under official scrutiny in Kathryn A. Edwards, "Inquiries on the Inquisition and a Burgundian Ghost," *Proceedings of the Annual Meeting of the Western Society for French History* 23 (1996): 219–29.

48. Certeau, *La possession de Loudun*, 29–32.

49. Sanson Birette, *Refvtation de l'errevr dv Vvlgaire, tovchant les responses des diables exorcizez* (Rouen, 1618), 4. Here again Birette is invoking the "vulgar" as both the perpetrators and the victims of this belief.

50. That is not to suggest that saintly ecstatics themselves were seen as unproblematic. See the discussion of the dilemmas of ecstasy in Alison Weber, "Between Ecstasy and Exorcism: Religious Negotiation in Sixteenth-Century Spain," *Journal of Medieval and Renaissance Studies* 23 (1993): 221–34.

the suffering which certain of the demon-possessed endured while attempting to live a good life.[51] This new accent on the virtue of the suffering possessed can be associated with two principal developments. The first is the increasing likelihood in this period that possession would be accounted for by an accusation of witchcraft, which deflected (without removing entirely) the likelihood of guilt on the part of the possessed. This feature of possession was almost universal in cases in early modern France. Second, a growing emphasis on the imitation of martyrs in pursuit of holiness became a benchmark of religiosity in the "century of saints."[52] The suffering possessed thus became in some cases, in effect, church-sanctioned witches, who divined under the guidance of exorcists.[53]

Marthe Brossier, for example, was reported to have performed as an oracle during a yearlong tour of exorcisms in the Loire valley, prior to her arrival in Paris. According to a woman named Anne Chevriou, whom Brossier had accused of causing her possession through witchcraft, Brossier fielded questions from onlookers about whether the souls of their deceased parents were in heaven or purgatory, whether husbands would come home safe from the fields, whether people with whom they had disputes would be damned when they died, and in Chevriou's words "a thousand other frivolous questions."[54] According to Chevriou, Brossier tailored her answers to the questioners' wishes and drew on her own knowledge of the deceased's lives.[55] For the possessed peasant Marie des Vallées (1590–1656), a profound desire to suffer graced her with the capacity for her soul to separate from her body during her lifetime and to enter hell and witness the suffering of the damned. There, she

51. Jean Benedicti, *La triomphante victoire De la vierge Marie, sur sept malins esprits, finalement chassés du corps d'vne femme, dans l'Eglise des Cordeliers de Lyon* (Lyon, 1611), 46.

52. See Jacques Le Brun, "Mutations de la notion de martyre au XVIIe siècle d'après les biographies spirituelles féminines," in *Sainteté et martyre dans les religions du livre*, ed. Jacques Marx (Brussels: University of Brussels, 1989), 77–96.

53. The arresting expression "God's witch" is used to describe a similar woman in Italy: Gabrielle Zarri, *Le sante vive: Cultura e religiosità femminile nella prima età moderna* (Turin: Rosenberg & Sellier, 1990), 12.

54. Bibliothèque Nationale, Paris, MSS fds fs 18453, fol. 8v. Anne Chevriou was later exonerated of the witchcraft charge in 1605. (Personal communication, Alfred Soman, n.d.).

55. Bibliothèque Nationale, Paris, MSS fds fs 18453, fols. 8v–9r. Chevriou also disparaged Brossier's "demon's" claim that the soul of one of her own exorcists, now dead, had gone straight to heaven (ibid., fol. 7r). It might also be noted, if this commentary was indeed dictated by Chevriou, that we see in it a peasant under accusation of witchcraft, dismissing as "frivolous" activities which were being promoted by senior members of the clergy. Here again the reality behind the model of the uneducated as the purveyors of exorcism may be open to challenge.

reported, she saw the sufferings of the damned, in particular the suffering of witches, which she undertook to share with them.[56]

For Jeanne des Anges, the superior of the Ursuline convent at Loudun, her initially demonic clairvoyance carried through to her assumption of a more mainstream identity as a mystic and spiritual leader. When possessed, she had testified against the priest Urbain Grandier, who was executed for witchcraft in 1634. But the personal cult around Jeanne, which began with the "spiritual tourism" of Loudun, grew over the next three decades, and her clairvoyant capacities augmented. Following the death of the wife and daughter of Baron de Laubardemont, Grandier's chief enemy and a promoter of Jeanne's cult, the baron sought news of their fate from Jeanne. Jeanne affirmed to Laubardemont that his wife and daughter were saved.[57]

In a letter of 1660 to her spiritual director, the Jesuit Jean-Baptiste Saint-Jure, Jeanne described a series of conversations she had with the spirit of a deceased nun, the subprioress of the convent, Mother Gabriel de l'Incarnation. Jeanne was aware of the possibility of devils disporting themselves as the dead; therefore, she first confirmed her vision by asking the help of Jesus and recommending herself to her guardian angel, a protective guide who served as something of an internal spiritual director to Jeanne and whose views she regularly relayed by letter to Saint-Jure. She described her experience of this revenant of Mother Gabriel to him:

> When I first saw her near to me, I had a great natural fear; but as there was nothing frightening about her, I was quickly reassured. I crossed myself and asked our Lord that I not be deceived in this encounter and I recommended myself to my holy guardian angel.

56. Bibliothèque Mazarine, MS 3177, 22.

57. Michel de Certeau, "Jeanne des Anges" (1966), in Jeanne des Anges, *Autobiographie* (1886; repr., Grenoble: Jérôme Million, 1990), 301–47, at 340. In a significant example, however, the friend and former exorcist of Jeanne des Anges, the Jesuit Jean-Joseph Surin urged Jeanne not to "run a sort of advice shop" [*tenir comme une boutique*], where her guardian angel responded to inquiries about marriages, lawsuits, and the like (339). Surin nonetheless related approvingly the story of a sister at Loudun who read minds. He tells of many nobles' being at the exorcisms and "their lackeys' being in the parlour with a secular girl, a pensioner in this convent," who was also possessed. The lackeys asked the girl to tell them their thoughts to divert themselves. They gave her a "dragée" (a kind of sweetmeat) for the whole evening, and she told them their thoughts. All of them said she had guessed right: Jean-Joseph Surin, *Histoire abrégée de la possession des Ursulines de Loudun et des peines du Père Surin* (Paris, 1828), 31. For Surin, such a display was clearly satisfactory in the case of a lesser sister in the presence of inconsequential employees, but for Jeanne as the superior, it would not do.

Then I prayed that this Mother tell me what state she was in and if I could render her any service. She replied: "I am satisfying divine justice in purgatory."[58]

The nun told Jeanne of the minor sins she had committed regarding convent life, and she chided Jeanne as her superior for having let them pass, begging her to "work to destroy all partialities in the community from the start." When her face approached Jeanne's, Jeanne felt as if "a burning coal had scalded her" even though Mother Gabriel's specter did not touch her. A month later, Mother Gabriel appeared "all clear and luminous" to Jeanne in the evening and bade her farewell as she passed through to heaven.[59] In the case of another nun who had died, Jeanne reported that she had spoken with the woman after her death, following a promise made by the woman to report to Jeanne on her fate once she had died. The woman thanked Jeanne for her contribution "to the glory that I possess."[60] In both cases the cult of the dead served to confirm Jeanne in her own quest for spiritual seniority by showing her to be a divinely appointed intermediary of the dead.

Jeanne's contact with the dead was a speculum held up to encourage personal betterment in this life, but it also reinforced the role of purgatory as a source of punishment. This lesson could work more than one way, and Certeau observed that Jeanne's interactions with the dead reflected her personal opinions of those whose suffering she described.[61] On at least one occasion, when Jeanne's reputation had be impugned, she found in her experience of purgatory vindication for her own contested spiritual authority. At Loudun, in 1662, critics had charged that she showed favoritism among her nuns and that the guardian angel and the famous holy names, miraculously inscribed on her hands following an exorcism, were diabolic illusions.[62] As a result

58. "Extrait des lettres que la mère Jeanne des Anges, supérieure des ursulines de Loudun, a écrites au révérend Père Saint-Jure de la Compagnie de Jésus," in Anges, *Autobiographie*, 234–89, at 283.

59. Anges, *Autobiographie*, 284–86.

60. Anges, *Autobiographie*, 287. This instance resembles the pact made between the shaman of Oberstdorf, Chonrad Stoeckhlin, and his drinking companion, Jacob Walch, in Behringer, *Shaman of Oberstdorf*, 11. Francesco Guazzo also reported that Marsilio Ficino had made a similar pact with a friend, Michele Mercatis: Guazzo, *Compendium Maleficarum*, 67–68.

61. Certeau, "Jeanne des Anges," 340.

62. "La vie de la vénérable Mère Jeanne des Anges…recueillie de ses propres écrits, et des mémoires des Révérends pères Seurin et Saint-Jure, jésuittes, et de ceux de nostre vénérable soeur du Houx," MS in Archives de la Visitation, Mayenne, 866. I thank the Sister Archivist Thérèse-Edith Barré for her gracious assistance in making the collection available.

there were moves to establish a commission under the bishop of Poitiers to examine her life, mores, and "the extraordinary things" that happened within her. The commission came to nothing, however, after a priest who had worked to build up the dossier against her died suddenly and unconfessed.[63] Jeanne offered to render satisfaction to God for his soul in purgatory, and it is recorded that Jeanne endured terrible pain on his behalf for a long time, implicitly showing him to have been a sinner. "This dead man," she wrote, "now sees the truth of what he opposed so heatedly," apparently referring to his actions in relation to her. Reflecting on the failure of the commission to follow up its investigations, Jeanne related simply that the death of the priest "had given [people] pause to reflect."[64] Thus, Jeanne's holiness, as a recovering possessed woman in a new climate of intense spiritual enthusiasm, was amplified through the medium of the dead and purgatory.

At the Hospitaller convent of Saint Louis and Saint Elizabeth in Louviers, Normandy, during 1643 a *mise-en-scène* unfolded similar to that at Loudun, again following the death of a convent's spiritual director, Mathurin Picard. In this case, it was one of the most depressing and sordid possession stories from this period. The alleged power of the deceased to bring about possession through his dead body and magic charms he had made in life led to the outbreak of possession. Picard, an elderly priest who had been an author of uncontroversial moral tracts,[65] died in September 1642 and was buried at his own request in the convent chapel. Around the end of 1642, disturbances began in the convent, and the nuns became unable to take communion, suffering "internal and external torments" caused by "visions of witches at night." Under exorcism the nuns said the cause was the presence of Picard's body in the chantry of the convent chapel.[66] The nuns did not see Picard's ghost, nor did they say it had entered their bodies, yet his power reached back to them from the world of the dead. According to the possessed nuns, Picard had seduced one of their sister nuns, Madeleine Bavent, into witchcraft and had also seduced her sexually. Together, the nuns said, Picard and Bavent had

---

63. "La vie de la vénérable Mère Jeanne des Anges," 864, 866.

64. "La vie de la vénérable Mère Jeanne des Anges," 865–67.

65. *L'arsenac de l'ame d'ov elle tire trois sortes d'Armes pour triompher plainement de ses communs Ennemis, savoir, Du ieusne, De l'Aumosne, de l'oraison* (Rouen, 1626), and *Le Fovet des Paillairds, ov Iuste punition des voluptueux et charnels, conforme aux arrests diuins & humains* (Rouen, 1628).

66. *Recit veritable de ce qui s'est fait & passé à Louviers touchant les Religieuses possedées Extraict d'vne Lettre escrite de Louviers à vn Evesque* (Paris, 1643), 5.

confected evil charms, using various obscene bodily by-products, including aborted fetuses from Bavent.[67]

The matter remained for some months within the convent's walls. A priest named Ravaut exorcised the nuns by day, and in a novel twist, some of the senior nuns "by the privilege of their eminent sanctity, although quite incapable of the order and function of exorcists" exorcised them by night.[68] In March 1643 the bishop of Evreux, François Péricard, moved to investigate and swiftly passed sentence on the memory of Mathurin Picard, ordering that his body be exhumed and thrown into a pit known as Le Puits Crosnier in the lands of the archbishop of Rouen.[69] The exhumation was carried out in secret, for fear of scandal, and in order to preserve the honor of "priesthood [and] religion" and to avoid prejudice to the convent.[70] Bishop Péricard also threatened to excommunicate anyone who revealed the secret.[71] It was noted at the time of the exhumation that the body of Picard, six months after burial, was "healthy and whole." One account said that, while this would normally be taken as a sign of sanctity, the demons offered the unusual explanation "that the flesh of the excommunicated cannot rot in holy ground."[72] Madeleine Bavent was stripped of her veil and locked up in the ecclesiastical prison of the *Officialité* of Evreux.[73] These moves proved inadequate, however, to stem the power of Picard's and Bavent's witchcraft, and the nuns remained possessed. Around 20 May 1643, children found the dumped body of Picard, and the

67. *Sentences et arrests servans a la ivstification de la calomnieuse accusation faite contre Soeur Françoise de la Croix, cy-deuant Superieure des Religieuses & Conuent des Hospitalieres de la Charité Nostre-Dame, proche la Place Royale* (Paris, 1654), 8; "Copie en forme de Recveil De ce qui se fait de jour en jour dans le Monastere des filles Relligieuzes Saint Louis dont la pluspart sont folles, maleficiez & tourmentez des Diables. En ceste Année 1643," in *Recueil de pièces sur les possessions des religieuses de Louviers*, (Rouen, 1879), 2.

68. [Madeleine Bavent and Charles Desmarets], *Histoire de Magdelaine Bavent, Religieuse du Monastere de Saint Loüis de Louviers... Ensemble l'Interrogatoire de Magdelaine Bavent: De plus l'Arrest donné contre Mathurin Picard, Thomas Boullé & ladite Bavent, tous convaincus du Crime de magie, l'vn brulé vif & l'autre mort* (Paris, 1652), 43. On female exorcists, see also David Lederer's essay in this volume. Mary O'Neil noted that Menghi allowed for the possibility of "devout persons" without priestly office performing exorcisms: O'Neil, *Discerning Superstition*, 336. As ordination is not a prerequisite for successful exorcism, since the rite is a sacramental not a sacrament, this view is theologically sound.

69. *Sentences et arrests*, 6; and *Recit veritable*, 6.

70. *Sentences et arrests*, 9.

71. Esprit Du Bosroger, *La pieté affligee ov discovrs historiqve & Theologique de la Possession des Religieuses dittes de Saincte Elizabeth de Louuiers* (Rouen, 1652), 383.

72. *Recit veritable*, 6. The same inversion of a usual sign of sanctity applies in the cases of vampires: Finucane, *Appearances of the Dead*, 155.

73. *Sentences et arrests*, 8.

bishop's actions were exposed. Picard's relatives complained to the Parlement of Rouen. The body was again removed, this time by a *sergent royal*, before a reported crowd of two thousand people.[74] To defend Bishop Péricard, allies in Paris organized a royal commission to investigate the case and, in effect, to find in his favor.[75] Legal machinations surrounding the case continued for around eleven years, during which time numerous exorcists found in this case a means to promote a range of devotional and polemic agendas. One of these exorcists, Father Thomas Le Gauffre, brought another dimension of beliefs about the cult of the dead to the case in the promotion of a reputed saint.

In March 1643, just as news of the exorcisms of Louviers was breaking, Le Gauffre and his companion, a layman known as "Brother" Jean Blondeau, traveled to Louviers from Paris in order to confront the devils with the supernatural power of their late friend, another recently deceased priest, the famous Paris preacher Claude Bernard. Bernard, known as "le pauvre prêtre," had died in 1641.[76] According to Le Gauffre, Bernard had successfully performed an exorcism on a possessed girl at Reims by applying his diurnal to her. Le Gauffre published booklets about the success of Bernard's exorcisms which tell that "demons" accused Bernard of persecuting them. According to Le Gauffre, Sister Bonnaventura, possessed by the demon "Arfaxa," "began to cry out against the relics of Father Bernard," making specific mention of his breviaries.[77] He recorded:

> I was surprised to hear mention of the breviaries of Father Bernard…and I conjured him to tell me more…and the harder it was for him to speak of it the more I pressed him by the merit of the relics. [The devil said]: "You know very well, dog, I have told you, he is a dog of a priest like you, a bigot who chased one of his companions with his breviary." And then he started to cry out: "Dog Bernard, you persecute us everywhere, the devils are powerless since you got involved."[78]

74. "Copie en forme de Recveil," 4.

75. *Attestation de Messievrs les Commissaires enuoyez par sa Majesté pour prendre connoissance, auec Monseigneur l'Euesque d'Eureux, de l'estat des Religieuses qui paroissent agitées au Monastere de Saint Louys & Sainte Elizabeth de Louuiers* (1643).

76. Albert Garreau, *Claude Bernard: Le Pauvre prêtre, parisien du Faubourg Saint-Germain* (Paris: Editions du Cèdre, 1965).

77. Thomas Le Gauffre, *Recit veritable De ce qui s'est fait & passé aux Exorcismes de plusieurs Religieuses de la ville de Louviers, en presence de Monsieur le Penitencier d'Evreux, & Monsieur le Gauffre* (Paris, 1643), 36, 29.

78. Le Gauffre, *Recit veritable*, 32–33.

Bishop Péricard also sought Claude Bernard's intercessory powers to deliver the Hospitaller convent nuns. In a letter to Le Gauffre in April 1644, Péricard wrote that he had vowed a novena at the altar of Bernard's burial place in order that "the sanctity of good Father Bernard...end the evil that a wicked priest had committed."[79] Through the agency of one dead priest, in effect, the exorcists pressed back the powers of another. Thus the cult of the dead was set on a collision course. The miraculous powers of the priest Bernard in death serve as an ironic counterpoint to the effects of the buried body of Mathurin Picard, and each contributes in its way to the cult of a thaumaturgic priesthood. A magic charm is, after all, just a bad or tainted relic. In the end, the Parlement of Rouen issued an *arrêt* on 21 August 1647 which ordered that Picard's bones be burned, together with a living priest, the young vicar Thomas Boulle, who, tragically, had also come to be accused of witchcraft by the same nuns. These mirror aspects of the cult of the dead bring into focus two preoccupations of the era of Catholic renewal: the standing of the priesthood and the sexual morality of Christians, particularly among nuns. The cult of the dead in this, as in other possession cases, was not itself the object of reform, but rather it operated as part of its armory, as a medium of zealous persecution.

CONCLUSION

This essay has attempted to illustrate two related arguments. First, it is not possible to assume that the notion of the "superstitions of the vulgar" refers to the behavior of a discrete social entity. Rather, such a notion in French possession cases functioned as a touchstone whereby elites sought to distinguish their position from that of their presumed inferiors. This essay attempts to show that the identity of social groups can be less important than the way in which the idea of them is mobilized. The retention of class distinction was not the primary aim here; rather, it was a way of enforcing the function of hierarchy within religion because of the essentially contestable nature of sacramental forms. The use of the term "vulgar" can be distinguished both from the reality of class relations, which was more complex, and the reality of elite practices. In that era, elites swooped on possession and exorcism and made them their own in the quest for a pure and purifying priesthood and in order to promote spiritually gifted women. The power to assign arbitrarily value systems to the vulgar remained, of course, largely the prerogative of the elite.

79. BN MSS fds fs 18695, fol. 189 r–v.

The second section of the paper sought to draw attention to innovations in the cult of the dead in possession cases. It shows that the cult of the dead was a viable and productive medium for the elites, one which was open to innovation and expansion even as its retention in Catholicism was qualified officially by reference to its "superstitious" uses.

More broadly, this essay seeks to examine the nature of Tridentine Catholicism as characterized by a fundamentally sacramental, ritualist, and immanent religiosity. Emphasis on the notion of accommodation, while it accounts for certain aspects of reform, tends to reinforce a view of Catholicism in which sacramentals, rituals, and immanence can be considered marginal. Yet because sacramentals, for example, have been the subject of perennial division, it does not mean they are in essence marginal; certainly they are not essential to salvation, as the sacraments are, but that does not mean that they are not central to the institutional identity of Catholicism.[80] In choosing to "ride the tiger" of a sacramental religion, people refashioning the early modern French church ensured the proliferation of activism and enthusiasm among the learned and the vulgar to equally good effect. Sacramental forms not only represented something whose persistence was tolerated in a revamped and supervised form, with the excesses pared down. Rather, their uses were highly innovative and took firm root among the elites, excesses or no excesses. Tridentine reform, however, had sharpened both the need and the taste for division, and in so doing it opened up the possibility of different versions of reform working at cross-purposes, leading to both innovation and fragmentation at the elite level.

---

80. Ramsey, *Liturgy, Politics, and Salvation*, 3.

REVISITING EL ENCUBIERTO

*Navigating between Visions
of Heaven and Hell on Earth*

Sara T. Nalle

For centuries the story of El Encubierto has repelled or fascinated those who have come across it. In March 1522, during the general uprisings in Valencia known as Las Germanías, a man claiming to be The Hidden One, a type of messianic figure, appeared out of nowhere and, until he was assassinated two months later on 18 May, was able to lead several villages in southwestern Valencia into battle against the forces of the crown and local nobility. In the decades that followed, chroniclers favorable to the monarchy and Valencian elites sought to discredit El Encubierto and erase all memory of his rebellion. Hundreds of years later, during the nineteenth century, El Encubierto became the focus of Valencian writers looking for romantic subject matter to support regional aspirations for autonomy within the Spanish state. Their fanciful renderings of the few facts known about the revolt obscured the true nature of the events which transpired.[1] In reality, Valencia had witnessed a millenarian revolt, but no one in the sixteenth or nineteenth centuries would acknowledge the fact. In the sixteenth century, religiously inspired utopian revolts were the most feared forms of social unrest; in the nineteenth century, progressive liberals did not want to admit that popular demands for freedom from oppression could be motivated by religious extremism. While there are several cases of self-declared messiahs and prophets in late medieval Spain, none seems to have had the impact on his contemporaries that El Encubierto did.[2] However, because of the revolutionary situation in Valencia during the

---

1. Ricardo García Cárcel, *Las germanías de Valencia*, new ed. (Barcelona: Península, 1981), is the best account available; see 30–32 for a summary of the romantic bibliography.

2. Outbreaks of Jewish messianism periodically swept through the converso communities of Spain and Portugal but did not result in revolts, unless one counts El Encubierto himself as a Jewish

Germanías, El Encubierto was able to succeed where others had failed: he alone, among the Spanish cases I have been able to document, garnered a following of believers who took to the streets and even bore arms in his cause, believing that El Encubierto would lead them to a millennial heaven on earth. Precisely because of El Encubierto's success it was necessary afterward for authors to discredit thoroughly the man and to obscure the currents of religious fervor that inspired his followers, for in their minds, El Encubierto's Promised Land was their earthly hell.

The campaign to discredit El Encubierto was so successful in its day that no unbiased accounts of the episode survive. Thus, while the story of El Encubierto is well known to specialists, they are forced to rely on hostile chroniclers who systematically distorted or even fabricated El Encubierto's story and refused to acknowledge the millenarian and messianic aspects of the revolt for what they were. Even Ricardo García Cárcel, who is perhaps the best informed modern historian to write about the Germanías revolt, could not avoid mixing the hostile accounts with more neutral ones, producing a contradictory analysis of El Encubierto. Fortunately, the antagonistic chroniclers are not the sole source for the history of El Encubierto. The Hidden One's patently heretical statements won the interest of the Inquisition, whose records preserve the only eyewitness testimony relating to the case. By carefully sifting through the Inquisitorial record, it is possible to recover the voices of El Encubierto's followers as well as those of his enemies and see the revolt through their eyes, without the subsequent distortions of the chroniclers. By comparing the chroniclers' descriptions of El Encubierto, we can see how the sketchy facts of the case became the basis for hostile counterhistories that sought to suppress all memory of the rebellion's true nature.

El Encubierto's brief but extraordinary career was made possible by the several years of civil unrest and outright war in Valencia known as *Las Germanías*, which began in late 1519. The causes and course of the revolt are

---

messianic leader, as have Américo Castro, *Aspectos del vivir hispánico: Espiritualismo, messianismo, actidud personal en los siglos XIV al XVI* (Madrid: Alianza, 1970), 42–60, and Julio Caro Baroja, *Los judios en la España Moderna y Contemporánea*, vol. 1 (Madrid: Editions Arion, 1962), 411–12. I do not believe El Encubierto was a Jewish messianic leader. See below, and Haim Beinart, "Inés of Herrera del Duque: The Prophetess of Extremadura," in *Women in the Inquisition: Spain and the New World*, ed. Mary E. Giles (Baltimore: Johns Hopkins University Press, 1999), 42–52; Elias Lipiner, *O sapateiro de Trancoso e o alfaiate de Setubal* (Rio de Janeiro: Imago Editora, 1993); Lea Sestieri, *David Reubeni: Un ebreo d'Arabia in missione segreta nell'Europa del '500* (Genova: Marietti, 1991); and the pamphlet by Antonio R. Rodríguez Moñino, *La muerte de David Reubeni en Badajoz, 1538* (Badajoz: Deputación Provincial, 1959).

complex and require some explanation before El Encubierto's story can be understood. Over the course of several centuries, during the Middle Ages Valencia had been reconquered from the Muslims by Christians from Catalonia and Aragon. In contrast to Castile, where the *Reconquista* had led to the disappearance of most of the Muslim population, Valencia continued to harbor large numbers of Muslims whose agricultural skills were needed to farm the fertile irrigated lands on the coast. The Muslims, protected by their noble landlords from outside pressure to assimilate, were generally hated by their Christian peasant neighbors. This hatred was exacerbated by the regular appearance of Turkish and North African corsairs off the coast of Valencia later in the fifteenth century. The corsairs attacked Valencian shipping, raided the coast, and captured Christians for the purpose of enslaving them and holding them for ransom.[3]

The tension between Muslims and Christians was only the beginning of problems. In the late fifteenth century, as part of the kingdom of Aragon, Valencia had been joined with Castile in the famous union of crowns created by the marriage of Ferdinand of Aragon and Isabella of Castile. To govern Valencia, Ferdinand imposed the institution of a viceroy, which was seen as a violation of local rights. Economically, while the city of Valencia prospered in the fifteenth century, the immigration of many artisans to the city had led to a general weakening of the guild system. Both the guild artisans and farmers felt victimized by the nobility, many of whom engaged in banditry and various acts of violence.[4] Social conditions were generally chaotic and moral standards were low. Instead of setting a higher standard of conduct, the Valencian clergy and friars lived dissolute lives, for which they were despised. Finally, Valencia was home to a large minority of conversos, Christians of Jewish descent who had converted over the course of the fifteenth century to avoid persecution and the expulsion of 1492. Valencia had its own tribunal of the Inquisition to deal with conversos, many of whom, in their desperation, nursed vague messianic hopes of escape to the Holy Land.[5]

---

3. For this summary of the causes and events leading up to the Germanías, I am indebted to García Cárcel, *Las Germanías*, 39–103.

4. Renaissance Valencia's high crime rate has been studied in Pablo Pérez García, *La comparsa de los malhechores: Valencia 1479–1518* (Valencia: Deputació de Valéncia, 1990).

5. An English-language study of the Valencian Inquisition is Stephen Haliczer, *Inquisition and Society in the Kingdom of Valencia, 1478–1834* (Berkeley: University of California Press, 1990), esp. 245, where Haliczer mentions El Encubierto in connection with Christian attacks on the moriscos during the Germanías.

In 1519, the foreign-born Charles I, Spain's new ruler, was touring the kingdoms and meeting with their various parliamentary bodies. In the midst of the tour, in June he received word that he had been elected Holy Roman Emperor. Now, his only goal was to raise as much money as possible from his Spanish subjects and return quickly to northern Europe to claim his title. In a concession to Valencia, where Charles's scheduled visit was canceled, the monarch granted the city the right to organize its own militias to defend itself from ongoing corsair attacks. The concession was interpreted locally to mean that the city's guilds should arm themselves. In the same month Valencia was also stricken by the plague. The nobility and magistrates fled the city, leaving it without leadership. In the absence of any higher authority, the guilds established militias (*germanías*) under the direction of their own Council of Thirteen and began issuing directives, much to the disgust of the nobility. Sporadic acts of violence followed in the next year 1520 while the viceroy, Don Diego Hurtado de Mendoza, sounded out the nobility for support. These were difficult times, for simultaneously the cities of Castile were progressively becoming more alienated from the caretaker government of Adrian of Utrecht, and over the summer of 1520 they joined in a rebellion against the monarchy, known as the Comunero Revolt.[6] In the spring of 1521, the city of Valencia as well as various localities near the coast finally revolted outright. Most of the rebels were members of the artisan or farming classes, who loudly expressed their hatred for Viceroy Mendoza, the nobility, and their Muslim serfs. After six months of warfare, the viceroy and nobles eventually regained control of the kingdom. Early in March 1522, royal forces had recaptured the last Germanías stronghold, the city of Xátiva, and all of the Germanías' leaders had been killed in battle or executed. Then, at the darkest hour of the revolution, when all appeared lost, The Hidden One walked into a rooming house belonging to Pedro Novercas in Xátiva.[7]

The myths and hostility surrounding El Encubierto require us to tread carefully if we hope to understand the situation as it was experienced at the time. This essay emphasizes how the rebellion and its leader appeared to eyewitnesses such as the Franciscan friars who recorded El Encubierto's public

---

6. The Comunero Revolt has an extensive literature, including Stephen Haliczer, *The Comuneros of Castile: The Forging of a Revolution, 1475–1521* (Madison: University of Wisconsin, 1981), and Joseph Pérez, *La revolución de las Comunidades de Castilla (1520–1521)* (Madrid: Siglo Vientiuno de España, 1977).

7. Details are recorded in Martín de Viciana, *Cronica de la inclita y coronada ciudad de Valencia, libro cuarto* (Barcelona, 1566).

sermon in Xátiva and some of El Encubierto's followers who were interrogated by the Inquisition several years later. Those who heard The Hidden One speak in Xátiva or lived in the village where he visited briefly were very clear about what to call him: he was The Hidden One, The Brother (another messianic term), or more descriptively, the man with the sailor's cape, after the thick mariner's cloak (*bernia*) which he always wore. About his origins and purpose, in a sermon delivered on 21 March 1522, El Encubierto said only that he was illiterate, and that one day while he was tending his sheep and cattle, Enoch and Elijah had appeared to him and told him to board their ship, and they would take him to a land where he was to accomplish much good and exalt the faith of Christ. One of the Franciscan friars noted that he had heard that the man, who spoke in Castilian to his Valencian-speaking audience, was a converso from Andalusia.[8] In other words, from the eyewitnesses almost nothing creditworthy about the man's true origins comes to light, since the converso identity was hearsay and El Encubierto easily could have adopted the shepherd's identity for its religious resonances. People would more likely believe that Elijah and Enoch chose to appear to a humble shepherd in a wilderness, for God prefers to make his will known through unsophisticated seers.

In fact, the witnesses were viewing or reporting about El Encubierto exactly in the manner in which he doubtless wished to be seen: as the messianic savior speaking in Castilian as prophesied by John Alamany's book, *De la Venguda de Anticrist* [The Coming of the Antichrist], republished in Valencia in November 1520.[9] As the research of Alain Milhou demonstrates, it is almost certain that the man who assumed the identity of The Hidden One knew something of the prophecies in this book. Alamany envisioned The

---

8. The transcript of the Inquisition testimony is reproduced in Manuel Dánvila y Collado, "El Encubierto de Valencia," *El Archivo* 4 (1889): 123–37: "...dixo que estando guardando las vaquas y ouejas le vino Elias y Enoch y le pidieron que se enbarquase y que ellos lo desenbarquarian y le traherian en la tierra do hauia de hazer mucho provecho y justicia y exalçar la fe de Christo" (124, col. b) and "habia hohit dir e sermonar en Xativa a un home lo nome del qual no sap el dit testis salvo que dihuen es natural de la Andalucia e ha ohit dir en Xativa que seria convers" (126, col. a).

9. Fr. Johan Alamany, *De la Venguda de Anticrist e de les coses que se han de seguir, ab un reprobacio de la secta mahometica* (Valencia, 1520). Valencia was the hometown of Saint Vincent Ferrer, whose sermons on the Apocalypse were well known. Sunni and Shiite Muslims hold a similar folk belief in the *mahdi*, "the divinely guided one" who will appear at the end of the world and usher in a period of prosperity. In the Shiite twelve-imam doctrine, Imam Mahdi, the last imam, will be hidden until the end times. While it is possible that Spanish Muslims, who were Sunnis, knew of *al mahdi* (I have not found any references in Spanish sources), they hardly would wish for their own destruction, as advocated by El Encubierto.

Hidden One along the lines of the timeworn prophecies of the Emperor of the End Times, who would lead a crusade of the poor in Spain that would culminate in the conquest of the Holy Land. Along the way, the Moors were to be annihilated, battle with the Antichrist would be joined, and the millennium would ensue, just as the book of Revelation and other texts promise. Alamany prophesied that El Encubierto would be a shepherd and went on to describe his appearance: "Know that he has a shapely form, is fair-haired with a pink and white complexion, [and] his word is good and true. He is a lover of justice and enemy of evildoers. He has beautiful eyes, a handsome face, and well-formed limbs."[10]

El Encubierto's intentions can be fleshed out by further examination of the content of the sermon he gave on 21 March and the memories of the villagers of Alcira. Quickly drawing together a following of some three hundred to four hundred armed men, on 21 March 1522 El Encubierto announced he would deliver a sermon in the cathedral square of Xátiva. The town's friars were rounded up at musket point and forced to listen, and fortunately for posterity, several of the scandalized brothers immediately wrote down what they heard and sent a copy of their record to the Inquisition in Valencia.[11] The Hidden One stood on a platform, flanked by two trumpeters (one of whom was a Negro artisan), and brandished a naked sword, which he called his sword of virtue. Unimpressed by his performance, the friars pointedly called The Hidden One the "man with the sailor's cape alias 'Lo Encubert.'" What he was about to say did not win their love.

The Hidden One took as his theme the contemporary belief that the Antichrist and a social revolution in Valencia were at hand. For good measure, he threw in a strong dose of anticlericalism directed at the religious orders. Two of the friars remembered that the man with the sailor's cape foretold that many clergy would follow the Antichrist and lose their souls and that the viceroy of Valencia, who had just defeated the Germanías, was the second Antichrist. The friars were further warned that if they did not turn away from this second Antichrist and stop speaking badly of the revolution, they would be burned in the town square. To prepare for the coming Day of Judgment, El Encubierto ordered the wealth of the church and of the nobility

---

10. Alain Milhou, "La chauve-souris, le nouveau David et le roi caché (trois images de l'empereur des derniers temps dans le monde ibérique)," in *Melanges de la Casa de Velázquez* 18 (1982): 70.

11. Dánvila y Collado, "El Encubierto de Valencia," 124. The friars also gave information about the number of armed men following El Encubierto, as well as details about his performance, such as the trumpeters, sword, and guards.

in Xátiva to be confiscated, heaped up in the main square, and sold by his legal agents. The proceeds would be used to support the Holy War (that is, the Germanías, now seen as a crusade) and the starving poor ("God's little sheep"). The Hidden One concluded by addressing his enemies directly: "That one, *your* king Don Carlos," he admonished them, waving his sword, would only become as much as God wished and with his approval ("I will demonstrate how he is king and not king").[12]

The man with the sailor's cape was clever. Without any discernible education he put together various eschatological notions, added some folklorisms and popular prejudices, and came up with a sermon that convinced the non-clerics in his audience of the truth of his mission. Nothing he said recalled textually *La Venguda del Anticrist*, but his audience was certainly reading *him* as the embodiment of Alamany's prophetic tract, published less than two years before. One strategy used by El Encubierto to lend authenticity to his message was to imitate the prophets' penchant for numerology, in this case the number four. Four was the true number of components in the godhead; four was the number of religions, judgments, and incarnations; four were the arquebusiers who rounded up the friars; and four was the number of trumpets at the End in Jerusalem. El Encubierto even apologized for not having four trumpeters to accompany his sermon.

The idea of a quaternity was widely diffused in late medieval Spain.[13] Normally, what was meant was a foursome of God the Father, the Son, the Virgin, and the Holy Spirit, but El Encubierto's version of the quaternity was the Father, Son, Holy Spirit, and the Holy Sacrament. His concept of the four religions, judgments, and incarnations could be derived from the Joachist preaching of the three ages of the spiritual development of the world, each associated with a religious figure, and culminating in an age of perfection. Joachism was widespread enough in Catalan-speaking lands that, given the circumstances of the 1520s and the reprinting of Alamany's book, some understanding of the Joachist eschatology would have spread to popular levels.[14] Although El Encubierto announced there were four religions and four incarnations, he had only thought through the Judgments, which he explained

---

12. Dánvila y Collado, "El Encubierto de Valencia," 125, col. a: "dix que esse vuestro Rey Don Carlos sera quanto Dios quisiere e yo os demostrare como es rey y no es rey."

13. Alain Milhou, *Colon y su mentalidad mesiánica en el ambiente francisanista español* (Valladolid: Casa-Museo de Colón, 1983), 83–86.

14. Marjorie Reeves, *The Influence of Prophecy in the Later Middle Ages: A Study in Joachimism* (Notre Dame: University of Notre Dame Press, 1993).

thus (as recalled by Fray Francisco Vicario de Leon): "The first Judgment God gave us was the creation of Adam [and exile from Paradise]; the second was Noah's Ark [the Flood]; and the one which He has made today is the third, and the other we will make in Jerusalem."[15]

Here El Encubierto includes his listeners in the millennial enterprise by presenting the third judgment in Xátiva as a fait accompli and by inviting them to join with him capturing Jerusalem. Several references to Enoch and Elijah showed that El Encubierto also was familiar with the general outlines of medieval popular apocalypticism—that Enoch and Elijah would fight with the Antichrist and ultimately kill him in Rome and the two were to be found in the earthly paradise on a dark mountain.[16] El Encubierto's special twist was that the two had revealed everything to him.

Finally the sermon contained some populist elements and what the friars called "idiocies," such as "Christ on this holy day, which is [Good] Friday, would come down from heaven to earth except that he did not want to tire himself out." Was this a dodge to explain His absence? El Encubierto said that the Virgin Mary should be addressed not by the familiar "thee" but by the formal "you," as is fitting for the Queen of Heaven. Several friars noted the fanciful story that El Encubierto told explaining why the mule is a sterile animal: when the Virgin Mary gave birth to Jesus in the stable, there were several animals there, including the mule, which began to eat the hay in Jesus' manger. Christ cursed it, and as a result it and all its kind became sterile. A story fit only for a child—but such is its durability and popular appeal that it is told to this day in Latin America.[17] The disparate nature of these various statements, as compared to the coherent eschatological message of most of the sermon, almost suggests that El Encubierto, once he delivered the essence of what he wanted to say, did not know when to stop and included everything else of a religious nature that he could think of. Unfortunately, given the manner in which his sermon has been recorded, we cannot even guess how it was delivered.

15. "de los quatro judicios que Dios nos ha dado el primero fue en la creacion de Adam el segundo en la arca de Nohe y este quell ha hecho hoy es el tercero y quel otro haremos en Hierusalem" (Dánvila y Collado, "El Encubierto de Valencia," 124, col. b). "Qu'ell ha hecho" in the text is ambiguous; the "he" could refer to God or El Encubierto.

16. In addition to the information provided in *La Venguda del Anticrist*, there was the popularizing work by M. Martínez Ampiés, *El libro del Anticristo* (Zaragoza, 1495).

17. Personal communication from Asunción Lavrin.

Xátiva's Franciscans were skeptical, but the man with the sailor's cape effectively revived the smoldering revolt. During March and April he led his followers into action against the royal forces, conducting a sort of guerrilla war well suited to the mountainous terrain of the southern part of the kingdom. In an ambush laid at Xátiva itself, his forces wounded the duke of Gandía and count of Oliva, but El Encubierto was injured as well and he retreated to the village of Alcira to recover. The testimony of these villagers, collected three years later by the Inquisition, is the only other eyewitness testimony that survives concerning El Encubierto. Indeed, it is the only account that we have of him given by his followers and not by his enemies.

In Alcira, El Encubierto gave another sermon, which a woman called Marguarida Colomina went to hear. She arrived to find a large crowd surrounding El Encubierto, so large that she could not get close enough to hear him. Afterward, people told her what he apparently had told them or had led them to believe: that he was an angel sent by God and they had to follow him to Jerusalem. The sea would part for them and they would pass through the middle.[18] At Alcira, The Hidden One achieved the status of a full-blown messiah. There, according to the Inquisition testimony, the villagers believed that the man could bring prosperity, perform miracles, defy death, and redeem them.

For example, Johan Rodes, a barber surgeon, believed everything he heard about El Encubierto: that the man was sent by God, that Enoch and Elijah had appeared to him, and that he came to relieve the people of their poverty. Rodes believed El Encubierto would give them so much that they would no longer have to work. When the rumor spread that El Encubierto had been killed, Rodes refused to believe it because he had seen El Encubierto in Alcira. While Rodes was sick the man had come to his house, made the sign of the cross three times on his forehead, and told him to say a Pater Noster and Hail Mary. The barber was convinced that The Brother would lead a crusade to Jerusalem and win the Holy House, and they all had to follow him with a cross from their parish church. A true believer, Rodes even told one man who was gravely ill, "Do not worry because The Hidden One who they say is dead is alive in Xátiva and *you should believe that he is the Messiah and he will free us*" [emphasis added].[19]

---

18. Dánvila y Collado, "El Encubierto de Valencia," 135, col. b: "la plaça estava plena de gent huynslo e ella conffesant no pogue entendre la preycacio salvo que per lo que hui dir a les gents ço ess que ere enviat per deu y que era angel y que havia de adar a Hierusalem y que les gents lo havien a seguir y que la mar se obriria y per mig pasaria la gent...."

19. Dánvila y Collado, "El Encubierto de Valencia," 135, col. a.

Miguel Johan Botoner, another resident of Alcira, believed that just the mere proximity of El Encubierto could heal him. After Miguel was wounded at the battle of Bellus, he was brought back to Alcira to recover. Hearing that El Encubierto was going to pass by his doorway, he swept it clean and sat there. Someone asked him why he had done that to the doorway since God was not going to pass by there, and Botoner hastened to correct him. El Encubierto *was* God and he knew it to be true because he had heard the Prophecies of Saint Isidore (also contained in the *Venguda del Anticrist*), which predicted the arrival of El Encubierto.[20] He had heard El Encubierto say that he and his followers would conquer Jerusalem, and if the pope opposed him in anything, El Encubierto would punish him. Botoner believed that El Encubierto could not die, even if he were poisoned with arsenic.[21]

Another follower, Anthoni Auger, heard that El Encubierto was covered by the Holy Spirit and had been sent to save the world from its sins. Echoing the prophecies about the so-called New David, Auger asserted that Emperor Charles V would take El Encubierto to Rome and make him the pope so he would reform the church. Anthoni was so convinced of the truth of El Encubierto that he told some people that he would make them see El Encubierto in the consecrated host; others he told that they did not need to go to mass, because just to see El Encubierto was to see the face of Jesus Christ.[22]

Finally, Bernat Climent, a tailor from the village of Enguera, actively promoted the cause of El Encubierto by telling people that they must believe in El Hermano. He told people that El Encubierto could not be killed in battle by any weapon except in Jerusalem, after they had won the Holy House. Climent

---

20. The "Lament for Spain Made by the Glorious Doctor Saint Isidore, Archbishop" bewailed the fact that the Christians permitted the Jews and Moors to reside in Spain and promised that all sorts of misfortunes would beset Spain, including civil war, until the arrival of the Encubierto. See Ramón Alba, *Acerca de algunas particularidades de las Comunidades de Castilla tal vez relacionadas con el supuesto acaecer Terreno del Milenio Igualitario* (Madrid: Editoria Nacional, 1975), 197–200. Yet another publication spreading the ideas of El Encubierto was *Las coplas de fray Pedro de Frias* (Valencia, 1520); see Yves-Marie Bercé, *Le roi caché: Sauveurs et imposteurs: Mythes politiques populaires dans l'Europe moderne* (Paris: Fayard, 1990), 320.

21. Dánvila y Collado, "El Encubierto de Valencia," 134, col. b.: "aço crehia ell conffesant perque havia huyt dir de les profecies de sent Isidro y que havia de venir hun encubert dehia quel havia de guannyar la casa sancta … y que crehia que lo encubert no podia morir encara que li donasen arcenich…."

22. Dánvila y Collado, "El Encubierto de Valencia," 133, col. b.: "el los faria veure lo hermano alias lo encubert en la hostia consagrada … no teniu necessitat de anar a missa puix es açi lo hermano çoes lo encubert que si mirau la sua cara veureu que es la cara de Jhesus crist…."

had prayed with El Encubierto in Saint Felix's church in Xátiva. There, a fantastic thing had occurred:

> While El Encubierto was praying…it seemed to me that El Encubierto was more than a foot above the ground in the air, and his lance and shield hung down without touching anything, and since I believed it I made it public to others who were also believers.[23]

Extraordinary testimony, made all the more interesting by Climent's qualifying remark that he spread news of the miracle only among those who were believers, that is, people who already were inclined to be receptive to the improbable news of El Encubierto's levitation. Some of the eight converts tracked down by the Inquisition three years later were simply repeating what they had heard in the streets; others had direct contact with the Brother. Whatever their individual experience, all admitted to believing everything they had heard and none expressed more than the most perfunctory remorse for having done so. No one tried, retrospectively, to suggest that they had doubts and were just following along. No, these were true believers, ready to pick up their swords and do whatever El Encubierto ordered, even three years later.

Judging by the testimony of both the friars and the villagers about the origin of this mysterious man and his purpose, the man with the sailor's cape never claimed much more for himself than the story about Elijah and Enoch. Bernat Climent remembered a conversation in which El Encubierto told him that when Elijah and Enoch found him on the mountain he had also encountered the Virgin and overcome the devil. He expressed the hope that he would become a holy father and have a wife and child.[24] Rather modest expectations for a messiah! No one recalled hearing the man actually say that he was "El Encubierto"; instead this is what they called him, in fulfillment of the prophecies swirling around Valencia, which as the testimony of Botoner demonstrates, had reached into the distant countryside. In the excitement of the movement, the traditional expectations about El Encubierto as a restorer of

---

23. Dánvila y Collado, "El Encubierto de Valencia," 134, col. a.: "estant lo dit encubert fent oracio en la sglesia de sent Feliu de Xativa li paregue a ell conffesant que lo dit encubert estava mes de dos palms alçat de terra en lo ayre al qual la lanca y adargua seguien sens tocarla algu y axi com ell conffesant o crehia lo publicava a altres que tenian la meteixa crehença…."

24. Dánvila y Collado, "El Encubierto de Valencia," 134, col. a: "li dix com quant Elies y Enoch lo trameteren de una alta montannya encontra en lo cami ab la verge Maria y parla ab ella y que en apres encontra ab lo dimoni y lo vence e que lo dit encubert havia de esser pare sant, y tenir muller y fills lo quall ell confesant crehia…."

Spain were forgotten and the man with the sailor's cape was elevated to a status equal to God himself.

Just as important is what the witnesses, particularly those in Alcira, did not say about El Encubierto. Except for the one Franciscan, no one suggested he was converso. In Alcira, although the barber and tailor may well have been conversos, from their testimony, El Encubierto's followers saw him as a Christian messianic figure. He variously was equated with Jesus Christ, the Eucharist, and the Holy Spirit. His ambitions were similar to the stories told about the Last Emperor, who would reform the papacy and recapture Jerusalem. El Encubierto's followers did not see him as an earthly king, nor did he claim to be one. They did not call him "El Rey Encubierto," but simply "El Encubierto" or "El Hermano." The immediate documentary evidence produced by royal officials also referred to the man as "El Encubierto."[25] And, most importantly, no one repeated the story that appeared in the later histories, that El Encubierto claimed to be a long-lost child of the crown prince Juan, who would have inherited the throne but for his untimely demise in 1497.

The remaking of El Encubierto's story by his enemies began immediately after the Germanías were over. In one of the first chronicles of the Germanías, written by the notary Miquel Garcia, who fought with the royalists, the story of El Encubierto acquired the trappings of a well-crafted tale, tapping into all the prejudices of a sixteenth-century audience. First, according to Garcia, El Encubierto was a Jewish adventurer, which automatically made him the villain of the piece. In Oran (present-day Algeria), he converted to Christianity for the love of a woman, but the conversion was both treacherous and sacrilegious since El Encubierto converted only for the purpose of seducing his employer's

---

25. Royal officials writing at the time also refer to the heretic as El Encubierto, a further indication that the appellation "El Rey Encubierto" gained currency later among hostile chroniclers. A few days after El Encubierto's assassination, the city government of Valencia wrote to the viceroy to inform him of El Encubierto's death and the fact that his head would be sent to the viceroy ("per la enita del corren qui porta lo cap del encubierto lo qual lo illustre marques tramet a su illustre senoria"): Dánvila y Collado, "El Encubierto de Valencia," 138. Later the same year the viceroy rewarded the murderers. The letter summing up their service reads, "Con el zelo que tuvieron al seruitio de la dicha Cesaria Magestat sabiendo que el heretico que se dezia Encubierto entendia con muchas sacasses suyos. ...": García Cárcel, *Las Germanías*, 244. One document, collected by Dánvila y Collado and published in *La Germanía de Valencia: Discursos leídos ante la Real Academia de la Historia por Manuel Dánvila y Collado* (Madrid, 1884), 365, records the execution of El Encubierto's chaplain in 1524: "A viii de agost de MDXXIIII sentenciaron a Mossen Johan lo portugues, prevere home de cinquanta cinch anys poch mes o menys que era stat gran caxador en Xativa en les coses y dans de la Germania e en lo fet del encubert": Libro de Antiguitats, fol. 36, Archivo de la Catedral de Valencia.

daughter. After he was discovered and expelled, El Encubierto came to Spain, and taking advantage of the revolts against Charles V, he became an impostor for a second time, claiming to be the son of the much-lamented Prince Juan, whose death had paved the way for Charles's unwelcome succession to the Spanish crown. Garcia related that El Encubierto had said that out of envy he had been kept in captivity until by God's will he escaped and came to restore Spain, which was lost. The people of Xátiva proclaimed him the *Rey Encubert*, and he incited them to rebellion and heresy. Garcia then repeated, without commentary, the essence of El Encubierto's eschatological message. A certain vagueness in Garcia's report is reminiscent of the nature of rumors, which he may well have been repeating. In the story, the impostor was given no name or physical description, and no one in the royal court was blamed for his mysterious captivity in an unnamed location.[26]

Here, according to Miquel Garcia's story, was a true king who literally had been hidden from sight and his rightful throne. It was the inquisitors, one of the friars, and hostile chroniclers who used the phrase, the Hidden King. A small detail perhaps, but one that grows in significance upon further reflection. "El Rey Encubierto," a variation of the messianic term used in the prophecies, as far as the direct testimony goes, was not used by the followers of the man with the sailor's cape: they preferred to say simply in Catalan, "Lo Encubert." The revolutionaries were not interested in the political structures of monarchy, and by the time El Encubierto arrived on the scene in the wake of the failed political revolution, some people were ready for an even more radical, millenarian solution. The ruling classes understood that the first phase of the Germanías had been a movement to overthrow the legitimate royal authority of Charles V and the nobility. The second millennial phase was beyond comprehension; they could not or did not want to imagine that the rebels were not interested in having a king at all, at least in a sense that they understood. Thus, in their accounts, El Encubierto was transformed into "El Rey Encubierto," a false pretender come to muddy the waters and

26. Eulàlia Duran, *Croniques de les germanies de Guillem Ramon Català i de Miguel Garcia (segle XVI)* (Valencia: E. Climent, 1984), 394: "vegué a ella [Xativa] un juheu que s'era fet chrestià en Orà, ciutat de Africa, per amor de una christiana…diç que era rey de Espanya, perquè era fill del príncep don Johan, fill del rey don Fernando, e que l'avien llançat per embeja, e que era stat cativ tants anys, e que llavons era eixit per la voluntat de Déu de cativ, per reparar Espanya qu'estava perduda." One chronicler/historian who does not repeat the story is Juan Maldonado, who sympathized with the Comunero cause. Maldonado writes simply: "[El Encubierto] was so skilled in making miracles with marvelous artifices and in creating a new religion that in Algeciras and Jativa he was almost adored as God," Juan Maldonado, *La revolución comunera* (Madrid: Editions del Centro, 1975), 228.

put doubt in the popular mind about the legitimacy of Charles's monarchy. Hidden or no, they saw El Encubierto as operating within the framework of the monarchical system that they knew.[27]

This way of thinking becomes clearer in the chronicle by Martín de Viciana, who also lived through the Germanías as a young man, although, like Garcia, he did not witness the events directly related to El Encubierto. In his account, Viciana immediately made clear his hostility by declaring that El Encubierto was sent by the devil who "presented the *agermandos* with a new way to sin." He also gave an unflattering physical description of El Encubierto, in some respects the opposite of the ideal description of The Hidden One given in Alamany's prophecy in *La Venguda del Anticrist*: "a man of average size, muscular, with a scant reddish beard, thin face, blue eyes, aquiline nose, short and thick hands, likewise his feet, chestnut-colored hair, a very small mouth, bow-legged, aged twenty-five years, he spoke Castilian very well and in the style of the palace."[28] Viciana acknowledged that El Encubierto's sermon on 22 March had been a pivotal event but gave no details of its content. He did record that some "not very sane persons" said that El Encubierto was a person sent by God to redeem Xátiva. Viciana reproduced a variation on the story of El Encubierto's origins. In his account, there is no mention of the suspect North-African Jewish origins of the impostor, but there is a bit more palace intrigue that would appeal especially to his Valencian readers, that the evil Cardinal Mendoza had sequestered Princess Margaret, Prince Juan's wife, until she gave birth to a baby boy and then sent the baby to Gibraltar, where he was raised by a shepherdess under the false name of Don Enrique Manrique de Ribera. Valencians would appreciate the reference to Cardinal Mendoza because his relative, Viceroy Mendoza, was widely hated by the rebels.[29]

The Castilian chroniclers of the time barely noticed the Germanías so El Encubierto received even shorter notice in their accounts. Alonso de Santa Cruz, quite far removed from the events, wrote that El Encubierto controlled

27. Except García Cárcel, the modern historians who deal with El Encubierto (Julio Caro Baroja, Américo Castro, and Joan Fuster) accept the veracity of the chroniclers' stories to prove their own points. Baroja and Castro want to prove the influence of Judaism in Spanish history, while Fuster maintains that the rebels really wanted a king: Joan Fuster, *Rebeldes y heterodoxos* (Barcelona: Ariel, 1972). Fuster's work was published before Milhou's work on *encubertismo*.

28. Viciana, *Cronica*, 411: "hun hombre de mediano cuerpo, menbrudo, con pocas barvas y roxas, el rostro delgado, los ojos garzos, la nariz aguilleña, las manos cortas y gruessas, los pies muy gruessas sobre manera, cabellos castaños, boca muy chiquita, las piernas coruadas, la hedad de veinteicinco años, hablaua muy bien castellano y del palacio...."

29. Viciana, *Cronica*, 412.

Valencia for two *years*, during which time no king was so well obeyed as was El Encubierto. Santa Cruz seems to have combined Garcia's account with Viciana's. Noting El Encubierto's origin in Oran, he wrote that "since [El Encubierto] was a Jew, smart and hypocritical, he avoided showing himself to be harsh, greedy or vicious" (traits believed to connote Jewishness). Santa Cruz then repeated Viciana's story of palace intrigue but added an even more salacious detail: Cardinal Mendoza had not merely whisked away the true heir to the throne, but had substituted his own illegitimate child in his place. Amazingly this was supposed to have happened without the knowledge of anyone else in the palace.[30]

The last important history of the period is Gaspar Escolano's *Decadas de la Historia de la Insigne y coronada ciudad y reino de Valencia* (1611). Escolano, almost one hundred years removed from the events, used published and documentary sources and added a slightly different perspective to El Encubierto. Dropping the story of Jewish origins, Escolano maintained that El Encubierto was a hermit of Castilian origin who lived outside of Valencia and was held to be simple-minded ("un hombre falto"). The rest of the story Escolano borrowed from Viciana, but he added the Inquisitorial notes of the Franciscans' report of El Encubierto's sermon on 22 March. In Escolano's narrative El Encubierto and his movement are reduced to madness. El Encubierto is simple-minded, his sermon is nothing but "heretical nonsense," and his followers are dupes who "swallowed" the whole thing.[31]

El Encubierto's intervention in the Germanías proved to be short-lived. In May 1522, emboldened by his successes, El Encubierto showed up on the outskirts of Valencia and entered into secret negotiations to murder the marquis of Zenete, brother of the viceroy. Instead, El Encubierto was betrayed and assassinated in Burjasot on 18 May; his head was delivered to Viceroy Mendoza, and ultimately it joined those of other traitors displayed over one of the city gates, while his body, given over to the Inquisition, was tried for heresy and burned.

The millenarian experiment in Valencia was over. The villagers of Alcira carried on with their lives and nurtured their memories, to be recovered several years later by the inquisitors, who decided to be forgiving. With the cessation of hostilities, we can imagine that the various participants drifted back to their homes, taking with them their memories and stories. The millennial

30. Alonso Santa Cruz, as cited in Castro, *Aspectos del vivir hispánico*, 50.

31. Gaspar Escolano, *Decadas de la Historia de la Insigne y coronada ciudad y reino de Valencia* (1611; repr., Valencia, 1879), 2:700–9.

hopes that El Encubierto embodied, however, were far from dead. In Valencia and the Balearic Islands, several more "encubiertos" would take the place of the slain one, only to be quickly discredited. In Castile, millenarian and religious speculation was alive and well in some of the palaces of the kingdom's great lords. But never would another messianic leader take up arms in Spain, and El Encubierto's promise was effectively transformed from one of earthly salvation to living hell.

W ORMS AND THE JEWS

Jews, Magic, and Community
in Seventeenth-Century Worms

Dean Phillip Bell

$\mathcal{S}$ ince 1976 a great deal of scholarship, drawn particularly from a variety of social science themes and methodologies, has been produced in relation to the interpretation of popular religion, magic, and witchcraft in early modern Europe. Creative and diverse research has unearthed and interpreted fascinating sources and employed innovative historiographical methodologies. The scholarly discussion produced by such new research has simultaneously examined anew the position and treatment of Jews in the early modern period, built upon earlier, largely internal Jewish scholarship, and ignored the vast corpus of Jewish sources, often in Yiddish.

Many of the sources (such as Inquisition records) and methodologies (for example, microhistory) have been applied to Jewish studies of the early modern period in only select ways. Of course, the relationship between magic (or superstition, as some see it) and religion, which has been explored notably by Keith Thomas and Carlo Ginzburg among others,[1] was noted some sixty years ago by Joshua Trachtenberg, in his now famous *Jewish Magic and Superstition: A Study in Folk Religion*. Trachtenberg referred to the biblical condemnation of sorcery but also pointed out that the notion of magic was in many ways tempered and redefined in the Talmudic period, giving way to a distinctly Jewish magic in the Geonic period.[2] According to Trachtenberg's sociological and folkloristic approach:

---

1. See for example, Keith Thomas, *Religion and the Decline of Magic: Studies in Popular Beliefs in Sixteenth and Seventeenth Century England* (New York: Oxford University Press, 1971); and Carlo Ginzburg, *The Cheese and the Worms: The Cosmos of a Sixteenth-Century Miller*, trans. John Tedeschi and Anne Tedeschi (Baltimore: Johns Hopkins University Press, 1980).

2. See Joshua Trachtenberg, *Jewish Magic and Superstition: A Study in Folk Religion* (1939; repr., New York: Antheneum, 1987), 19, 11. See also Abraham Cohen, *Everyman's Talmud* (1949; repr., New

alongside this formal [internal religious] development there was a constant elaboration of what we may call "folk religion"—ideas and practices that never met with the whole-hearted approval of the religious leaders, but which enjoyed such wide popularity that they could not be altogether excluded from the field of religion. Of this sort were the beliefs concerning demons and angels, and the many superstitious usages based on these beliefs, which by more or less devious routes actually became a part of Judaism, and on the periphery of the religious life, the practices of magic, which never broke completely with the tenets of the faith, yet stretched them almost to the breaking-point. If we call these "folk religion" it is because they expressed the common attitude of the people, as against the official attitude of the Synagogue, to the universe.[3]

In stories of Jewish magic, Trachtenberg and others have seen both the confluence of popular belief and religious dogma and the interaction of Jewish and non-Jewish culture and thought. Stories in the famous medieval *Sefer Hasidim*, for example, replicated stories in non-Jewish works, while simultaneously incorporating uniquely Jewish elements.[4] For over a decade now, specialists in Jewish studies have indicated that the history of Jewish magic beckons, and the juxtaposition of Jewish and non-Jewish sources is of extreme importance in the development of Jewish history.[5] The insights of specialists in Jewish history combined with the methodological tools of many early modern historians offer tremendous opportunity to explore issues of popular *mentalité*. This is particularly significant given recent findings about the

---

York: Schocken, 1975), 260, where Cohen argues: "So firm was the belief in evil spirits, both among the educated and uneducated classes, that the Talmud legislates for it. In their legal decisions the Rabbis prescribed for circumstances which presuppose the actuality of demons."

3. Trachtenberg, *Jewish Magic*, vii–viii.

4. Trachtenberg, *Jewish Magic*, 13.

5. Ivan Marcus pointed out with great wit that "above all, the rite of passage includes an incantation to ward off the demon of forgetfulness, and the entire field of the history of Jewish magic beckons." In response to Marcus, Hava Tirosh-Rothschild argued that "the future of Jewish social history in the medieval period lies in juxtaposing information gleaned from internal Jewish sources with documentary evidence taken from non-Jewish sources." See Ivan Marcus, "Medieval Jewish Studies: Toward an Anthropological History of the Jews," in *The State of Jewish Studies*, ed. Shaye J. D. Cohen and Edward L. Greenstein (Detroit: Wayne State University Press, 1990), 113–27; and the response of Hava Tirosh-Rothschild, 128–42.

complexity of Jewish communal life at the end of the Middle Ages, and relations between Jews and non-Jews as well as Jewish and non-Jewish culture.[6]

Within the world of Jewish scholarship, there has been a great deal of scholarly literature on well-trodden topics such as the Golem legend,[7] Jewish views about magic, medicine,[8] science,[9] and a variety of cabalistic issues,[10] as well as Christian accusations of Jewish ritual murder.[11] There has been much less scholarly attention given to the description of magical occurrences as an integral part of Jewish communal history. This essay offers a brief contextual introduction to the history of the Jews in Worms and examines selected writings of Jepthah Joseph Juspa, b. Nafthali Hirz Ha-Levi (1604–78), or simply Juspa, who served for many years as community scribe in Worms and who wrote a variety of materials relating to community events, customs, legends, and legislation. In particular, this essay focuses on specific incidents reported by Juspa, in his own time or as a part of Worms Jewish lore, that involve magic associated with the larger communal body. It explores select stories that deal with issues of communal salvation. It is hoped that in this way the reader can begin to penetrate into Jewish views of magic, the process of acculturation between Jews and Christians, and the communal history of the

6. In particular, to what extent can we characterize Jews as cultural mediators of European folklore? See Israel Zinberg, *A History of Jewish Literature*, vol. 7 of *Old Yiddish Literature from Its Origins to the Haskalah Period*, trans. and ed. Bernard Martin (Cincinnati: Hebrew Union College Press, 1975), 174. The case of *Ma'ase Nissim* examined here seems different from other such works before or after. As Peter Stallybrass and Allon White have argued, citing E. R. Wolf: "to define societies as autonomous and bounded structures discourages 'analysis of intersocietal or intergroup interchanges, including internal social strife, colonialism, imperialism, and societal dependency'"; Peter Stallybrass and Allon White, *The Politics and Poetics of Transgression* (Ithaca: Cornell University Press, 1986), 38.

7. See for example, Gershom Scholem, "The Idea of the Golem," in *On the Kabbalah and Its Symbolism* (New York: Shoken, 1965), 158–204, and Moshe Idel, *Golem: Jewish Magic and Mystical Tradition on the Artificial Anthropoid* (Albany: State University of New York Press, 1990).

8. See David Ruderman, *Science, Medicine, and Jewish Culture in Early Modern Europe* (Tel Aviv: Tel Aviv University, 1987). An older work is Hirsh Jacob Zimmels, *Magicians, Theologians and Doctors: Studies in Folk Medicine and Folklore as Reflected in the Rabbinic Responsa, 12th–19th Centuries* (1952; repr., Northvale, N.J.: J. Aronson, 1997).

9. A recent example is Raphael Patai, *The Jewish Alchemists: A History and Source Book* (Princeton: Princeton University Press, 1994).

10. For examples of recent and important studies see Moshe Idel, *Kabbalah: New Perspectives* (New Haven: Yale University Press, 1988), and Elliot R. Wolfson, *Through a Speculum That Shines: Vision and Imagination in Medieval Jewish Mysticism* (Princeton: Princeton University Press,1994).

11. See R. Po-chia Hsia, *The Myth of Ritual Murder: Jews and Magic in Reformation Germany* (New Haven: Yale University Press, 1988), and idem, *Trent 1475: Stories of a Ritual Murder Trial* (New Haven: Yale University Press, 1992).

Jews—complete with sociological and religious distinctions—by integrating a variety of traditional sources, local stories, and customs.

WORMS IN THE EARLY MODERN PERIOD

The early modern city of Worms[12] offers an intriguing context in which to assess questions of religious interaction, community development, and magic, given its multiconfessional nature, the interaction of a variety of sources of political and legal authority, and its rich medieval legacy. Since the second half of the sixteenth century Lutherans, Catholics, and Jews all inhabited Worms, even if antipathies against any group never disappeared completely.[13] Worms was a free city since the eleventh century, and its inhabitants possessed tax privileges, freedom from tolls, and the right of fortification, among other privileges granted by the emperor. Although the bishop maintained the title of *Stadtherr*,[14] the city had over the course of the later Middle Ages slowly removed itself from his yoke. By the beginning of the sixteenth century, the city had denied the bishop his right to install the *Burghermeister*, and the council members had even reconstituted the city council. In the same year, 1505, in a Jewish ordinance, the council usurped the bishop's right to install (and to collect a fee for that installation) the Jewish council.[15] Still, the bishop did retain some force in the city, as did the emperor and the local *Schutzherr*, the elector of the Palatinate.[16] The city, a regional trading center of around six thousand inhabitants, was governed by a small oligarchy of wealthy citizens, many of whom comprised the thirteen-member city council. In the

12. Among the synthetic overviews, see Fritz Reuter, "Mehrkonfessionalität in der Freien Stadt Worms im 16.–18. Jahrhundert," in *Städtische Randgruppen und Minderheiten*, ed. Bernhard Kirchgässner and Fritz Reuter (Sigmaringen: J. Thorbecke, 1986), 9–48; and Christopher R. Friedrichs, "Anti-Jewish Politics in Early Modern Germany: The Uprising in Worms, 1613–17," *Central European History* 23:2, 3 (1990): 91–152.

13. Consider for example the variety of legislation of the interim council between 1548 and 1552 regarding evangelical worship or the string of attempted expulsions of the Jews throughout the sixteenth century. See Fritz Reuter, *Warmaisa: 1000 Jahre Juden in Worms* (Worms: Verlag Stadtarchiv Worms, 1984), 21, 26.

14. For the late-tenth- and early-eleventh-century transfer of power from the emperor to the bishop, see *Germania Judaica*, ed. Zvi Avneri, Marcus Brann, et al., vol. 1, *Von den ältesten Zeiten bis 1238;* vol. 2, in 2 bks., *Von 1238 bis zur Mitte des 14. Jahrhunderts;* vol. 3, in 3 bks., *1350–1519* (1917–34; repr., Tübingen: J.C.B. Mohr, 1963–), 1:437-38.

15. Reuter, *Warmaisa*, 58.

16. See Leon J. Yagod, "Worms Jewry in the Seventeenth Century" (diss., Yeshiva University, 1967), 7–12; and, Reuter, *Warmaisa*, 57.

seventeenth century there was a deep and widening social and economic gulf in the city, and complaints were lodged through the guilds, which expressed antipathy to the ruling elite as well as the Jews.

THE JEWS IN EARLY MODERN WORMS

Jews may have lived in Worms[17] already in the Roman period; however, the first reliable report of Jews in Worms comes from the beginning of the eleventh century. The Jewish population seems to have grown dramatically in the eleventh century, and in a 1074 privilege granted to Worms by the emperor in return for the city's support, the Jews are mentioned. A number of prominent rabbis are found in Worms at the end of the eleventh century. In 1090 the Jews were granted privileges, similar to those granted to the Jews in Speyer, by Henry IV; these privileges were later renewed by Frederick I Barbarosa in 1157 and then extended to all Jews in the empire by Frederick II in 1236. Among the privileges granted the Jews were that they should live undisturbed inside or outside of the city walls, that they were free to serve as merchants and businessmen, and that they paid no tolls. The privilege also dealt with a host of legal issues and allowed the Jews a good deal of internal legal autonomy.[18]

During the First Crusade, many of the Jews of the community fled to the bishop's palace. On 18 May 1096 (10 Iyar) the crusaders overran the Jews still in their houses; some Jews took their own lives, while others were forcibly converted and murdered. The Jewish houses were plundered and destroyed. On 25 May (1 Sivan) the crusaders, with the help of citizens, began to seize the Jews holed up in the bishop's palace, and a large proportion of the thousand-member community was murdered.[19] In 1097 those forcibly converted were allowed by Henry IV to return to Judaism. Not until 1112, however, do we again find mention of Jews in Worms. By the end of the thirteenth century the Jewish community in Worms had again risen to prominence as one of the most significant communities along the Rhine and throughout Germany; it remained so until the time of the Black Death in the middle of the fourteenth century,[20] when the Jews of Worms were again slaughtered en masse—the *Memorbücher* record the names of more than 580 martyrs.[21] After the 1349

---

17. See *Germania Judaica*, 1:437–74.

18. Reuter, *Warmaisa*, 24–25.

19. *Germania Judaica*, 1:445, suggests 800; Reuter, *Warmaisa*, 60, assesses the number at 400.

20. See *Germania Judaica*, vol. 2, pt. 2, pp. 919–27.

21. *Germania Judaica*, vol. 2, pt. 2, p. 923.

persecution Jews first returned to Worms in 1353.[22] By 1377 there were thirty-six married Jewish men, or a community of about two hundred Jews.[23] This number grew to about 250 by 1495/96.[24] Like other Jewish communities in the second half of the fourteenth century, the community in Worms was assessed numerous and weighty taxes.[25] In the period before 1350 the community was governed by a *Judenrat* of twelve members, including the *Judenbischof.* That number was reconstituted in 1505 to thirteen.[26]

In the fifteenth century the Jews of Worms faced numerous challenges: in 1410 a ritual murder accusation;[27] in 1431 a peasant uprising in the surrounding areas which turned against Jews in the city; the cancellation of debts owed to Jews; conversions (reported in 1476, for example); internal strife; and attempts at expulsion, as in 1487/88 and again in 1515, that were not allowed by the emperor.[28] Yet the Worms Jewish community continued to be significant not only in size, but also in the production of customs and legends. Already by the early sixteenth century a "Wormser Legende" was composed in Yiddish.

Throughout the sixteenth century the Jews were affected by the political and religious instability of the times, and numerous iterations of Jewish ordinances dictated the position of the Jews within the civic community. Though the Jewish ordinances did not differ from one another greatly, they

22. See *Germania Judaica*, vol. 3, pt. 2, pp. 1671–97.

23. According to Reuter, *Warmaisa*, 63, there were only 180.

24. Including: 57 adult men (40 family heads, 13 not living in households, 10 Talmud students, and 7 others); 74 adult women (37 married women, 13 not living in households, 5 independent women, and 19 maidservants); and 113 children.

25. A special tax of 20,000 G was, for example, assessed by Graf Emich von Leiningen; see Reuter, *Warmaisa*, 63.

26. On the community structure, see Yagod, "Worms Jewry," 83–84. Yagod notes that: The council consisted of 23 electors, a council of 12 plus an additional 11 residents. The 12 parnasim of the council were elected for life. When one died the others voted in a replacement in secret. The rabbi, though appointed by the council, acted independently and received an annual salary from the Worms community as well as the surrounding Jewish communities and any additional sums for marriages, divorces, etc. He also served as the rector of the local yeshiva, the supervisor of elementary education, the head of the judiciary and communal enactment committee, and principal teacher and religious guide. He may have preached some as well. There were five tax assessors (two from the council) and seven enactment offices (three from the council). Two council members were appointed to prevent foreign Jews from moving into the homes of local members without formal reception. Acceptance into the community required possession of at least 500 fl. ratables and the favorable recommendation of six parnasim.

27. For details see Yagod, "Worms Jewry," 35–36.

28. Reuter, *Warmaisa*, 63–67.

did evince a marked trend toward increased legislation against allowing foreign Jews in the city, particularly in 1584 and then again in 1594.[29] Nonetheless, imperial legislation from 1544 extended a privilege to the Jews of the empire to lend at interest and at higher rates than Christians, recognizing that Jews were forbidden from owning land and practicing most trades and that they often paid higher taxes. By midcentury attempts were again made to expel the Jewish community,[30] which at that point numbered about three hundred members. In the seventeenth century, the Jews lived on one street in the northern part of the city, separated from the rest of the city by two gates.[31] By 1610 there were 103 house lots—110 by 1620, with ninety houses of varying quality.[32] Jews numbered around 650,[33] constituting something like 10 percent of the total city population. Worms had one of the four largest Jewish communities in the empire (behind Prague, Frankfurt, and Vienna) and one of the five central Jewish courts established by the synod of 1603 (the others

29. Yagod, "Worms Jewry," 36.

30. In 1558 the city obtained a privilege from Ferdinand I to expel the Jews; the attempt was again thwarted, this time by the bishop and his powerful vassals, the Dalbergs; see Friedrichs, "Anti-Jewish Politics," 103, 101.

31. Friedrichs, "Anti-Jewish Politics," 96.

32. Compare the dramatic growth in the number of Jewish houses in Frankfurt in the sixteenth and early seventeenth centuries: Isidor Kracauer, *Geschichte der Juden in Frankfurt am Main (1150–1824)*, 2 vols. (Frankfurt am Main, 1925–27), 1:311–12.

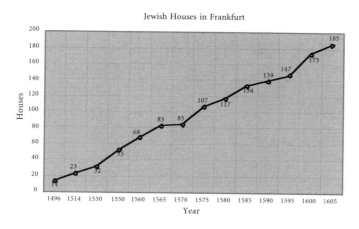

Jewish Houses in Frankfurt

33. Reuter, *Warmaisa*, 96; Friedrichs, "Anti-Jewish Politics," 96–97, claims 700 with houses including multigenerations and inhabited by an average of seven people per household.

being Frankfurt, Fulda, Friedberg, and Günzburg).[34] Plagues in the early 1630s and late 1660s affected the Jews as they did the other inhabitants of Worms; so too did the ravages of the Thirty Years' War and the entrance of French troops toward the end of the seventeenth century. It is in this complex historical context of at times volatile and at other times normal Jewish and Christian relations that the tales related in the work of Juspa need to be considered.

Juspa of Worms and the *Sefer Ma'ase Nissim*: Magic and the Jews in Worms

Juspa was born in Fulda in 1604 and lived there until he was at least thirteen. At Fulda he attended the yeshivah of Rabbi Pinhas Hurewitz, who had previously served as head of the court of appeals in Prague. By 1623 Juspa had left Fulda for Worms where he became a student of Rabbi Elijah Loans, who was both the head of the Worms yeshivah and a noted cabalist. It is from Loans that Juspa may have heard some of the tales he later wove into his *Ma'ase Nissim* (literally, miraculous or wondrous events).[35] After living as a bachelor in the house of the wealthy councilman David Oppenheimer, Juspa married, at the age of twenty-one, a woman by the name of Faierchen from a good Worms family, and was appointed as Shammash, a position which he held for over forty years.[36] Juspa served as community scribe, where he wrote divorce documents, transcribed cases before the rabbi, recorded important events in the "Pinkas Hakehila," and signed documents as a witness to their legality. He was also mohel, shohet, and principally, sexton (custodian of the synagogue property, rabbi's secretary, and administrative assistant of the charity overseer).

Juspa authored the *Ma'ase Nissim* in 1670. The twenty-five stories included in this volume, which went through nine editions between 1696 and 1788,[37] cover a variety of themes and undoubtedly were collected from numerous sources over many years. There is no unified theme in the book, though the majority of the stories focus on local legends and Worms's Jewry.[38] The stories

34. Yagod, "Worms Jewry," 37.
35. Yagod, "Worms Jewry," 205–6.
36. Yagod, "Worms Jewry," 206; and Shlomo Eidelberg, *R. Juspa, Shammash of Warmaisa: Jewish Life in Seventeenth Century Worms*, a translation of idem, *R. Yuzpa Shamash di-kehilat Vermaisa: 'Olam Yehudeha ba-me'ah ha-17* (Jerusalem: Magnes, 1991), 10. Juspa had three sons and two daughters; his most famous son was Eliezer Lieberman, who later translated the *Ma'ase Nissim* from Hebrew to Judeo-German.
37. Yagod, "Worms Jewry," 210.
38. Zinberg, *History of Jewish Literature*, 7:198; Eidelberg, *R. Juspa*, 40, in the Hebrew section.

typically portray close relations between the Jews and the city council members and, conversely, poor relations between the Jews and some of the citizenry, in particular the wandering students.[39] According to one synthetic interpretation there are two central motifs in the *Ma'ase Nissim*: "terror and dread before the hostile environment, before the slanders and persecutions that could break out at any time and bring enormous destruction, and on the other side, ignorant superstitions, unshakable belief in magic and incantations, in transmigrations and all kinds of demons." The collection does not seem to borrow heavily from the earlier *Ma'aseh Book* of the sixteenth century, nor does it contain significant Talmudic or Midrashic themes.[40] Some of the tales do, however, borrow from earlier Jewish lore, particularly regarding the actions of certain well-known and pious Jewish heroes, such as Judah the Pious in the medieval *Sefer Hasidim* and the *Ma'aseh Book* (published no earlier than the 1580s) and Rashi, the famous medieval exegete (who had an important synagogue in Worms in the eleventh century), as presented in tales from the *Shalshelet Ha-Kabbalah* of Gedaliah Ibn Yahya, also published around the end of the sixteenth century,[41] or the use of holy names as presented in the medieval *Megillat Ahimaaz*.[42] Some of the tales do bear resemblance to non-Jewish tales, such as "The Queen of Sheba," which has elements of "The Fisherman and His Wife" tale intermingled with peculiarly Jewish elements.[43] Certainly a number of the tales in the *Ma'ase Nissim* reappear in later Jewish folklore as well. By and large the *Ma'ase Nissim* does not seem to have borrowed heavily from any Christian sources, certainly not the famous medieval exempla of Caesarius of Heisterbach or Jacques de Vitry.

Ma'ase Nissim is, of course, not a chronicling of events, even if many of its stories offer apparent discussion of historical occurrences.[44] Rather than

39. Zinberg, *History of Jewish Literature*, 7:198–99. For other early modern German tales and legends, see Herman Pollack, *Jewish Folkways in Germanic Lands (1648–1806)* (Cambridge: Harvard University Press, 1971).

40. Zinberg, *History of Jewish Literature*, 7:198. For assessments of the *Ma'aseh Book* and *Ma'ase Nissim*, see the following older studies: Zalman Merkin (M. Erik), *Di Geshikhte fun der yidisher Literatur* (Warsaw: n.p., 1928), and Jakob Meitlis, *Das Ma'asebuch: Seine Entstehung und Quellengeschichte* (Berlin: n.p., 1933).

41. Eidelberg, *R. Juspa*, 53, in the Hebrew section; see Zinberg, *History of Jewish Literature*, 7:187. Regarding Gedaliah Ibn Yahya, see Abraham David, "R. Gedalya ibn Yahya's *Shalshelet Hakabbalah* (Chain of Tradition): A Chapter in Medieval Jewish History," *Immanuel* 12 (1980): 60–75.

42. Howard Schwartz, *Lilith's Cave: Jewish Tales of the Supernatural* (San Francisco: Harper & Row, 1988), 252.

43. Schwartz, *Lilith's Cave*, 241–42.

44. Eidelberg, *R. Juspa*, 52, in the Hebrew section.

examine each of the twenty-five tales offered in *Ma'ase Nissim* (the majority of which have now been rendered into English by Shlomo Eidelberg), this essay examines the few tales that both tell communal history and integrate elements of magic, in particular tales 3, 9, and 10.

Before a review of these three tales, however, let us look at a number of other stories that deal with the use of magical powers by non-Jews against the Jewish community or against particular individual Jews. In story number 4, for example, an idle fellow has a tailor sew a mandrake with magical power into the cloak of the beautiful daughter of a Worms parnas. The daughter falls madly in love with the idle fellow, does his bidding, and then steals her father's treasure for him on the Sabbath. In the end, the daughter realizes the sorcery being played on her and comes to hate the idle man. Her father succeeds in having the tailor arrested, and when the tailor confesses he is expelled and the idle fellow runs away. The girl marries an impoverished young man and both end their days wealthy and pious. Tale 4 clearly utilizes the biblical story in which mandrakes are chosen by Reuven for his mother because of their power to induce pregnancy (Gen. 30:14–16).[45] A somewhat similar tale is number 22 in which a wandering student passes by and informs a Jew's daughter that she will not be able to guard herself against him. The daughter informs her father, and she is placed in the middle of a room filled with ten rabbis studying through the night, since it is posited that in such an environment no harm could befall the girl. Utilizing a number of magical procedures, however, the student forces all but the girl to fall into a deep sleep. As the student approaches the girl, she stabs him to death. But only the perpetrator of the magic, who is now dead, is able to break the sleeping spell on the rabbis by extinguishing the magical candles he had lit earlier in the evening. In the end, through clever positioning of the dead body and depressing its stomach, forcing it to break wind and extinguish the candle, the girl is exonerated from the murder and the rabbis awake. The relation between a Jew's daughter and a wandering student are played out in Christian tales as well. In a carnival play (*Fastnachtspiel*) by Hans Folz, from the fifteenth century, *Der Falsche Messias* (1482), we hear of an eager student living next door to a Jew with the most beautiful of daughters. The daughter is pregnant after a secret affair with the

45. See *Legends of the Jews*, ed. Louis Ginzberg, trans. Henrietta Szold, vol. 1, *Bible Times and Characters from the Creation to Jacob*; vol. 2, *From Joseph to the Exodus*; vol. 3, *From the Exodus to the Death of Moses*; vol. 4, *From Joshua to Esther*; vol. 5, *Notes to Volumes 1 and 2: From the Creation to the Exodus*; vol. 6, *Notes to Volumes 3 and 4: From Moses in the Wilderness to Esther*; vol. 7, *Index* (1909–38; repr., Baltimore: Johns Hopkins University Press, 1998), 1:366–67.

student. Of course, the Christian presentation of the similar theme is quite different from the ruse played on the Jews by the malicious Christian in *Ma'ase Nissim* stories 4 and 22. A similar air of trickery is found in Folz's play, however, since the student stands outside the Jew's house in the middle of the night and in a strange voice suggests that the Jew's daughter will give birth to the Messiah. The father relays the news to a synagogue full of Jews, who are then lectured to by the rabbi, who thanks God for sending the redeemer after so long. Folz's description of the ruckus caused in the synagogue gives a detailed description of the Jewish prayers that sounded so foreign, so different from the reality that Folz and other Christians could understand, and of the ubiquity of the Jews who deny the divinity of Jesus and his miraculous conception but who secretly accept the virgin birth of their own Messiah.[46] As elsewhere in *Fastnachtspiele* Jews are portrayed as in league with the devil and with the Antichrist.

Other *Ma'ase Nissim* stories are directed at the larger Jewish community. In story number 5, for example, the mayor of Worms had a son who did bad things to the Jews. When the Jews complained to the mayor, his son was reprimanded and abandoned his attacks but secretly vowed to take his revenge on the Jews at a later date. He planned to attract the Jews to a presentation and kill them. When the moment came to act, however, he fainted. The Jews revived him and from then on he remembered them favorably. The Purim motif is evident here, but again the close relation between the Jews and the ruling authorities in the city is also demonstrated. In a similar vein, stories 16 and 18 involve ritual murder. In story 16, a Gentile approached a Jew in Worms and offered to sell his child for its blood, since, he claimed, he knew that Jews used Christian children for such purposes. The Jew cursed the Gentile for making such an accusation and offer and went to inform the parnasim. The parnasim in turn informed members of the city council, who decided to dress as Jews and approach the man looking to sell his child to determine if the information was correct. The information turned out to be true, the Gentile was captured and put to a harsh death, and the Jews were greatly honored.

These stories reveal the tenuous position of the Jews as well as the ability of the tales to portray Jewish and Christian relations in diverse ways. Now let us turn to the three *Ma'ase Nissim* stories that summon up historical events and paint them in legendary colors.

---

46. Hans Folz, "Der Falsche Messias," in *Die Reimpaarsprüche*, ed. Hanns Fischer (Munich: Beck, 1961), 94.

THE TWO VISITORS

Story 3, which also appears in the custom book of Liwa Kirchheim, elucidates the reason why two candles are kindled in the synagogue in memory of two strangers who gave their lives to save the Jews of Worms. According to the story, shortly before Passover a Jew, unaware that a Christian procession was passing through the Jewish quarter, cast "waters of urine" from his window and it landed upon the cross. "They [the Christians] immediately said that the Jews did this and provoked [them], and the Jews stood in great danger."[47] The Christian authorities demanded that the culprit confess or all of the local Jews would be killed. If the confession came before the seventh day of Passover the Jews would not be harmed. On the morning of the seventh day of Passover the Gentiles assembled in arms to exact revenge on the Jews. "On the morning of the seventh day of Passover, the shammash called everyone to prayer. When opening the gate of the Jewish section, two visitors [literally guests] were standing before him." The Shammash inquired who these visitors were and why they had come to Worms on Yom Tov, the festival. He informed them that "because of our sins, a decree has been issued against the community: [a decree] to murder all of us at the conclusion of the festival." The two visitors replied that they surely knew all this and that they had come to nullify the evil decree by declaring in the town square that the Jews are guiltless—"no man from the street of the Jews emptied or poured waters of urine upon the cross"; rather, both of them were present and it was they who committed the act. The burghers put these two visitors to death under extreme torture, the evil decree was annulled, and the Jews were not harmed. The story concludes: "From that time on, memorial prayers were established on the seventh day of Passover for the souls of the two visitors, but until this day it is not known who these two visitors were. Perhaps God sent two angels in the form of two humans to annul the evil decree."[48]

This is a curious story at many levels. In other cultures there are tales of salvation delivered through the hands of strangers, and there is widespread belief in "guardian angels,"[49] yet there is no equivalent to this story. As Eidelberg points out, the seventh day of Passover was certainly not a lucky one for

---

47. Eidelberg, *R. Juspa*, 61, in the Hebrew section. Unless otherwise noted I have included my own translation from Eidelberg's Hebrew text. While Eidelberg's English translation is quite good, it sometimes lacks precision in terminology that is useful for this paper.

48. All quotes are from Eidelberg, *R. Juspa*, 62.

49. See Stith Thompson, *Motif Index of Folk Literature*, 6 vols (Bloomington: Indiana University Press, 1975), motif no. R 169.15; for guardian angels see Thomas, *Religion and the Decline of Magic*,

the Jewish community in Worms. It was on the same day in 1615 that the Jews were expelled from the city (see tale 9 below). We should note at the outset that this story is offered as an explanation for a custom in use in Worms that apparently was not found elsewhere.

The scenario for tale 3 is highly probable, given the fact that there was much legislation in place throughout Europe that forced Jews to remain inside during *Karwoche* (the week of Easter). It is also in keeping with accusations of Jewish blasphemy and desecration of Christian symbols and religious items to accuse the Jews of such an act. In this vein, however, a number of questions naturally arise. One wonders why a Jew would not be cognizant of the fact if he was shut up in his house for that reason. One also wonders why the Christians did not act immediately against the Jews, as often occurred in popular uprisings, and why the date chosen for the final confession was the seventh day of Passover. Could the Christians not deduce who the culprit might be based on the location of the house? What this tale does suggest is that although severe action could be taken against the Jews, the civic authorities seem to have been rather even-tempered in their relations with the Jews. No mobs were formed, until the last hour, when the confession was demanded, and although the Jewish community was held accountable, once the individual culprit came forward the community was not to be punished. In fact, the authorities—secular and ecclesiastical—are presented in rather positive terms, and seem to be referred to as "Christians," while the mob are described simply as Gentiles, "goyim." Of course, the parnasim saw the matter slightly differently and attributed it to punishment for communal sins. Odd as well is the fact that nowhere in the tale is it implied that the Jews are innocent and have been framed by the Christians, as in ridiculous accusations of ritual murder and host desecration. The Jews are not truly vindicated in the end.

Who exactly were these guests, these "orchim"?[50] The text implies that these guests were Jews or at least appeared as Jews—after all they came to the Jewish gate and the parnasim asked them why they were traveling during a festival, when such travel would have been prohibited. On the other hand, the guests state that "no man from the street of the Jews" cast the "waters of urine."

---

472. For Jewish motifs, see Dov Neuman, "Motif-Index to the Talmudic-Midrashic Literature" (Ph.D. diss., Indiana University, 1954); and Haim Schwarzbaum, *Studies in Jewish and World Folklore* (Berlin: de Gruyter, 1968).

50. There is an event reported in *Ma'aseh* books where one story reports three local Jews who go into the furnace to save the community, and are not injured. See Moses Gaster, *Ma'aseh Book: The Book of Jewish Tales and Legends*, 2 vols. (Philadelphia: Jewish Publication Society, 1934), 2:430–31.

If they were Jews, then, these Jews were foreign Jews, who would have been forbidden from the city by the end of the sixteenth century. The answers to the obvious questions that the parnas asks—who they are and why they have come—are that the guests were really angels, sent to abolish the evil decree. Contributing to the assumption that these guests were otherworldly is the notion that they surely know about the evil decree and that they have come to annul it. Such a suggestion makes some sense, since we know that in Jewish thought angels are sent typically for one mission and that they are able to take human form and have appeared as guests, as for example, in the Genesis story of Abraham and the three visitors (Gen. 18).[51] Indeed, Joshua Trachtenberg has argued that the functioning of angels, as God's agents, was a characteristic and distinguishing feature of medieval Jewish magic.[52] This situation where outsiders save the community is particularly significant, for it has been argued that there is a tradition in Ashkenazic stories that the heroes are of the community and that they rely on the traditions of their forefathers. In Sephardic stories, on the contrary, heroes are from outside the community and rely more on their own skills than on community tradition.[53]

The timing of this miraculous event—the final events transpired on the seventh day of Passover—also deserves some note. There is a tradition of Jews' gaining salvation on this day, as when the Egyptians were drowned after pursuing them.[54] It is interesting in the end that salvation has to come from outside the community—whatever that might mean—either divinely or through the assistance of outsiders. Is there a moral lesson here about kindness to strangers? Does this story suggest that the larger federation of Jews and Jewish communities are eternally bound and must support one another, particularly at times of grave danger? In this case, the two strangers are memorialized in

51. See Ginzberg, *Legends of the Jews*, 1:81, 241. See Trachtenberg, *Jewish Magic*, 31, regarding the idea that angels could transform themselves into any object, including men.

52. "The characteristic and distinguishing feature of medieval Jewish magic was the function which it assigned to the angels, the agents of God. The magical use of angels was of course predicated upon the assumption that the world is very thickly populated with them, and that they play a unique role in nature.... These 'deputies' are the agents through whom the universe operates—in fact, the activities that go on in the world are nothing more than reflections of their acts." Trachtenberg, *Jewish Magic*, 61.

53. See Elisheva Carlebach, "Between History and Hope: Jewish Messianism in Ashkenaz and Sepharad" (Third Annual Lecture of the Selmanowitz Chair of Jewish History, Touro College, New York, 1998), 20 n. 13, where she cites Sara Zfatman, *The Jewish Tale in the Middle Ages: Between Ashkenaz and Sepharad* (Jerusalem: Magnes, 1993), 150–52.

54. Ginzberg, *Legends of the Jews*, 6:12.

much the same way that deceased kin are on the last day of Passover, Shavuot, and Sukkot as well as on Yom Kippur, through the Hazkarat Neshamot service, perhaps sacralizing the day through local achievements.

In the end, the memorialization of a particular and local event by a religious means, creates a sacralized center within the community, which absorbs the holy act of the guests. It is common for Jewish communities to establish fast days in commemoration of suffering[55] or feast days in commemoration of salvation. As Moshe Idel has recently suggested, Jewish "historical" sources frequently combine a variety of visions and uses of time and history. In this case, the linear depiction of the events as they unfolded combines with a circular and ritual approach to memorialization, using the recurrent remembering of an event, or at least its representation, in time to inform Jewish religion, culture, and in this case as well, community.[56]

THE EXPULSION OF THE JEWS OF WORMS IN 1615

Tale 9 of the *Ma'ase Nissim* begins historically by noting that in 1614 (5374) the burghers of Frankfurt expelled the Jews living in the city. The burghers in Worms, the tale continues, had plotted the same in 1614 after the Frankfurt example, and hordes of Gentiles assembled on the night of Tisha b'Av (5374) to plan the expulsion. "However, the Gentiles who lived in the vicinity of the street of the Jews cried out against the Gentiles assembled, and they said that the street of the Jews was full of armed men. And there was fear that the Jews would become the masters! A great fear then fell upon them, and they [the mob] dispersed." But, the story continues, on that night there had not been a single man in the Jewish street; it was, rather, "the Ba'alei Shemot" (literally masters of the divine names), and they said that the Ba'alei Shemot appeared to them [as armed warriors].[57] The leader of these mystics was Rabbi Gedalia,

55. In an interesting responsum, Jair Bacharach notes that it is permissible to transgress the Sabbath by decreeing a fast on the congregation *(tsibur)* because of the sins of the community *(kahal)*. See Jair Hayyim ben Moses Samson Bacharach, *Sefer She'eilot v'teshuvot Havot Ya'ir*, 2 vols. (Ramat-Gan: Mekhon 'Eked sefarim,1997), responsum no. 236.

56. See Moshe Idel, "Some Concepts of Time and History in Kabbalah," in *Jewish History and Jewish Memory: Essays in Honor of Yosef Hayim Yerushalmi*, ed. Elisheva Carlebach et al. (Hanover, N.H.: University Press of New England, 1998), 153–88. Idel notes that "In contradiction to Eliade's assumption, I propose that in Judaism the ritual elements are not just 'traces' that 'survive' from ancient doctrine but an integral component of this religion, which, far from representing an attempt to escape the terror of history, was conceived as shaping the direction of the linear by means of the circular approach to time" (155).

57. Eidelberg, *R. Juspa*, 72.

a leading cabalist of the generation. Still, the Gentiles continued to plot against the Jews and finally expelled them on the morning of the seventh day of Passover, 1615 (5375), while they prayed in the synagogue. The Jews were forced to leave their possessions and to cross over the Rhine where they were abandoned.

The story next describes the fate of the Jews who found themselves in the province of Pfalz. Previously, Jews had not been allowed there. The new duke, however, took pity on the Jews when he heard of the burghers' actions, and after God "instilled mercy in the heart of the duke," the duke "allowed the refugees to settle in his land, to travel in it and to conduct business wherever they desired." A similar welcome was extended by the Kurfürst of Mainz and the Landgraf of Darmstadt. "The Jews clearly saw the blessed Creator's protection over His nation. He metes out punishment with one hand, while with the other, He extends relief."[58] The princes of Mainz and Darmstadt protected the Jews of Worms and Frankfurt and interceded with the emperor on their behalf. Tale 9 notes that not all of the burghers (*ironim*) were guilty of persecuting the Jews; some attempted to hide the Jews, but the rebellious hordes (*ha-mordim*) prevented them. This mob also attacked the burghers themselves, attempting to wrest their power. In the end, the Frankfurt rebels were eventually defeated and executed, and a particularly gruesome fate awaited the ringleader Vincent Fettmilch. The tale returns to the events in Worms, where immediately after the Jews were expelled, the rioters and some burghers destroyed the synagogue. Although warned by some citizens and a certain (Christian) scholar to abstain from such destructive action or suffer punishment—we assume that the scholar was referring to the emperor—the rioters continued in their destruction.

The Jews sent two parnasim to the emperor, who appointed emissaries. The city was conquered, the burghers were summoned, and all the property taken from the Jews was recorded. The rioters were vanquished and the Jews received redemption on Rosh Chodesh Shevat, 1616 (5376). Most property, it seems, was still intact. The day preceding Rosh Chodesh Shevat was established as a fast day. The synagogue had, however, been destroyed and the cemetery desecrated. With the assistance of the wealthy parnas David Oppenheimer, as well as the monetary and physical contributions of the entire community, the synagogue was rebuilt by 1620 (5380). The story ends with a general call for the speedy arrival of the redeemer.

58. Eidelberg, *R. Juspa*, 72.

Tale 9 relates a series of somewhat interconnected events and associates the Fettmilch uprising against the Jews and the city council in Frankfurt with the eventual actions taken against the Jews in Worms. While rather historical in presentation—dealing with the plotting and final execution of the plan to expel the Jews, the confiscation of Jewish property, the assistance of the nobility and emperor, and the final vindication of the Jews and the rebuilding of their synagogue—the tale also includes important distinctions between various groups within the city and the Jews' relations with them.

Both the Fettmilch uprising and the revolt in Worms have been seen within a broad political context, in which a variety of concerns and relations were played out. Both riots seem to have been more political and economic than religious in nature and both had a long history. Among the issues of disaffection among the populace in Frankfurt were high taxation rates, rumors of corruption among the magistrates, and the obvious presence of a very large Jewish population.[59] Throughout the initial phases of the revolt the council sought to moderate the demands of Fettmilch and his followers. When it was demanded that all but the twenty wealthiest Jewish families be expelled, the council agreed in principle to some sort of expulsion but countered with a suggestion to expel only the poorest sixty families.[60] A similar situation arose in Worms, where the rioters, under the leadership of Dr. Chemnitz, argued for the reduction to 5 percent for the amount of interest that Jews could charge on money they loaned. The council discussed this proposal but noted that the Jews should be allowed to charge a higher interest rate since they could not support themselves in other traditional ways.[61] Chemnitz then demanded that the council expel the Jews, since the council held the political authority to do so through an earlier imperial grant. Chemnitz was later granted permission to inspect the book of charters and discovered that Emperor Rudolf had, in 1582, confirmed the city's control over the Jews. In the meantime, the Jews, who were accused of numerous crimes and of libeling the city in 133 ways, appealed directly to the emperor. Combined with the emperor's protective stance regarding the Jews, the failure of Fettmilch in Frankfurt forced the Worms council to distance itself from any overt mistreatment of the Jews.

59. Christopher R. Friedrichs, "Politics or Pogrom? The Fettmilch Uprising in German and Jewish History," *Central European History* 19 (1986): 186–228, here 190–91.

60. Friedrichs, "Politics or Pogrom?" 192.

61. Friedrichs, "Anti-Jewish Politics," 110–11.

The event in Worms is rather complicated. It demonstrates the intersection of numerous sources of authority and the conflagration of myriad issues. Local, regional, and imperial discussions about the Jews, their status, and their privileges evolved throughout the sixteenth century and the early part of the seventeenth. The dispute also continued after the events played out in Frankfurt and Worms, when, for example, the Kurfürst in Cologne demanded compensation from the Jews in 1619 and proceeded to enter into legal battles at the imperial courts.[62] The general contours of the event follow much like the Jewish accounts.[63] The incident of the destruction of the synagogue deserves one final note, however. According to one official city account, when the "members of the council appeared in the Judengasse, demanding to know by whose authority the synagogue was being destroyed, 'It is the command of the whole citizenry,' they were told, 'that idolatry should be eradicated so that not a single stone remains on top of another.'"[64]

Like tale 3, tale 9 unfolds on the seventh day of Passover and ends with fasting and feasting. As in other tales, this one utilizes the magical skills of the mystical Ba'alei Shemot, and in particular the powers of a leading cabalist, Rabbi Gedalia. Gedalia's invocation of divine names is a common theme in Jewish tales both earlier and later, particularly amongst the Ashkenazic hasidim. According to Trachtenberg "the primary principle of medieval Jewish magic was an implicit reliance upon the Powers of Good, which were invoked by calling upon their names, the holy Names of God and His Angels." For medieval Jews, the Jewish magician was, therefore, a scholar who used the divine names to cast his invocations.[65]

It appears that Juspa's account was based on one version of the event retold in Liwa Kirchheim's *Book of Customs*. Still, Kirchheim's account adds a number of details worth considering at length. In the first of several accounts offered by the eyewitness Kirchheim, a different language is used to describe the rioters. Kirchheim refers to them as "bubim" (arrogant ones) and writes that there were more than six hundred of them. Kirchheim also includes an account of the scholar warning the mob to abstain from destroying the synagogue, which is also quite different because it refers to the initial plot against

62. See Volker Press, "Kaiser Rudolf II und der Zusammenschluß der deutschen Judenheit: Die sogenannte Frankfurter Rabbinerverschwörung von 1603 und ihre Folgen," in *Zur Geschichte der Juden im Deutschland des Späten Mittelalters und der Frühen Neuzeit*, ed. Alfred Haverkamp (Stuttgart: Hiersemann, 1981), 243–93, esp. 279–80.

63. See Friedrichs, "Anti-Jewish Politics," 132–33.

64. Friedrichs, "Anti-Jewish Politics," 135.

65. See Trachtenberg, *Jewish Magic*, 15–17.

the Jews on Tisha b'Av (the ninth day of the month of Av, a historically tragic day for the Jews), where he mentions the magic of the Ba'al Shem. According to his account:

> As they broke down the small gate, our hearts melted. A number of frightened people, including men, women, youths, and children, hid themselves.... The remainder of the people bravely mustered their courage and armed themselves with sticks, stones, and barrels which they filled with dirt. They placed these in front of the gates so that the enemy would not be able to enter the Jewish street. The enemy then locked the gates on the outside with an iron chain so that not even one could escape. They began to speak harsh, wicked words...and we were afraid.... From the smallest to the oldest, everyone cried, wept, and prayed to the Lord of heaven and earth. He hearkened to our prayers and delivered us from their hands. Fear fell upon them, for in our midst was a great leader of the generation, the sage Rabbi Gedalia, who was a Cabalist. By uttering Divine names, he caused the Jewish street to be filled with soldiers marching with armor and all types of weapons. When the enemy saw these soldiers upon the wall, they became afraid. This Divine salvation protected us from becoming their prey and placed a different mind in the learned Chemnitius [Chemnitz] who was a foe to the Jews, seeking to destroy us.... Day and night, his conduct was concentrated upon killing, despoiling, and plundering.... Since he was a wealthy man, he greatly feared the Kaiser's authority, and so...he came with two witnesses into the midst of the throng and bitterly cried aloud to the arrogant mob: "My brothers, my friends, Guard your lives and your money! Do not harm the Jews either bodily or monetarily.... Do not do this evil...for there will be no means of expiation before the Kaiser for harming the Jews. However, I promise you that I shall wage a legal battle against them to insure that all their possessions shall be transferred to you and your children...but do not harm them now." As he spoke, one by one, his friends retreated and went home, for the fear of the Kaiser had fallen upon them....[66]

66. Liwa Kirchheim, *Book of Customs*, MS 153a, translated in Eidelberg, *R. Juspa*, 92–93; for the Hebrew see also Abraham Epstein, *Die Wormser Minhagbücher* (Breslau, 1900), xii–xiii.

The story is retold in other accounts as well, particularly, for example, in the *Zemak David*, written by David Gans (1541–1613) at the end of the sixteenth century and then expanded by David ben Moses of Reindorf in a second edition printed in Frankfurt in 1692 that included historical events through the seventeenth century as well. Divided by year, *Zemak David* begins by describing the revolt against the duke of Brandenburg in Berlin in 1615 (5375) and how the duke took revenge on the rebels (*Zemak David* employs the same term used by Juspa—"mordim"). *Zemak David* next discusses the situation in Worms, noting that the crowd of people heard the news of the events in Frankfurt and determined to expel the Jews from Worms as well. *Zemak David* repeats that the Jews were forced to leave their possessions, that they had to cross the Rhine, and that they were received warmly by the duke from Heidelberg. *Zemak David* does not mention the emperor—the duke seems to have sent his three thousand armed warriors independently—nor does it mention the magical incantations of Rabbi Gedalia. To be sure, the account in *Zemak David* is a more solemn historical chronicle than a "wonder book." Nevertheless, once shorn from its local context the story is also shorn of its magical components, yet reveals a great deal about the use of storytelling and the role of magic in creating and defining community.

THE FALSE ACCUSATION OF WELL-POISONING

A story similar in some details to tale 9 is presented by Juspa as tale number 10. In this story, which retells the events related to the Black Death attacks against the Jews in 1349 (5109), we find some parallel and some quite different themes at work. The tale notes that a false accusation was brought against the Jews in 1349 because many non-Jews died but not one Jew. False witnesses testified that Jews had been seen leaving the Jewish street in the middle of the night and that they had poured poison in the well. An evil decree was passed that the Jews would be killed on the tenth day of II Adar. The Jews received little comfort from the bishop, who divined that he had no power to break the enemy. The Jews decided to avenge themselves on the day when the decree was to be carried out, since they knew they would die anyway. When the twelve parnasim were summoned to the courthouse to hear the sentence they carried concealed weapons with them. As the councilmen were about to pronounce judgment, one parnas cried that the justice of the council was false and the parnasim killed all the councilmen. In the meantime, "while the Parnasim were in the council chambers, ten or twenty mysterious figures armed with swords and spears surrounded it outside and attacked the burghers who passed by. They ignited the storehouses of grain, causing fires that could not be extinguished. But all this did not avert the threat to the Jews, and almost all of them were killed."[67]

Several burghers took pity on the remaining Jews and hid them. However, evil burghers took to black magic and summoned a goose that flew to the houses in which Jews were hiding. Finally, a Jewish visitor came to town who was acquainted with the local priest. The visitor, fluent in Latin and secular and evangelical works, was held in high esteem by the priest. But, when the priest heard of the goose he was afraid lest the Jew be found in his house. The visitor suggested that the priest dress him in priestly garments, introduce him as a fellow priest, and allow him to deliver the sermon in the church. The visitor rebuked the audience for spilling Jewish blood and told them they had sinned by invoking sorcery through the goose. At that moment the goose perched on the church roof. The congregants were amazed at the sight and regretted their trust in divination. The tale notes that the "evil 'goose' decrees" were annulled. A communal fast was instituted on the tenth of Adar.

The general scenario of this tale is common in German and European literature since the fourteenth century, namely that Jews caused the Black Death by poisoning wells. The false accusations as well as the assumption that Jews were somehow less affected by the plague are also typical. This tale is, however, somewhat surprising and improbable. In many cities the attack against the Jews in 1348–50 was planned, but was carried out in surprise. The attack against the Jews in Augsburg, for example, was planned for a Saturday, when the Jews' defenses would be down.[68] Tale 10 also offers a surprising twist—the Jews fight back and take the lives of all of the city council members—and although the tale gives the impression that the Jews were on good terms with some good citizens and some of the clergy, it presents the relations between the Jews and the authorities in uncharacteristically bleak terms. Nevertheless, despite the fact that the tale mentions that most Jews were killed, it does not go into any details, suggesting that a conciliatory film may have been added to the story. Perhaps, too, the historical distance of the event being described (from some three hundred years earlier), with its tensions between the Jews and the councilmen, throws into relief the much more positive relations that Juspa seems to find in his own day.

---

67. Eidelberg, *R. Juspa*, 75.

68. See Bernhard Schimmelpfennig, "Christen und Juden im Augsburg des Mittelalters," in *Judengemeinden in Schwaben im Kontext des Alten Reiches*, ed. Rolf Kießling (Berlin: Akademic Verlag, 1995), 23–38, at 32.

As in tale 9, we find the presence of mysterious armed figures protecting the Jews. Unlike story 9, however, there is no mention of a Ba'al Shem's invoking them and they fail to protect the Jews, most of whom are killed. In tale 9 the armed warriors scare off the crowd, and so save the Jews, at least at first. In tale 10 the protection is much less obvious. As in other tales, magical devices are employed against the Jews, in this case the magical goose that locates the Jews. Shlomo Eidelberg notes that in the First Crusade chronicle of Rabbi Solomon ben Samson it is stated that "there was a Gentile woman who desired to accompany the crusaders. She owned a goose that would follow her everywhere she went,"[69] but this does not imply any great power, only a possible connection in the compiler's mind. In different cultures, there are also tales of a cackling goose spreading alarm.[70]

As in tale 3, it is again a visitor that saves the community. In this case, the visitor has the qualities of a hero who outwits enemies through his cunning—he is no angel. Nonetheless, the close relationship between the guest and the local priest seems surprising, as does our hero's familiarity with Christian and secular learning. This familiarity is rather striking and needs to be examined more closely. As in other stories, the tale ends by noting that a communal fast was established in memory of the massacre of many members of the community. Here as elsewhere there is an important connection between the communal customs, particularly those of a religious nature, and the fate of the community. In this case, as well, the community, or what is left of it, suffers at the hand of magic. The relationship between magic and memory, therefore, also deserves more complete attention.

Jewish Community, Magic, and Sacral Identity

The rituals of purity and impurity examined by Mary Douglas have important similarities to the use of magic noted in Juspa's text. Douglas noted long ago that rituals of purity and impurity forge unity in experience by creating, developing, and publicly displaying symbolic patterns.[71] Pollution ideas function to influence others' behavior, while crafting analogies for expressing general

---

69. Cited in Eidelberg, *R. Juspa*, 77 n. 34. The story of this woman is also mentioned in Robert Chazan, "The Mainz Anonymous: Historiographic Perspectives," in *Jewish History and Jewish Memory*, 54–69, at 61.

70. See Stith Thompson, motif type B 521.3.2; cf. James George Frazer, *The Fasti of Ovid*, 5 vols. (London: Macmillan, 1929), 3:175 n. 5.

71. Mary Douglas, *Purity and Danger: An Analysis of Concepts of Pollution and Taboo* (New York: Praeger, 1966), 2–3.

views of the social order. They create order by exaggerating internal and external differences. Like Douglas's dirt, magic too is part of a larger and certainly not isolated system.[72] The use of magic in the *Ma'ase Nissim* is fairly traditional. The valence of magic itself is dependent upon its use; negative or bad magic is presented in Gentile attacks against the Jews; more positive representations of magic occur, in almost a religious sense, when Jews employ magic, almost entirely in conscious self-defense. The magic depicted throughout by Juspa is of a protective nature, and what is perhaps more intriguing, it is not always successful, in the long run anyway. As in most uses of magic, we find combined the holy and the mundane, the combination of the divine names to create real or illusionary effects in this world. Often the magic, in its use or limitations, seems to hint at the concern with particular religious values (for example, the hasidei Ashkenaz and their pious behavior) or particular moral meanings (such as how to treat strangers). Anthropologists have, in fact, known for years that there is no clear-cut evolutionary development from magic to religion; these two concepts are intimately interconnected.[73] The magic represented by Juspa may also serve as a useful tool for assessing cultural relations between Jews and Christians in the early modern period. If Jews were viewed as magical and diabolical by some Christians, some Christians were also seen as purveyors of black magic by the Jews. The extent to which Jews and Christians borrowed from one another's magic and discourse about magic is difficult to assess in the limited stories from Juspa's account, but certainly the question needs to be investigated more fully.

The magic in the *Ma'ase Nissim*, in particular the stories upon which I have chosen to concentrate, reveals a great deal about the relationship between magic and Jewish historical memory and definitions of community. As noted above, the sacralization of local events, the act of transforming historical occurrences into the realm of the holy, is a significant tool in the development of Jewish memory, Jewish reflections on historical experience, and development of a conscious and autonomous Jewish communal sensibility. The external formulation of religious experiences, in this case through clearly magical

72. Douglas, *Purity and Danger*, 35.
73. See Douglas, *Purity and Danger*, 22–23. For a discussion of this theme as it pertains to the early rabbinic period, see Michael Fishbane, "Aspects of Jewish Magic in the Ancient Rabbinic Period," in *The Solomon Goldman Lectures*, ed. Nathaniel Stampfer (Chicago: Spertus College of Judaica Press, 1979), 2:29–39. See also Stephen Sharot, "Religion and Magic in the Traditional Jewish Community," in *Messianism, Mysticism, and Magic: A Sociological Analysis of Jewish Religious Movements* (Chapel Hill: University of North Carolina, 1982), 27–44.

acts and divine intervention, is an important means of religious and communal identification and expression.[74] Magic is employed by Juspa as a means to explain customs, and it is magic that creates the context for the commemoration of specific acts of salvation and rebuilding.

The dating of the narrative and the events represented is difficult to ascertain and the accuracy of how we understand the meanings within the texts and construct the larger contexts in which we view the tales is less than clear. Nevertheless, we can see in the tales a vision of community that has real echoes in what we know of the history of the Jews in seventeenth-century Germany. This is not surprising since it has been argued, after all, that "culture, in the sense of the public, standardized values of a community, mediates the experience of individuals."[75]

Magic, therefore, relates to and explains communal customs at the same time that it fits into a life cycle of Jewish religion, the Jewish community, and individual Jewish experiences. Magic helps to create the opportunity for the reconstruction of the Jewish community after many and diverse setbacks, attacks, and massacres. Communal boundaries are also set, in part, through miraculous events and the employment of magic. The magic of the Ba'alei Shemot reveals the dependence of the community upon particularly learned men. The use of magic effectively delineates the relationship of Jews to a variety of non-Jews in the city as well as to a multitude of sources of authority. Magic and subsequent salvation, as evident in the assistance of angels and visitors, also reveal the interdependency of Jewish communities, in a period when regional associations were taking on more significant roles in Jewish communal and constitutional history.

The magical tales reviewed here also reflect well the position of and relation to the Other in early modern German culture. The shifting position of the Jews in the early modern city, and in particular the seemingly favorable view of the city's ruling classes and, at times, religious authorities, is strikingly contrasted with the common multitudes and in particular the guilds that represented groups seeking to undermine traditional structures of authority and relations of power. In a certain sense, the use of magic, by creating non-human warriors, for example, allows Jews to engage Christians without having to take a position of open confrontation. As Giovanni Levi has argued in his interpretation of an exorcist's activities as part of an attempt to secure political authority:

74. Douglas, *Purity and Danger,* 62.
75. Douglas, *Purity and Danger,* 36–37.

It may seem to us that the laws of the modern state were imposed despite a resistance that was powerless and, in the long run, historically irrelevant. It did not happen that way, however. Normative systems, both long established and in process of formation, left gaps, interstices in which both groups and individuals brought into play consequential strategies of their own. Such strategies marked political reality with a lasting imprint. They could not prevent forms of domination, but they did condition and modify them.[76]

Did tales of magic afford the Jews of Worms in the seventeenth century such opportunity to confront authority? Curiously, the one story reviewed here that has the Jews taking direct action into their own hands and attacking the city councilmen is a tale of a noticeably earlier period in the history of the Jews in the city. Elisheva Carlebach has noted, regarding Josel of Rosheim's depiction of the expulsion of the Jews from Regensburg, that "by his elevation of apostates to the status of primary hostile Other, Josel deflected the ultimate responsibility for oppression of Jews from the highest power in the land, where responsibility manifestly resided, to an internal malefactor."[77] The magical tales allow for a complex construction of non-Jewish identity which simultaneously records both the positive and negative relations between Jews and Christians. The tales reveal the inherent complexity of the non-Jewish society, but this construction, mediated through magical and wondrous tales, allowed Jews to challenge the traditional system, or rather contest domination, by asserting and defending their own position through a third party. It is in this mediated construction that the boundaries of Jewish community, both internal and external boundaries, take on important shape.

In the end, the magical stories of early modern Jewry combine elements of traditional religious culture, in its legal and mystical or magical components, along with glimpses of the social, political, economic, and cultural realities in which the Jews found themselves. A more thorough reading of these

76. Giovanni Levi, *Inheriting Power: The Story of an Exorcist*, trans. Lydia G. Cochrane (Chicago: University of Chicago Press, 1988), xv.

77. Elisheva Carlebach, "Between History and Myth: The Regensburg Expulsion in Josel of Rosheim's *Sefer Ha-Miknah*," in *Jewish History and Jewish Memory*, 40–53, at 46. This is Yosef Hayim Yerushalmi's notion of the "profound internalization and concomitant glorification of the myth of the royal alliance" amongst Jews noted by David Myers; see David N. Myers, "Of Marranos and Memory: Yosef Hayim Yerushalmi and the Writing of Jewish History," in *Jewish History and Jewish Memory*, 1–21, at 6.

Jewish sources together with other non-Jewish materials may, as suggested at the beginning of this investigation, eventually allow us to reconstruct a much fuller and more satisfying picture of Jewish culture in a period somehow both medieval and modern together.

A Nun-Witch in Eighteenth-Century Tuscany

Anne Jacobson Schutte

From the late sixteenth century on, witches were as scarce as hen's teeth in Italy. Giovanni Romeo has explained why. Soon after it was founded in 1542, the Roman Inquisition managed to wrest jurisdiction over witchcraft from the secular authorities. By the 1580s, a majority of the cardinals on its governing body, the Congregation of the Holy Office, had come to doubt the possibility of pacts with the devil and periodic flights to gatherings of witches featuring abundant food, drink, and sex. Hence, the Congregation decided on "a partial depenalization of the sabbath": no longer were inquisitors to prosecute people named by witches as accomplices unless there was independent evidence suggesting that they had perpetrated *maleficia*.[1] Beginning in the 1620s, as John Tedeschi has shown, this policy was publicized through the wide circulation in manuscript of Cardinal Desiderio Scaglia's authoritative *Instructio pro formandis processibus in causis strigum, sortilegorum et maleficiorum*.[2]

From then on, inquisitors in the field, whose operations were closely monitored by the Congregation in Rome, prosecuted thousands of women

A preliminary, very different version of this essay appeared previously: "My Satanic Spouse: Nuns and Sexual Possession in Early Modern Italy," *Civic* 21 (1997): 163–75.

1. Giovanni Romeo, *Inquisitori, esorcisti e streghe nell'Italia della Controriforma* (Florence: Sansoni, 1990), 25–108, 247–74; quoted phrase at 54.

2. John Tedeschi, *The Prosecution of Heresy: Collected Studies on the Inquisition in Early Modern Italy* (Binghamton, N.Y.: Medieval & Renaissance Texts & Studies, 1991), 205–27. On Scaglia, a Dominican friar and inquisitor before he was named commissioner of the Holy Office and then cardinal, see also *Hierarchia catholica medii et recentioris aevi: Sive Summorum pontificum, S.R.E. cardinalium ecclesiarum antistitum series* (hereafter *HC*), ed. Konrad Eubel et al., 7 vols. (Padua: Typis et sumptibus Domus Editorialis "Il Messaggero di S. Antonio," 1913–68), here vol. 4, ed. Patricius Gauchet, 14–15.

accused of engaging in simple sorcery and a smaller number of male sorcerers and magicians, but they neither sought out nor attempted to persuade sorceresses that they were witches in league with the devil. For these reasons—the handling of sorcery and magic by a centralized ecclesiastical court with highly trained personnel and that court's rejection of diabolical witchcraft—Italy did not experience the witch craze that afflicted northern Europe and British North America in the seventeenth century.[3]

✢ ✢ ✢

Nonetheless, the occasional "classic" witch came to the Roman Inquisition's attention. A team of experts has closely examined the case of a Tuscan woman, Gostanza da Libbiano, tried by the Inquisition for witchcraft in the late sixteenth century. As an introduction to the case of Asmodea, Gostanza's story is worth recounting briefly here. In the late fall of 1594 this sixty-year-old widow, who practiced healing and midwifery, was denounced as a witch by her neighbors in San Miniato following the deaths of several infants and children who had been in her care. After the vicar of the bishop of Lucca had interrogated a number of witnesses, the case was taken in hand by the young Franciscan friar Mario Porcacchi, the bishop's inquisitor in San Miniato.[4] Unlike most Italian inquisitors of the late sixteenth century, Porcacchi evidently believed in the modern heresy of witchcraft. Convinced by the testimony already gathered and circumstantial evidence that seemed to point to murder, he subjected her immediately to torture.[5]

Under physical duress, Gostanza was quick to admit that she had used her knowledge to harm as well as to heal. When asked whether she "had ever gone out at night with other women in the same profession," she realized

3. As scholars of the Iberian and Latin American inquisitions too numerous to mention here have established, the same was the case in Spain, Portugal, and their overseas dependencies.

4. The tiny independent republic of Lucca was the only state on the Italian peninsula to resist successfully the introduction of the Roman Inquisition. See Simonetta Adorni-Braccesi, "La Repubblica di Lucca e l'aborrita' Inquisizione: Istituzioni e società," in *L'Inquisizione romana in Italia nell'età moderna: Archivi, problemi di metodo e nuove ricerche*, ed. Andrea Del Col and Giovanna Paolin (Rome: PAS, 1991), 333–62; and eadem, *"Una città infetta": La repubblica di Lucca nella crisi religiosa del Cinquecento* (Florence: Olschki, 1994).

5. Silvia Mantini, "'Et chi vi andava una volta vi sarebbe tornata sempre': Una storia di streghe," in *Gostanza, la strega di San Miniato: Processo a una guaritrice nella Toscana medicea*, ed. Franco Cardini (Rome: Laterza, 1989), 5–25; and eadem, "Gostanza da Libbiano, guaritrice e strega (1534–?)," in *Rinascimento al femminile*, ed. Ottavia Niccoli (Rome: Laterza, 1991), 143–51.

what the inquisitor had in mind and promptly fulfilled his expectations. Yes, she replied: thirty years earlier, a devil named Polletto had transported her to the witches' sabbath on about six occasions. There she had sworn allegiance to the Great Devil and feasted in his magnificent palace, but she had never participated in the orgies following the banquets. At the beginning of the second interrogation, she refused to authenticate her previous testimony. Put to torture again, she declared, "If you want me to tell lies, I'll tell them." In subsequent sessions she confirmed everything she had said before and offered a host of new details.[6]

Claiming to be the illegitimate daughter of a Florentine patrician, Gostanza asserted that she had been abducted from her father's country villa at the age of eight by a shepherd, who raped her and then forced her to marry him.[7] The devil, she averred, was a much better sexual partner than her husband. Not only was he very handsome, well dressed, and lusty; he was a considerate lover who tenderly caressed and kissed her, the favorite member of his harem. Gostanza's description of the devil's headquarters was not the temporary throne set up in a mountain meadow that is mentioned in most accounts of the sabbat. According to her, it was located in a city "more beautiful than Florence, with everything in gold, and there were beautiful palaces…and whoever went there once wanted to stay forever."[8]

This creative exercise in wish fulfillment, triggered by torture, drew on at least two sources. Gostanza's familiarity with traditional lore about the sabbat—the sacrilegious acts required of the devil's disciples, but above all the abundant food, drink, and good sex—probably stemmed from acquaintance in her youth with four witches of San Miniato who had been tried and burned by the secular authorities in 1540. For the urban component of her vision, she could draw on her childhood in Florence, not in a patrician palace but in the humbler abode of her real father, one Michele da Firenze. Once the inquisitor general of Florence, Fra Dionigi da Costacciaro, took charge of her case, Gostanza benefited from treatment in accordance with the moderate, skeptical approach to witchcraft recently endorsed by the Congregation of the Holy Office. On 24 November, encouraged to confess that her story was a tissue of lies, she promptly complied. After releasing her from prison, Fra Dionigi

6. Mantini, *Gostanza*, 152–54.
7. On sexual abuse as a precipitant of fantasies about a pact with the devil, see Anita M. Walker and Edmund H. Dickerman, "Magdeleine des Aymards: Demonism or Child Abuse in Early Modern Europe?" *Psychohistory Review* 24 (1996): 239–64.
8. Mantini, *Gostanza*, 154–57.

admonished his imprudent young colleague in San Miniato not to believe all the tales told by witnesses and, especially, by defendants under torture.[9] Release from confinement and physical torment must have come as a relief to Gostanza. Still, one may wonder whether during the remaining years of her life she recalled nostalgically the earthly paradise she had constructed during the trial.

A century and a quarter later, another Tuscan witch came before the Inquisition. She was of higher estate and considerably younger than Gostanza—and she was a nun. Given the passage of time and the different social and religious status of the defendants, their stories are quite dissimilar in many respects, as we shall see. From a historian's point of view, the biggest difference lies in the sources available for re-presenting their Inquisitorial adventures. For Gostanza, we have a firm documentary base on which to operate: the record of her trial.[10] For Asmodea, our main source is a naive, sensationalistic account of the case in its early stages. In the absence of transcripts of interrogations, we can hear various investigators talking about her, but she never speaks directly. Despite this serious limitation, the story of Asmodea sheds considerable light on witchcraft, the Inquisition, and the condition of women in early modern Italy.

✠ ✠ ✠

In 1721 a team of Fathers of the Mission based in Forlì was hard at work in the Tuscan Romagna, a region of mixed jurisdiction subject politically to the grand duchy of Tuscany and ecclesiastically to the bishopric of Faenza.[11] They learned that five years earlier, the inhabitants of a convent in Marradi had

---

9. Mantini, *Gostanza*, 157–60. For the handling of similar cases in seventeenth-century Tuscany, see Adriano Prosperi, "Inquisitori e streghe nel Seicento fiorentino," in *Gostanza*, ed. Cardini, 217–50. On torture in an "irregular" trial, Prosperi's discussion of the case of Maddalena Serchi (225–37) is particularly instructive.

10. The trial record is published in *Gostanza*, ed. Cardini.

11. They almost certainly belonged to the Congregation of Priests of the Mission, founded by Vincent de Paul in 1625 and usually called Lazarists after their first house in Paris, Saint-Lazare. By the early eighteenth century the congregation had fourteen houses in Italy. Like members of many other orders and congregations founded during the early modern era, notably the Society of Jesus, the Lazarists devoted much effort to evangelizing in the rural areas of Italy, known to missionaries as "our Indies." *Enciclopedia Italiana* (1929–39), s.v. "Lazzaristi" and "Vincenzo de Paul"; and *Storia della Congregazione della Missione*, 5 vols., ed. Luigi Mezzadri and José María Román Fuentes (Rome: CLV-Edizioni Vencenziane, 1992–99), vol. 1, *Dalla fondazione alla fine del XVII secolo* (1625–97), esp. 197, 203, 247–92.

begun to suffer from strange maladies. Since neither medical treatment nor exorcism had sufficed to cure the affected sisters, the bishop of Faenza, Cardinal Giulio Piazza, appointed one of the missionaries to serve as extraordinary confessor to the nuns and ordered him to conduct a thorough investigation. This credulous emissary soon discovered to his horror that the infestation was due to the machinations of "an out-and-out witch" (*una solennissima strega*) inside the convent.[12] Written in 1722, almost certainly by the investigating missionary, the account provides abundant information about the nun. When the missionary interrogated her, the woman revealed that at the age of nine she had been introduced by a witch servant to the devil in the guise of a handsome young man. Taking her as his wife, he appointed her "second queen of the nether regions, with the name Asmodea."[13] He endowed her with powers in the upper world as well: every month she could cause eleven people to fall ill and one to die. When she reached the age at which her father had to decide whether to find her a husband or make her a nun, her satanic spouse persuaded her to enter a convent in Marradi. Responding to her objection that she would prefer some religious house in Florence, closer to her home in Borgo San Lorenzo,[14] the devil assured her that she would not find

12. Bologna, Biblioteca Universitaria (hereafter BoBU), MS Ital. 6, no. 19, "Caso seguito in Maradi [*sic*], diocesi di Forlì, di una monacha che sino da fanciulla sposò un demonio" (hereafter *Caso*), 155r–56r. The writer gives the nun's age as thirty-two; in fact, she was twenty-five at the time he discovered her alleged witchcraft. Other copies of the account include BoBU, MS Ital. 22 (9L), no. 35; BoBU, MS Ital. 304, no. 57; and Bologna, Biblioteca Comunale dell'Archiginnasio, MS B.324, no. 31 bis. Italian libraries and archives hold numerous miscellaneous manuscripts containing Inquisition sentences and summaries of cases. Since many of the cases include sexual components, the miscellanies may have been compiled not only to inform inquisitors but also to titillate lay readers: John Tedeschi, personal communication. As suggested below, the probable author of *Caso* is the missionary who conducted the investigation; he did not give his name or specify his intended audience. Giulio Piazza (1663–1726), the only person named in the report, served as a papal diplomat before being appointed bishop of Faenza on 21 July 1710; he was elevated to the cardinalate in 1712: *HC*, vol. 5, ed. Remigius Ritzler, and Permin Sefrin (Padua: Messagero di S. Antonio, 1952), 199, 282, 233; *Stemmi dei vescovi e vescovi cardinali di Faenza* (Faenza: F. Lega, 1925), 40–41.

13. *Caso*, 156r. Her name is the feminine form of Asmodeus (first mentioned in the apocryphal book of Tobit 3:8, 17), whom writers on exorcism identified as the demon of lust. See, for example, Girolamo Menghi, *Fustis daemonum*, in *Thesaurus exorcistarum* (Cologne, 1608), 538; and Francesco Maria Guazzo, *Compendium maleficarum*, 2d ed. (Milan, 1626), 175. It seems likely that the name Asmodea was suggested to the nun by her learned interrogator. Later in the account, Asmodea is reported to have said that "the Queen of Hell, who is not as we describe her but the exact opposite, is still alive." *Caso*, 157v.

14. Or nearby; see below at p. 132. On the modern railroad line, Borgo San Lorenzo lies 32 km southwest of Marradi and 54 km northeast of Florence, but in the eighteenth century the route

confinement in Marradi difficult to endure, "for he would take her anywhere she wished."[15]

The Evil One fulfilled his promise. In her imagination, Asmodea was escorted on an itinerary recalling that of a twentieth-century fictional traveler, Virginia Woolf's Orlando:

> She had herself transported to Naples, to France, and then to Constantinople, where she saw everything that was great and beautiful in those courts, learned about treaties concluded in ministers' cabinets, and fomented great discord among potentates. She attracted the attention of the Grand Turk, joined his seraglio, became one of his concubines, and satisfied her insatiable and libidinous desires with him. As evidence of this, she claimed that he had given her a superb tapestry, which in fact was found in her house.

On other excursions she attended the coronation of the emperor at Frankfurt in the guise of a handsome little dog, killed the emperor's son, witnessed the battles of Temisvár and Belgrade, and took a hand in causing an outbreak of plague in Marseille.[16]

Not all of Asmodea's journeys were deluxe tours of major cities. She also traveled to the preferred destinations of ordinary lower-class witches. On more than one occasion, she confessed, she had gone to the Walnut Tree of Benevento, a classic site of the witches' sabbat. There, in the company of twenty thousand witches and five thousand warlocks, she had received royal honors.[17] Closer to home, she had visited all but two of the houses in Marradi in order to provoke abortions, hurt children, and cause other kinds of harm.

---

running down to the Tuscan capital would have been easier to travel. Furthermore, as we shall see, the young woman had relatives in Florence. Therefore, she probably reasoned that even behind convent walls, living in a city was preferable to vegetating in a small hill town. In 1745 the population of Marradi was 1,577. Emanuele Repetti, *Dizionario geografico fisico storico della Toscana*, 6 vols. (Florence, 1833–45), 3:91. Her father undoubtedly sought to economize by placing her in Marradi; as he surely knew, convent dowries in Florence were much higher; see n. 50.

15. *Caso*, 156r–v.

16. *Caso*, 156v.

17. *Caso*, 156v. Here again, suggestive questioning may have elicited this place-name in Campania, which would have been less familiar to a Tuscan nun than to a cleric who had read treatises on witchcraft and magic. See, e.g., Girolamo Menghi, *Compendio dell'arte essorcistica et possibilità delle mirabili e stupendi operationi delli demoni e de' malefici* (Bologna, 1576; repr., ed. Antonio Aliani, postface by Ottavio Franceschini, Genoa: Nuova Stile regina editrice, 1987), 173; Guazzo, *Compendium Maleficarum*, 86.

During her long career as a witch, Asmodea alleged, she had killed nine thousand babies and caused injury and death to several clerics. Her claims were confirmed by the discovery in townspeople's beds of witchcraft materials that filled four sacks, which were burned in the main square of Marradi.[18]

Meanwhile, to all appearances until the missionaries' arrival, Asmodea remained behind convent walls, where she conducted herself in such an exemplary fashion that the other nuns believed her to be a budding saint. Little did they know that she secretly refrained from consuming communion wafers, which at the devil's order she crushed under her feet or conserved for use in casting spells. At first, despite their puzzlement when she was seen in two places at the same time and a good-looking young man with a peculiar wig was observed wandering around the convent, her sisters discounted such odd occurrences because they were convinced of her holiness. After they stationed themselves outside her cell at night and heard her saying "words of affection, as between husband and wife" and other "dirty things," they decided to inform their superior. The nuns' report was dismissed as the product of their "illusions and hypochondriacal afflictions."[19]

All this information emerged during the investigator's interrogation, conducted in strict secrecy. When he conveyed his findings to Bishop Piazza, he received authorization to strip the nun of her habit, put her in chains, and have her watched constantly by the only two nuns in the convent whom she had not yet managed to bewitch. Once the Holy Office was informed, she was taken to its jail in Faenza. Until then, she had remained "contumacious and obstinate in the horrendous promise that she had made to the devil, who had marked her as his own on several parts of her body." Her demonic consort urged her to cut out her tongue and did everything in his power to keep her out of the Inquisition's hands, but to no avail. Now that she was in a place where her demonic consort could not penetrate, the author of the account piously stated that everyone was hoping and praying that Asmodea would be illuminated by a ray of divine grace and persuaded to confess her many sins and crimes.[20]

18. *Caso*, 156v.

19. *Caso*, 156v. In the early modern period the term hypochondria did not mean imaginary illness. Physicians took the Greek word in its literal sense: the part of the stomach lying below (*hypo*) the short ribs (*chondros*). Here, one of them explained, "natural heat" is often "converted into a non-natural and foreign heat," a process that may be complicated by the intrusion of "vicious humors." Paolo Zacchia, *De' mali hipochondriaci libri tre* (1639; rev. ed. Venice, 1665), 1–5.

20. *Caso*, 156v–57r.

-|-|- -|-|- -|-|-

Why did the author of the account give only the nun's witch name, Asmodea? The reason is not difficult to determine. In his *Prattica per procedere nelle cause del S. Offizio*, written around 1635, Desiderio Scaglia had established guidelines for the diagnosis and treatment of heretical nuns. Like his *Instructio pro formandis processibus*, this work, in manuscript form, reached inquisitors and others concerned with the repression of heresy. Cardinal Scaglia identifies several problems that arise in female religious houses. First, women forced into convents, as well as those maltreated by their superiors, sometimes fall into desperation so deep that they come to doubt central doctrines of the faith. When this occurs, the convent's designated confessor, directly or via the ordinary, should notify the Holy Office and request papal permission to absolve the nun, which will be granted provided that she has no accomplices or disciples. If she does, she must be put on trial.[21]

The second, more common occurrence—a natural consequence of "womanish competition and rivalry"—is a nun's coming to believe that she is bewitched or possessed by the devil, a possibility about which Scaglia is obviously skeptical. With pungent sarcasm, he reveals how ineptly such cases are normally handled. The superiors call in exorcists, whose ministrations serve only to spread the malady among the other nuns. Then they conduct a trial, in which by suggestive questioning and torture they obtain spurious confessions. Inevitably and most unfortunately, the convent and the entire city are turned topsy-turvy. Scaglia recommends a more effective procedure: isolating the affected sisters (making sure, however, that they are always accompanied by a reliable companion) and bringing in a good confessor, who will reassure the other nuns and occupy them with the sacraments and prayer. Above all, the infestation must be kept secret, so that the reputations of the convent and its inhabitants' relatives are not damaged. In the event that the delusion is widespread, the chief perpetrators should be punished and the others reprimanded.[22] If the author of the report was not already familiar with the policy established by Scaglia, followed to the letter in the case of the nun of Marradi, Bishop Piazza or the inquisitor, Vincenzo Maria

---

21. Albano Biondi, "'L'inordinata devozione' nella *Prattica* del Cardinale Scaglia (ca. 1635)," in *Finzione e santità tra medioevo ed età moderna*, ed. Gabriella Zarri (Turin: Rosenberg & Sellier, 1991), 316–17.

22. Biondi, "'L'inordinata devozione,'" 317–18. Exorcists, however, did not disappear from the convent scene. On 22 June 1725, for example, the Congregation of Bishops and Regulars approved a

Ferrero, must have explained it to him.[23] Consequently, he refrained from revealing her secular or religious name.

Who was Asmodea? Fortunately, other sources enable us to identify her. As he was required to do, Inquisitor Ferrero promptly informed his superiors, the cardinals on the Congregation of the Holy Office, about the nun-witch. When that body's archive was opened to scholars in early 1998, it became possible to consult the *Decreta*, minutes of the Congregation's meetings. These reveal that Asmodea's name in religion was Suor Maria Deodata Fabri.[24] No record of her trial, a copy of which must have been sent from Faenza to Rome, survives in the section Stanza Storica of that seriously depleted archive. If the original has survived in Faenza, it is not available for consultation.[25] Fabri's *supplica* (petition) for release from her vows, presented to Pope Benedict XIII in 1725, however, takes us back to the beginning of her life. Since the Congregation of the Holy Office directed developments in the case, notations in the *Decreta* carry her story forward several years beyond 1722, when the missionary's account was written.

request forwarded by the bishop of Catania from Giovanna Grimaldi, abbess of San Benedetto in Castro, that a reformed Franciscan exorcist be sent to her house to deal with three "obsessed" nuns. Vatican City, Archivio Segreto Vaticano (hereafter VaAS), Congregazione di Vescovi e Regolari (hereafter SCVR), Positiones Monialium, 69 (1725, giugno-luglio).

23. Ferrero's name is not mentioned in any of the sources concerning Asmodea. This Dominican, a native of Nizza Monferrato, had served previously on the Inquisition of Ancona. He was named inquisitor of Faenza on 12 November 1712 and died in office on 6 February 1725. Bonaventura Maria Grossi da Savona, who arrived in Faenza on 12 May 1725, took his place: Faenza, Biblioteca Comunale Manfrediana, MS 88(I), loose printed sheet numbered XIV (last leaf of *Serie cronologica storico-critica dei vescovi faentini compilata dal canonico Andrea Strocchi*).

24. Vatican City, Archivio della Congregazione per la Dottrina della Fede (hereafter VaCDF), *Decreta*, 1721, 277v–278r (1 October). A short summary of the case gives her surname but misstates her first name as Teodora. Venice, Biblioteca Correr d'Arte e Storia Veneziana, MS Gradenigo 159, *S. Offitio: Inquisitione di Venezia et Magistrati delli Assistenti al S. Offitio et contro l'Eresia*, 414–15.

25. According to a local historian, the records of the Inquisition of Faenza "are today destroyed or impossible to find," except for a few now in the library of Trinity College, University of Dublin. Francesco Lanzoni, *La Controriforma nella città e diocesi di Faenza* (Faenza: F. Lega, 1925), 168, 174. Trinity College Dublin does not hold the record of Fabri's trial. Since in some episcopal archives Inquisition trial materials may be found among the criminal records, I sought on 28 May 1996 to inspect the series *Ius criminale* in the Archivio Vescovile of Faenza (hereafter FaAV) but was informed by the assistant director that his superior had excluded them from consultation.

Daughter of Gaetano di Francesco Fabri, a Florentine citizen, the future nun-witch was born on 31 March 1696 in Santa Maria a Vezzano, a hamlet northeast of Borgo San Lorenzo, and baptized the following day as Caterina Angela. On 2 April 1709, at the age of thirteen, she took the habit in the Dominican convent of Santissima Annunziata in Marradi, assuming the name Maria Deodata; she professed on 27 April of the following year. Both ceremonies took place almost two years earlier than the regulations of the Council of Trent allowed.[26]

Several considerations—Fabri's illegally premature vestition and profession, Cardinal Scaglia's analysis of the factors leading some nuns to believe that they were possessed by the devil, and the missionary's account of her career as a witch—strongly suggest that parental pressure, rather than a genuine calling to the religious life, led her into the convent. In other words, she was very likely a victim of forced monachization, a pervasive practice designed to preserve patrimonies and enhance families' honor.[27] Perhaps her father employed gentle conditioning by placing her in the convent very young as a boarder or *educanda* (pupil, often under the tutelage of an aunt), or perhaps he abruptly informed her where and how she would spend the rest of her life; the latter seems more likely. Whether before her profession, as the decrees of the Council of Trent required, the bishop of Faenza or his representative questioned her to determine if she was taking this important step voluntarily seems dubious, for

26. VaAS, Congregazione del Concilio, Positiones, 497 (1725, diebus 24 Martii pars secunda et 14 Aprilis pars prima), n.p. In routine fashion, Fabri's *supplica* was passed by the pope to the Congregation of the Council, which dealt with requests for release from vows submitted more than five years after a religious had professed; hers was discussed on 14 April 1725. Gaetano Fabri's Florentine citizenship is mentioned in VaCDF, *Decreta*, 1724, 228r (13 September). Her mother, who may have been dead by 1725, is not mentioned in the *supplica*. Since no baptismal registers for Santa Maria a Vezzano have survived in Florence, Archivio Arcivescovile (hereafter cited as FiAA), her mother's name cannot be determined; no wife of Gaetano Fabri appears in the death registers of either Santa Marie a Vezzano or Borgo San Lorenzo. It seems possible that Caterina Angela was an illegitimate child.

27. On forced monachization, see Giovanna Paolin, "Monache e donne nel Friuli del Cinquecento," in *Società e cultura del Cinquecento nel Friuli occidentale: Studi*, ed. Andrea Del Col (Pordenone: Edizioni della Provincia de Pordenone, 1984), 201–28; Enrico Cattaneo, "Le monacazioni forzate fra Cinque e Seicento," in *Vita e processo di Suor Virginia Maria de Leyva monaca di Monza*, ed. Umberto Colombo (Milan: Garzanti, 1985), 145–95; Francesca Medioli, *L'"Inferno monacale" di Arcangela Tarabotti* (Turin: Rosenberg & Sellier, 1990), esp. 111–35; and Giovanna Paolin, *Lo spazio del silenzio: Monacazioni forzate, clausura e proposte di vita religiosa femminile nell'età moderna* (Pordenone: Biblioteca dell'immagine, 1996). On monachization as a strategy to enhance family honor, see Jutta Sperling, *Convents and the Body Politic in Late Renaissance Venice (1550–1650)* (Chicago: University of Chicago Press, 1999).

surely the interviewer would have realized that she was too young to make her vows.[28] If she was interrogated, she was probably so thoroughly brainwashed or frightened, like many adolescents under pressure to profess as nuns, that she dared not respond in the negative.

Founded in the late sixteenth century, Santissima Annunziata, the only female religious house in Marradi, began operation under the guidance of two Dominican nuns brought in from the diocese of Fiesole.[29] Its location just above a riverbank proved insalubrious; "very bad vapors" from the Lamone caused most of the nuns to contract lung disease, of which many died.[30] Still, the foundation flourished. In 1603 the Congregation of Bishops and Regulars considered the nuns' request for expansion of the premises.[31] A few years later, the convent had twenty-five inhabitants.[32] What its population

28. Chapter 17 of the Decree on Regulars and Nuns, passed in session 25 of the Council of Trent on 4 December 1563, provided that before a young woman took the veil, "the ordinary, his vicar, or someone designated by them examine diligently the will of the virgin to determine whether she has been forced or tricked, [and] whether she knows what she is doing." *Conciliorum Oecumenicorum Decreta*, ed. Giuseppe Alberigo et al. (Bologna: Instituto per le Scienze Religiose, 1973), 781. Since Cardinal Marcello Durazzo, bishop of Faenza, died on the same day she professed (*HC*, 5:199), it is improbable that he himself conducted the interview, if indeed it took place. Unlike most *suppliche* for release from monastic vows, Fabri's does not allege that she was compelled *per vim et metum* (by force and fear) to enter the convent, only that she did so two years before the minimum age of sixteen.

29. FaAV, *Visite Pastorali*, Modigliana, fasc. Marradi (formerly S.S. 9, b. 3), 70r (Cardinal Marcantonio Maffei to Annibale Grassi, bishop of Faenza, Rome, 26 June 1582). Marradi was in an area of mixed jurisdiction: ecclesiastically in the diocese of Faenza (not Forlì as the title of Caso asserts), part of the papal state, but politically in the grand duchy of Florence. The Tuscan Deputazione de' Monasteri handled financial and some other matters concerning female religious houses. On her convent, still in existence, see Carlo Mazzotti, *Il monastero della SS: Annuziata delle domenicane di Marradi: Memorie storiche* (Faenza: Fratelli Lega, 1960). The nuns informed me that their archive contains nothing from the eighteenth century (letter, 27 March 1996). A small amount of information about Santissima Annunziata may be found in FaAV, *Visite pastorali*, Modigliana, cartella Marradi (produced in the twentieth century by the ill-advised dismembering of several series of documents); and Florence, Archivio di Stato (hereafter FiAS), *Conventi soppressi governo francese*, 157: SS. Annuziata di Marradi, b. 8.

30. FaAV, *Visite Pastorali*, Modigliana, fasc. Marradi (formerly S.S. 9, b. 3), 34r (petition to the Congregation of Bishops and Regulars from Suor Dorotea Paganini, who requested a temporary transfer to another convent for health reasons, 23 June 1586).

31. FaAV, *Visite Pastorali* (formerly S.S. 9, b. 4), 13r (Cardinal Antonio Maria Gallo to Cardinal Valenti, Rome, 3 Mar. 1603). Either the addressee's surname or the date of the letter is wrong: there was no Cardinal Valenti in 1603; Erminio Valenti got the red hat in 1604: *HC*, 5:203.

32. Angelo Turchini, *Inquisitori e pastori: Considerazioni su popolazione romagnola, articolazione territoriale, competenza dell'Inquisizione faentino all'inizio del Seicento* (Cesena: Società editrice "Il Ponte Vecchio," 1994), 68.

was in Fabri's time cannot be determined, but it was large enough to accommodate *educande*. According to the missionary's account, Fabri tried in vain to introduce one of them, who had expressed an inclination toward marriage, to a young devil—presumably in the hope that the girl would follow her example and become a nun-witch.[33]

Fabri's effort "to open a school" of witchcraft in Santissima Annunziata[34] came to light in the fall of 1721. When Suor Maria Giacinta Tamburini, no doubt prompted by the investigating missionary, denounced her to the Inquisition of Faenza,[35] Fabri was immediately confined to the convent prison. The Congregation of the Holy Office instructed its consultants to concern themselves first with Tamburini's denunciation, which they ruled invalid. Since the accuser had implicated herself as well, the Congregation ordered Bishop Piazza to interrogate Tamburini "about her intention and credulity." If she did not respond "in a Catholic manner," she must be required to abjure *de vehementi* (vehemently suspect of heresy)—after which, given that she had presented herself spontaneously, she should be assigned salutary penances rather than a more severe punishment.[36] Then the cardinal-members turned their attention to Fabri. Assuming, as seemed likely in terms of Scaglia's analysis of such cases, that she was deluded, they ordered Bishop Piazza to appoint an "expert, learned, and prudent confessor" authorized to absolve her in the "forum of conscience."[37] Thereafter, if the bishop considered it appropriate, she should be released from confinement and transferred to another convent.[38]

33. *Caso*, 157r.

34. *Caso*, 157r.

35. VaCDF, *Decreta*, 1721, 277v (1 October).

36. For details on sentences and other matters, see John Tedeschi, "The Organization and Procedures of the Roman Inquisition," in *Prosecution of Heresy*, 132–53.

37. On the "forum of conscience," a shadowy intermediate zone between the "internal forum" of confession and the "external forum" of the court first delineated by observant Dominican and Franciscan theologians in the late fifteenth century, see Elena Brambilla, "Confessione, casi riservati e giustizia 'spirituale' dal XV secolo al concilio di Trento: I reati di fede e di morale," in *Fonti ecclesiastiche per la storia sociale e religiosa d'Europa: XV–XVIII secolo*, ed. Cecilia Nubola and Angelo Turchini (Bologna: Il Mulino, 1999), 491–540, esp. 516–40. The issue of confessors' collaboration with inquisitors has received much attention in recent scholarship: see Romeo, *Inquisitori*, 191–98; Giovanna Paolin, "Inquisizione e confessori nel Friuli del Seicento: Analisi di un rapporto," in *L'Inquisizione romana*, ed. Del Col and Paolin, 175–87; Adriano Prosperi, *Tribunali della coscienza: Inquisitori, confessori, missionari* (Turin: Mulino, 1996), 219–57; and Giovanni Romeo, *Ricerche su confessione dei peccati e Inquisizione nell'Italia del Cinquecento* (Naples: La Città del Sole, 1997). Brambilla's article casts the subject in an entirely new light.

38. VaCDF, *Decreta*, 1721, 278r (1 October).

A few weeks later, a letter from Piazza revealed that the Congregation's initial benign hypothesis about Suor Maria Deodata had proven erroneous. The cardinals ordered him to move her to the Inquisition's jail and instructed Inquisitor Ferrero to open proceedings against her.[39] In the spring of 1722, the names of others in and around the convent of Santissima Annunziata implicated in witchcraft came to light: Fabri's fellow nuns Maria Fortunata Castrucci, Margherita Chiaretti, and Maria Giacinta Tamburini (who had spontaneously appeared again to confess that she had relapsed); Rosa Barbieri, perhaps a laywoman; the parish priest of Marradi, Iacopo Cesare Fabrini; someone identified only as P. Lavagna (most likely another cleric); and a Jew named Consolino Samuel Pesaro, who had supplied a vase of unguent "of the sort used by a surgeon in healing wounds."[40]

As usual in all but the most routine cases, the wheels of Inquisition justice in Fabri's trial turned very slowly. Throughout 1723 and into early 1724, the Congregation repeatedly reminded Bishop Piazza and Inquisitor Ferrero that Suor Maria Deodata must be attended by a competent confessor to assess and ameliorate her spiritual state and by physicians to cure her psychophysical ills (*morbosis affectionibus*). Interestingly, it was the confessor who evaluated her mental health; he declared her to be sane. Urging Ferrero to expedite the case, the cardinals discussed moving her out of jail into another convent but eventually decided against it.[41] In the spring of 1724, although the sentence had not yet been issued, she was back in Santissima Annunziata.[42]

Six months later, Fabri's father wrote to the Congregation asking that she be moved to another convent because her sisters in religion did not want her.[43] The search began for a suitable house in Florence. At first the hospital of San Bonifacio appeared to be a good possibility. The sisters there were willing to

---

39. VaCDF, *Decreta*, 1721, 328r (26 November).

40. VaCDF, *Decreta*, 1722, 237v, 135v–36r (29 April and 6 May). On 3 July the congregation requested that the inquisitor of Siena track down Consolino, who had reportedly moved to Monte San Savino. Ibid., 222r–v. Two years later the bishop and inquisitor of Faenza were ordered to investigate further the priest Fabroni's possible complicity in Fabri's witchcraft: ibid., 1724, 96v–97r (27 April). Evidently he encountered no immediate trouble, for in the following year the nuns of Marradi successfully petitioned to have him reappointed their confessor for another three-year term on the ground that they could not afford to pay a "foreigner" for confessional services: VaAS, SCVR, Positiones Monialium, 69 (1725, giugno-luglio), *supplica* approved 22 June 1725.

41. VACDF, *Decreta*, 1723, 168r, 180v, 211r–v, 279r, 396v–97r (13 May, 16 May, 23 June, 19 August, and 7 December); 1724, 32v, 58v–59r (2 January and 29 February).

42. VACDF, *Decreta*, 1724, 89v (19 April).

43. VACDF, *Decreta*, 1724, 228r (13 September).

have her, but it turned out that they were legally unable to accept any additional members. Next, Bishop Piazza approached the sisters of the hospital of the Incurabili, who declined to take her in. More and more desperate, the Congregation conceded that she could go into an unenclosed conservatory provided that she agreed to maintain cloister; if necessary, additional funds to supplement her convent dowry could be found.[44] Then the cardinals requested that Giuseppe Maria Martelli, archbishop of Florence, take the situation in hand. In late February 1725 he had her moved to the house of relatives in Florence, began to explore the feasibility of placing her among the oblates of the hospital of Santa Maria Nuova, and guaranteed that he and her relatives would supply any extra money needed for her support. Insisting that strict secrecy about this plan be maintained, the cardinals approved it.[45]

The Congregation's probable relief was short-lived. Two weeks later, Archbishop Martelli wrote to convey the shocking news that before being removed from the jail of the Inquisition in Faenza, Fabri had been raped. Soon he was able to name the perpetrator: Agostino Scozzi, an employee of the Faentine Holy Office, who had confessed the deed to the recently deceased inquisitor of Faenza claiming that he had acted under "diabolical suggestion." On 11 April 1725 Scozzi hanged himself in jail.[46] Having learned in late June that Fabri's appeal to have her religious profession annulled had been discussed in April by the Congregation of the Council, the cardinal-inquisitors asked Archbishop Martelli to determine whether she was in fact expecting a child.[47] She had not menstruated for several months, he replied.[48] Despite Fabri's probable pregnancy, negotiations for placing her among the oblates of Santa Maria Nuova proceeded. Requiring—as was normal when religious shifted from one order

---

44. VACDF, *Decreta*, 1724, 280v (8 November); ibid,1725, 3v, 15v (4 and 10 January).

45. VACDF, *Decreta*, 1725, 58v–59r (20 February). On the Oblates, founded in the 1280s by the servant Monna Tessa with financial assistance from her employer, Folco Portinari (father of Dante's Beatrice), see *Dizionario degli istituti di perfezione* (1974–), s.v.,"Oblate Ospedaliere di Santa Maria Nuova," by Guido Pettinati, 6:590–92. It is worth noting that all three Florentine institutions considered as possible destinations for Fabri were congregations of hospital sisters, not houses of the Dominican order, in which she had originally professed. Although subject to enclosure, these congregations certainly ranked lower in prestige than convents of regular orders.

46. VaCDF, *Decreta*, 1725, 73r–v, 90v–91r, 106r–v, 123r–v (7 and 14 March, 11 and 25 April).

47. VaCDF, *Decreta*, 1725, 187v, 203r (21 June).

48. VaCDF, *Decreta*, 1725, 203r (11 July). Fabri's *supplica*, which at first sight appears belated, may well have been submitted, like those of most petitioners, soon after her father died. My search in the death registers of Borgo San Lorenzo and Santa Maria a Vezzano (FiAA) for the record of his demise yielded nothing; perhaps he died elsewhere.

to another—that she must serve a novitiate and make a new profession, the Congregation of the Holy Office furnished 555 scudi 3s. 4d. to supplement her dowry. Martelli supplied an additional 37 scudi for her food and 80 scudi to pay a wet nurse.[49]

✢✢✢ ✢✢✢ ✢✢✢

Not surprisingly, it is rarely possible to discover anything about a defendant's life once his or her trial came to a close. Whether a sentence against Maria Deodata Fabri was eventually handed down, how the petition for annulment of her vows was handled, and what became of her and the baby she was probably carrying neither the *Decreta* of the Congregation of the Holy Office nor the records of the Congregation of the Council reveal.[50] Reconstructing the rest of her story, therefore, is just as impossible as exploring in depth the first three decades of her life. Making do with what we have, however, we can speculate responsibly about the role of witchcraft in her life.

Clearly Fabri had been forced to become a nun, an experience so devastating that she seems to have repressed all memories of the actual circumstances.[51] These she replaced with a complex fantasy built on two elements. First, using traditional lore of witchcraft probably imparted to her by a female servant, she imagined not the usual ceremony of homage and fealty to the devil, which would have rendered her just one of his many followers, but an exclusive marital pact with him made freely in childhood. Through this alliance she gained a new identity independent of family and convent, signaled by a new name, Asmodea, different from her first (Caterina Angela, given her at baptism) and her second (Maria Deodata, assumed when she professed as a nun).[52] Second,

---

49. VaCDF, *Decreta*, 1725, 218r, 244r–v, 236v, 342r (25 July, 9 and 30 August, and 28 November). The oblates of Santa Maria Nuova kindly informed me that their archive contains nothing on Fabri (telephone call, 2 September 1999).

50. The last allusion to Fabri's case in the *Decreta* is a request from Maria Bianca, Agostino Scozzi's widow, for a copy of his death certificate; the congregation ordered Inquisitor Grossi (see n. 23) to issue it: VaCDF, *Decreta*, 1726, 38r (30 January). After receiving her supplica on 14 April 1725 (see n. 26), the Congregation of the Council ordered that Bishop Piazza investigate her claim. I have found no further evidence in that body's manuscript records or in the printed series *Thesaurus resolutionum Sacrae Congregationis Concilii* (Urbino, 1739–), which begins in 1718, that indicates how they disposed of it.

51. As in the case of Gostanza, it is conceivable that Asmodea had been traumatized even earlier by sexual abuse.

52. One writer on witchcraft describes the pact with the devil as a counter-confirmation involving the renunciation of all previous promises to God and the assignment of a new name: Guazzo,

drawing on familiarity with recent historical events and foreign customs gained from conversations with visitors at the grate in the convent parlor, reading, and possibly correspondence,[53] Fabri envisioned vastly expanded possibilities for mobility and status. Although the imaginary world she inhabited was geographically broader and politically more sophisticated than Gostanza's, it served her in very similar ways. From her fantasy she obtained what was unavailable to her in real life: the emotional gratification of being cherished by an attractive and wealthy male, sexual satisfaction, and above all power.

For Fabri, access to power appears to have been particularly important. Its range was much broader than that exercised by Gostanza. Not only, she believed, did her special relationship with the devil enable her to escape from the narrow confines of the convent and make an impact on international affairs, it also empowered her to take revenge on her enemies—in her mind, practically everyone in her immediate environment. With her family, who had refused to marry her and then ignored her preference for a Florentine convent, she symbolically cut all ties by taking a new name. On her fellow nuns, who had spied on and denounced her to their superior, she wreaked bodily harm and mental confusion. Against the lay folk of Marradi, who enjoyed the privileges of marriage and parenthood denied to her, she retaliated by killing their progeny. Against the local clerics and missionaries who claimed control over her, she exercised her privilege of causing illness and injury, as well as challenging their monopoly on the sacrament of the Eucharist by finding alternative uses for consecrated communion wafers.

+⊹+   +⊹+   +⊹+

To Asmodea as well as to the missionary who wrote the report, all this "really happened." To the Congregation of the Holy Office and those who followed

---

Compendium Maleficarum, 36. Another likens the ceremony of the pact to that of monastic profession: Menghi, *Compendio*, 83.

53. On the convent *parlatorio*, see Anne Jacobson Schutte, "The Permeable Cloister," in *Arcangela Tarabotti: A Literary Nun in Baroque Venice*, ed. Elissa Weaver (forthcoming). On nuns' reading, see, for example, Danilo Zardin, *Donna e religiosa di rara eccellenza: Prospera Corona Bascapè, i libri e la cultura nei monasteri milanesi del Cinque e Seicento* (Florence: Olschki, 1992). On nuns' correspondence, see three essays in *Per lettera: La scrittura epistolare fremminile tra archivio e tipografia, secoli XV–XVII*, ed. Gabriella Zarri (Rome: Viella, 1999): Silvia Mostaccio, "Delle 'visitationi spirituali' di una monaca: Le lettere di Tommasina Fieschi O.P.," 287–311; Anna Scattigno, "Lettere dal convento," 313–57; and Manuela Belardini, "'Piace molto a Gìesù la nostra confidanza': Suor Orsola Fontebuoni a Maria Maddalena d'Austria," 359–83.

its instructions, it was as obvious as it is to us that, like her marriage to the devil, coronation in hell, and adventures on the road, her exercise of retaliatory power occurred mainly in her imagination. We cannot know whether the authorities succeeded in dismantling her fantasies. At the very least, they reduced her to complete silence. She was now bereft of even a hostile mouthpiece like the missionary.

Thus the enforcers of orthodoxy and discipline ended Fabri's career as a *mulier fabrix*, an active female subject able to exercise an extraordinary amount of agency—that is, to craft and express, albeit under pathological circumstances, a distinctive identity. Perhaps, under yet another name after she had professed again, the former Asmodea lived out whatever remained of her life in Florence as an oblate of Santa Maria Nuova. Or perhaps Archbishop Martelli's plan aborted, and she was put back into the convent in Marradi.[54] In either case, she returned to the condition from which most women of her era never made even a temporary escape: that of an object who was defined, assigned a status, and controlled by others.

---

54. It is remotely possible that she was the anonymous decedent mentioned in Santissima Annunziata's account book in January 1728; the convent spent the small sum of 0.3.6.8 ducats, "coins which were found in the deposit," on "five masses for the soul of *that nun*" (emphasis added): FiAS, *Conventi soppressi governo francese*, 157: SS. Annunziata, b. 8 (Libro uscita 1726–90). Commemorative rites for other deceased nuns of Santissima Annunziata, identified by name in the account book, ranged in cost from 5 to 21 ducats.

WHEN WITCHES
BECAME FALSE

Séducteurs *and* Crédules *Confront the Paris Police*
at the Beginning of the Eighteenth Century[1]

Ulrike Krampl

*D*uring the course of the seventeenth century, magic and witchcraft began to move from the forefront of the French judicial theater. The acts constituting an exceptional crime (*crime d'exception*) were penalized less and less, and in 1625 the Parlement of Paris confirmed a death sentence in such a case for the last time.[2] The royal edict of 1682 finally made this tendency official by separating magic and witchcraft from poisoning, which remained subject to the most severe sanctions, and assimilated astrology into the domain of magic.[3]

Translated from the French by Kathryn A. Edwards.

1. The terms *séducteur* and *crédule* have been retained to stress the nuances of those words in eighteenth-century French, a nuance that is essential for my argument. In contemporary dictionaries a *séducteur* is defined first as "the devil," then as Muhammad, a man who seduces a girl or sometimes young people more generally, and/or a person who seduces someone and the seduction leads to a morally bad action. All of these connotations exist in the eighteenth-century use of this term, particularly the link between deception and the devil. The *crédules* are essentially "easy believers"; not as naive as gullible people, the *crédules* are open to various beliefs, both positive and negative, that people with greater empirical tendencies would probably discount or at least challenge.

2. Robert Mandrou, *Magistrats et sorciers au XVIIe siècle* (Paris: Plon, 1968); Robert Muchembled, *La sorcière au village (XVe–XVIIIe siècle)*, 2d ed. (Paris: Gallimard, 1991); idem, *Le roi et la sorcière: L'Europe des bûchers XVe–XVIIIe siècle* (Paris: Desclée, 1993); Alfred Soman, *Sorcellerie et justice criminelle (16e–18e siècles)* (Hampshire: Variorum, 1992); Michel de Certeau, *La possession de Loudun* (Paris: Gallimard, 1990); Alfred Soman, "La décriminalisation de la sorcellerie en France," in *Histoire, économie et société* 4:2 (1985): 179–203.

3. In *Recueil général des anciennes lois françaises, depuis l'an 420 jusqu'à la Révolution de 1789*, 29 vols., ed. Jourdan, Decrusy, and Isambert, vol. 19, *1672–1686* (Paris, 1833), 369–401; also see Hervé Drévillon, *Lire et écrire l'avenir: L'astrologie au Grand Siècle (1610–1715)* (Seyssel: Champ Vallon, 1996).

This legislative gesture also closed the famous and disturbing *Affaire des poisons* which, from 1679 to 1682, affected the most intimate court circles.[4] The virulence of the threat seemed to have been moderated.

After a period of relative silence, at least in the capital, around 1700 a somewhat heterogeneous series of so-called false sorcerers (*faux sorciers*) and false sorceresses (*fausse sorcières*) arose under the purview of the police of Paris.[5] These false sorcerers and sorceresses were people suspected of being versed in the manipulation of all sorts of "secrets" including fortune-telling and preparing horoscopes, making gold and transmuting metals, looking for treasure, invoking spirits, as well as producing and selling talismans, philters, and recipes for love, gambling, and health. Focus on these men and women permits us to examine the knowledge, difficult to access elsewhere, and the stakes which are pursued in this way. Were they simply ridiculous traces of an archaic world in the process of being "forgotten" by the "progress" of the Enlightenment?[6] In Paris at the beginning of the eighteenth century, witchcraft could not necessarily be reduced to a popular activity, confined and immobile. Witchcraft was layered with multiple references difficult to classify according to the traditional dichotomies of tradition-modernity and superstition-reason.[7]

THE DIFFICULT CONSTITUTION OF THE OBJECT

Doubt formed the starting point for these investigations. The object of police interest is difficult to pin down. It seemed almost impossible to find a reliable common denominator to apply to the offense. The terminology for magic and witchcraft expanded: treasure hunters, people who used the philosopher's

4. For example see Arlette Lebigre, *L'Affaire des poisons* (Paris: A. Michel, 1989); Frantz Funck-Brentano, *Le drame des poisons* (1899; repr., Paris: Hachette, 1977); Georges Mongrédien, *Madame de Montespan et l'Affaire des poisons* (Paris: Hachette, 1973); Jean-Christian Petitfils, *L'Affaire des poisons* (Paris: A. Michel, 1977).

5. My ideas are based on documents produced by the Paris police which implicate or at least mention some 300 names between 1700 and 1760. These papers are conserved in the Archives de Bastille at the Bibliothèque de l'Arsenal (hereafter AB) and in part at the Bibliothèque Nationale (hereafter BnF). In this case *sorcier* and *sorcière* have been translated as "sorcerer" and "sorceress" to stress the gendered aspect of my argument; in most cases in this paper, I follow the traditional translation of "witch."

6. This is what the second lieutenant general of police, René Voyer, count d'Argenson, wanted in a letter to the king dated 9 October 1702, attached to his *Mémoire* about the question of witches; see BnF, Manuscrits Clairambault 983, 1–3 (copy), edited in Robert Mandrou, *Possession et sorcellerie au XVIIe siècle* (Paris: Fayard, 1979), 275–328.

7. See Jeanne Favret, "Sorcières et Lumières," *Critique* 287 (1971): 351–76; and also Elisabeth Claverie, "La Vierge, le désordre, la critique: Les apparitions de la Vierge à l'âge de la science," *Terrain* 14 (1990): 60–75.

stone, fortune-tellers (male or female), makers of horoscopes, soothsayers, magicians, and false witches (*faux sorciers*)[8] are the most frequent denunciations, sometimes combined or nuanced with additional terms. In 1709, Marie Madeleine du Colombier, widow of Jean Gaillard, saw herself thus placed under the truly vast heading of "false witches, [people who used the] philosopher's stone, treasure hunters, [those] suspected of poison and secrets in order to win at gambling"; later people were satisfied with calling her a *fausse sorcière*.[9] Finally, very particular, and doubtlessly disquieting, definitions combined as "swindler, treasurer hunter," or "[person who used the] philosopher's stone, swindler," or "false witches and swindlers." In the eighteenth century, was it necessary that an epithet be added to the word "witchcraft" in order to refine the designation? It seems that witchcraft is neither magic nor trickery; the meaning oscillates indecisively inside this new terminology.

The problem posed by this tension between the falseness of the witch and the truth of the swindler is at first that of the organization of knowledge. In the course of the seventeenth century, medicine and natural sciences placed themselves more and more at the heart of what determined the vision of the world—and that placement did not automatically result in an "enlightened" position. When confronting the marvelous, the natural sciences took it upon themselves to explore the astonishing margins of the explicable world.[10] Participating in this movement, the police verification procedures combined the experimental method with trusted experts, doctors, or apothecaries until a workable frontier between magic and cheating (*friponnerie*) developed and the criminal element was unmasked.

BEHIND THE HAZE

Behind this veil of marvels, more persistent and pragmatic matters became clear. In a more or less direct manner, the police turned its attention towards the eventual utility of knowledge and cleverness, however pursued. Thus, in a

---

8. Although this term is most commonly translated as "witches," it should not be read as meaning only female witches. Both men and women were designated by that term, and when the police or their witnesses felt that greater precision was necessary they distinguished between *sorcier* and *sorcière*. The significance of such distinctions will be developed throughout this article.

9. "faux sorciers, pierre philosophale, Chercheurs de tresors, Suspect de Poison et de Secrets pour faire gagner au Jeu": AB 10590, 1709.

10. Michel de Certeau, "La magistrature devant la sorcellerie au XVIIe siècle," in *L'Absent de l'histoire* (Tours: Mame, 1973), 13–39; Lorraine Daston, "Marvelous Facts and Miraculous Evidence in Early Modern Europe," *Critical Inquiry* 18:1 (1991): 93–124; Jean Ehrard, *L'idée de nature dans la première moitié du XVIIIe siècle* (1964; repr., Paris: Albin Michel, 1994).

case from 1715 that involved a philosopher's stone in which the accused gold-maker and chemist Heinrich Diesbach attested to his deceit, those responsible for order deliberated for a long time to decide if they ought to put the incriminating knowledge into the state's service so that the state could appropriate a potential fortune.[11] Another concern was the need to prevent the chemists, who were simultaneously roguish and exploitable, from falling into the hands of a perceived enemy. The mercantilist tone of this proposition is only one facet of the first central motif. A number of cases indeed were ordered around the subject of wealth. The attraction of treasure hunting like that undertaken by Marie-Anne de la Ville and the abbot Pinel in 1703, for example, varied often from one person to another. The priest in question wanted, among other things, to rid himself of his debts. Others, like the lord of Brederode or the merchant Desalles, were motivated by a certain greed for easy gain. Marie-Anne, for her part, looked to provide for her needs forever, to manage the bonds between the people around her, and especially to ensure the affection of her companion Pinel.[12] Sometimes the accused put "curiosity" or "amusement" first, which provided them with an explanation of as well as a defense for their activities. For others, their hope of simply being able to fashion a life to their tastes comes through in the testimony. A treasure was not simply envisioned as a distant, formless mirage. To the contrary, the guardian spirits of riches were subjected to quite precise claims: obtaining an office, the regular payment of a pension, or when it was a matter of sums of money, the desired amount.[13] Even the currency in which the money must be delivered was sometimes specified in order to be able to receive "good and useful money."[14]

Admittedly, these were often quite ordinary hopes. Nevertheless, they expressed the clear hope not to be obliged to accept as immutable the social and economic lines of estate or sex, indeed to be able to exercise a certain influence on the course of things here on earth, to advance on unforeseen trajectories in the public organization of the community. To make "hope" through "promises" was the specialty, it seems, of *séducteurs*.[15] Thus, certain men and women were designated *séducteurs* referring primarily to their moral status,

11. AB 10620, 1715, dossier Diesbach.

12. AB 10545, 1703.

13. AB 10545; BnF, MS Clairambault 983, fol. 102.

14. AB 10555, 1704, fol. 52.

15. At the end of the seventeenth century, this term, which likewise appears in an edict of 1682, retained a primarily moral sense but also designated an economic transaction with juridical value; see *Dictionnaire de l'Académie française* (1694), s.v. "*séducteurs*."

but also to their economic, indeed sociopolitical, potential. It was said that the *séducteurs* abused the simplicity of gullible (*crédules*) spirits, opposing the power of make-believe with susceptibility to belief. Social order was pursued at the same time as community cohesion, relations between subjects and royal power were arranged around control of secrets, among other things. Thus, it was the body which, in this order too, was the object of a number of secret knowledges elaborated and transmitted in the form of remedies for health, talismans for love, or sophisticated recipes to prolong life or, on the contrary, to shorten it. In sum, these powers were destined to intervene in the physical state of a person, that is to say to heal or to put to death. This essay touches on crucial questions which, throughout the modern era, have found themselves at the heart of writings devoted to witchcraft. The articulation between the pair *séducteur/crédule* and demonological thought, on one side, and the *Affaire des poisons*, on the other, will allow the suggestion of some explanatory perspectives and will provide a better understanding of the specific functioning of this new falseness of witches which, at the beginning of the eighteenth century, was established in the territory of the Paris police.

THE *DÉMON SÉDUCTEUR*

Toward the end of the fifteenth century, demonology as a specific subject of discourse became more and more consolidated, resulting in the first comprehensive summary in 1486, developed by the Rhenish inquisitors Jakob Sprenger and Heinrich Institoris in the *Malleus Maleficarum*.[16] This process had its roots in the crisis which crossed the Christian world at the end of the Middle Ages, confronting, among other things, questions about the relation between the body and the soul, free will, and the reformulation of differences between the sexes. In the framework of battles against medieval heresies, notably against the Waldensians, the decisive combination of two elements was accomplished: the demonological myth, forged in this context, of the pact with the devil, which allowed order to be reversed in the form of the nightime sabbat, and the belief in *malefice*. Bringing a series of ancient elements up to date through the prism of contemporary preoccupations gave birth to a new figure of alterity—diabolical witchcraft—thus opening the path to the persecutorial fury whose images mark modernity so strongly.[17]

16. Nicole Jacques-Chaquin, "La sorcellerie et ses discours: Essai de typologie du discours démonologique," *Frénésie* (summer 1990): 11–22.

17. Alain Boureau, "Le sabbat et la question scolastique de la personne," in *Le sabbat des sorcières en Europe (XVe–XVIIIe siècles)*, ed. Nicole Jacques-Chaquin and Maxime Préaud (Grenoble: Jérôme

Nevertheless, consolidation of demonological doctrine hardly showed a new certainty. On the contrary, doubt was rooted in even the foundations of such knowledge.[18] With violent diligence, demonologists and theologians attempted to probe this agitation, which touched on the order of knowledge as well as that of religion and politics, so as to control it better. The extension of persecution testifies to this tension, but it was reflected above all in the proliferation of "literature avid to know all the powers of the devil."[19] The first modernity was especially marked by the fearful but perfectly thought out suspicion of the existence of a countersociety which was escaping the influence of intelligible and admissible order that was guaranteed by God and delegated to his representatives on earth, who were the church and the state.

From the diabolical pact emerged a field of competition that concerned the legitimate community and the legitimate means of constituting it. It was in this community that the complex moment of apostasy was located. The human being took simultaneously the shape of the impotent victim succumbing to the seductive advances of the devil, and through his influence, the shape of the calculating sinner. In this way, the individual will disavowed the just path of God to open the fault by which, thanks to his illusory and illusionistic power, the devil managed to penetrate the imagination, that dubious space between the soul and the body. Even if the demon's room for maneuver was subject to God's permission, it nevertheless remained worrisome, gaining a more and more palpable reality during the modern era.[20] In a system based on religious logic, one could say the pact was considered an alliance between the deceptive demon, *séducteur*, and men with weak spirits and will who would transform themselves into sorcerers and sorceresses (*sorciers et sorcières*).[21] Defined as particularly weak, women often became the principal target of persecutory rage.[22] This configuration was doubtless maintained until the

---

Millon, 1993), 33–46; Robert Muchembled, ed., *Magie et Sorcellerie en Europe du Moyen Age à nos jours* (Paris: A. Colin, 1994).

18. André Vauchez, "La nascita del sospetto," in *Finzione et santità tra medioevo ed età moderna*, ed. Gabriella Zarri (Turin: Rosenberg & Sellier, 1991), 39–51.

19. Sophie Houdard, *Les sciences du diable: Quatre discours sur la sorcellerie* (Paris: Cerf, 1992), 217.

20. Diabolic action, which in the Middle Ages was thought of as a type of illusion, materialized and became "real" in the modern era. As such, it became possible to think of the sabbat as real and, later, witchcraft as pathology; see *Theologische Realenzyclopädie*, s.v. "Magie," as well as Michel Foucault, "Les déviations religieuses et le savoir médical" (1968), in idem, *Dits et écrits* (Paris: Gallimard, 1994), 1:624–35.

21. See also Certeau, *La possession de Loudun*, 10ff.

22. Ingrid Ahrendt-Schulte, "Hexenprozesse," in *Frauen in der Geschichte des Rechts: Von der Frühen*

beginning of the Grand Siècle.[23] Certainly, Henry Boguet's and Pierre de Lancre's great treatises yielded place to more scattered productions according to
fields of knowledge, and once the great cases of possession passed, a certain
calm seemed to assert itself in this domain.[24]

In the course of the seventeenth century, the demarcation between tolerated and sanctioned behaviors kept varying. The logic of sorting between
good and bad followed, less and less, the opposition God versus the devil.
Instead, societal behavior viewed as legitimate or illegitimate became the
frame of reference, thus passing from a religious system to the political and
economic system of the Enlightenment.[25] But the theme of the demoniac did
not disappear in one stroke. The eighteenth century had a protean literature
and did not hide its ambiguities.[26] Ways of presenting oneself as well as the
organization of knowledge were no longer regulated by the same principles,
and language started to function differently. Thus, a new rationality emerged
which demanded an opposite to grow stronger.[27]

Neuzeit bis zur Gegenwart, ed. Ute Gerhard (Munich: Beck, 1997), 199–220; Susanna Burghartz, "The
Equation of Women and Witches: A Case Study of Witchcraft Trials in Lucerne and Lausanne in the
Fifteenth and Sixteenth Centuries," in *The German Underworld*, ed. Richard J. Evans (New York: Routledge, 1988), 57–74; Eva Labouvie, "Männer im Hexenprozeß: Zur Sozialanthropologie eines
'männlichen' Verständnisses von Magie und Hexerei," *Geschichte und Gesellschaft* 16 (1990): 56–78;
Megan McLaughlin, "Gender Paradox and the Otherness of God," *Gender & History* 3:2 (1991): 147–
59; Jean-Michel Sallmann, "Sorcière," in *Histoire des femmes en Occident*, 4 vols., ed. Geores Duby, et
al., vol. 3, *XVIe–XVIIIe siècles*, ed. Arlette Farge and Natalie Zemon Davis (Paris: Plon, 1991), 455–67.

23. Houdard, *Les sciences du diable*; Nicole Jacques-Chaquin, introduction to Henry Boguet, *Discours exécrable des sorciers* (1602), ed. Nicole Jacques-Chaquin (Paris: Sycomore, 1980).

24. The principal cases are Aix-en-Provence (1609–11); Loudun (1632–40); Louviers (1642–47);
and Auxonne (1658–63). See, for example, Henry Boguet, *Discours exécrable des sorciers (1602)*, ed.
Nicole Jacques-Chaquin (Paris : Sycomore, 1980), and Pierre de Lancre, *Tableav de l'inconstance des
mavvais anges et demons, ov il est amplement traicté des sorciers, & de la sorcelerie* (Paris, 1612).

25. Michel de Certeau, "La formalité des pratiques: Du système religieux à l'éthique des Lumières," in *L'écriture de l'histoire* (Paris: Gallimard, 1975), 153–212.

26. Jean-Marie Goulemot, "Démons, merveilles et philosophies à l'Age classique," in *Annales ESC*
6 (1980): 1223–250; Max Milner, "Le discours sur la magie chez les gens d'Église (XVIIIe siècle)," in
Magie et littérature (Paris: A. Michel, 1991); for a general overview, see Kay Wilkins, "Attitudes to
Witchcraft and Demonic Possession in France during the Eighteenth Century," in *Journal of European
Studies* 3 (1973): 348–62; eadem, "Some Aspects of the Irrational in 18th-Century France," in *SVEC*
140 (1975): 107–201.

27. Jean Bazin, "Les fantômes de Madame du Deffand: Exercices sur la croyance," in *Critique* 529–
30 (1991): 492–511; Octave Mannoni, "Je sais bien, mais quand même...," in *Clefs pour l'Imaginaire
ou L'Autre Scène* (Paris: Seuil, 1969), 9–33.

WEAK AND CRÉDULE?

In this paradoxical apparatus, *crédulité* formed the second pole, evoking above all readiness to adhere to an idea or belief.[28] Doubtless, the denunciation as well as the responsibility of this attitude within the framework of the Counter-Reformation and Catholic Reform largely contributed to fix this meaning. It was probably with the *Affaire des poisons* that this concept solidified. The Great Ones of the court did not refrain from stating aloud their contempt for ridiculous activities like magic, alchemy, divination, and astrology, but they did not slow their passion for these occult operations. The marquis of Feuquières, an officer with a brilliant career but who was sometimes anxious that his vigor threatened its permanence, looked to get for himself from a certain Vigoureux, a tailor's wife who was well informed about chiromancy, a secret to make himself invulnerable in combat, along with other secrets. The marquis's inclinations could hardly be surprising at that time.

Accepted for a long time, the extremely widespread and stylish practice of having horoscopes told or of going to the city to buy love potions and remedies with miraculous effects lost its ludic character as soon as poison entered the scene.[29] In their denunciations, the diviners (*devineresses*) and magicians who were interrogated drew a picture of a court aristocracy avid for weapons that were not very orthodox but were effective to settle accounts between male and female rivals, to attract the affection of a beloved man or woman, to dissolve an unhappy marriage, and sometimes even to shorten the life of parents from whom they would inherit. The evocation of Louis XIV as eventually the target of murderous slanders, culminating in the accusation of his former mistress Madame de Montespan, finally made the smooth surface of this discourse break apart and revealed the duplicity of attitudes towards superstition, which ended by hindering the exercise of power. In addition, and this is not negligible, the frontiers between the two socially distinct spheres of the court and the common people proved less rigid than the official representation of the social and political hierarchy. This permeability was not only unheard of; it was unsustainable. A curious formula came in a royal declaration and underlined the difficulty of uprooting the activities of magicians and

28. Dictionaries at the end of the seventeenth century unanimously establish an equivalence between *crédulité* and the readiness to believe or the ease of belief, which was already an ancient parallel at that time. In medieval Latin the word had a positive value, indeed the value of *fides*; see also Jean Wirth, "La naissance du concept de croyance (XIIe–XVIIe siècles)," *Bibliothèque d'Humanisme et Renaissance* 45:1 (1983): 7–58, esp. 42 ff.

29. Archives de la Préfecture de Police, Affaire des poisons, série AA, 4.

witches [*sorciers*]: "when by dissimulation or by the number of guilty they become public crimes." To condemn *crédulité* thus amounted to condemning secrecy.[30] It was at that moment, at the latest, that the field of sorcery's reality "was transported into a moral and social world" and that it was thought of more "in relation to the order of the modern state."[31]

If, at the end of the century, the figure *séducteur-crédule* was not split apart, the distribution of roles had changed. Thus, the edict of 1682 proclaimed that the *séducteurs*, who from now on came from foreign countries "under the *pretext* of [making] horoscopes and divination, and by the means of the *prestige* of the operations of the so-called magic and other similar *illusions*…would have surprised diverse ignorant or *crédules* persons who would be gullibly involved with them…."[32] In this text, magic and witchcraft did not rise above the realm of superstition as opposed to other, more weighty crimes: sacrilege, impiety, poison. What was diabolical saw itself reduced to the status of pretext. Authorities continued to perceive a certain danger, less for its intrinsic evil than for its power to bring in the worst. From now on, the witch himself substituted for the demon and thus was invested with the position of the deceiver. Was it for this reason that the witch (*sorcier*) was no longer false, evoking by the term itself the distance from the demon? In any case, Satan did not fail to leave traces. The false witch (*sorcier*) inherited from the true devil his pernicious power of seduction. The devil still passed to him the taste for simulacra, but it was the false witch (*faux sorcier*), "counterfeiting the Devil," to whom the active role returned.[33] To the condemnable will to leave the right path was joined the power to give hope and to change the course of things—to the detriment of those who had the "weakness" to consult a witch, indeed to abandon themselves to the witch's enterprise.

THE ORDER OF THE CITY

Responsible for maintaining order in the city, the police used the idea of false witches (*faux sorciers*) as a tool to detect the abusive misdeeds to which the *crédules* would lend themselves so readily. They saw this role as less important among the elite but as essential among the common people who needed watching and directing. It was particularly around 1700 that the lieutenancy general of the police changed leaders—d'Argenson succeeded Reynie who had,

30. Drévillon, *Lire et écrire l'avenir*, 230.

31. Michel Foucault, "Médecins, juges et sorciers au XVIIe siècle" (1969), in *Dits et écrits*, 1:753–66.

32. Emphasis added.

33. BnF, MS frç., 8121, fol. 240, year 1713.

as a judge, examined the *Affaire des poisons* in the Chambre Ardente[34]—and, especially, that the concept of order was changing and enlarging.[35] The consolidation of the new police into a distinct body, outside of the traditional bodies of Old Regime society and conceived as necessary to the state, supported itself on the elaboration of a collection of rules about the penal nature as well as an administration founded on the principles of interference and secrecy. Its intervention was supported by a desire to make everything visible to the eyes of the city's residents through the proliferating diffusion of placards, but especially to the (secret) regard of the prince to whom the lieutenant was a direct emissary.[36] The maintenance of hierarchical and interdependent relations (father-son, master-apprentice) apparently no longer sufficed to assure control over political and social cohesion. This attempt to restructure order was supposed to reinforce the attachment of the subjects to their sovereign. The new order tended to replace relations of the same type on a small scale. In this unstable territory, we find certain resonances with demonological witchcraft and its overlap with poison. Perhaps it was in this very unusual encounter that one of the key moments of judicial and social reformulation of the magical universe at the dawn of the Enlightenment was situated.

A long memoir about "false diviners" and "alleged witches" (*sorciers*), collected by the lieutenant general of police d'Argenson in 1702, traces the contours of this changing and uncertain world.[37] In this text addressed to the king, the magistrate expressed disquiet in the face of the "great disorder,"

---

34. This was an extraordinary court of justice, called the Chambre de l'Arsenal, established by letters patent of 7 April 1679 and dissolved 21 July 1682, from which the cases were not subject to appeal and which was called on to judge those accused of poisoning. The appellation was due either to the color of the tapestries hanging from the walls or to the torches lighting the hall.

35. See among others, Arlette Farge, *La vie fragile: Violence, pouvoirs et solidarités à Paris au XVIIIe siècle* (Paris: Hachette, 1986); Paolo Piasenza, *Polizia e città: Strategie d'ordine, conflitti e rivolte a Parigi tra sei e settecento* (Bologne: Mulino, 1990); Alan Williams, *The Police of Paris, 1718–1789* (Baton Rouge: Louisiana State University Press, 1979).

36. Notable for the abundant use of *lettres de cachet* and of secret informers, called "flies." Paolo Piasenza, "Opinion publique, identité des institutions, 'absolutisme': Le problème de la légalité à Paris entre le XVIIe et le XVIIIe siècle," *Revue historique* 290 (1994): 97–142; on the use and appropriation of royal orders by the city's inhabitants, see Arlette Farge and Michel Foucault, *Le désordre des familles: Lettres de cachet des Archives de la Bastille* (Paris: Gallimard, 1982).

37. *Memoire qui contient en détail les noms et les intrigues des Faux Devins, des pretendus Sorciers, de ceux qui promettent la découverte des Trésors, ou la Communication des Genies, qui distribuent des Poudres, vendent des Talismans, consacrent des Bouquets & des Pantacles*, 1702, BnF, MS Clairambault 983, 5–58, edited in Mandrou, *Possession*, 282–328; the term *faux sorcier* is used in a number of cases examined by police agents.

which d'Argenson said then reigned in Paris and which he was determined to combat. To do this, he proposed a reclassification of suspects by "troops" or "sects," each of whom would be directed by a "chief." Not only did d'Argenson work to name and number the suspects in great detail—he accounted for nineteen—but, beyond that, he furnished a very detailed characterization of their respective practices.

Disorder seemed omnipresent seeing that the number of "cabals" did not stop growing, almost outstripping "our communities of arts and crafts."[38] The comparison with economic space, whose supervision equally fell under the vast duties of the police, was not soothing because it allowed the exercise of magic to be considered a semiprofessional activity, later even called a craft.[39] Witness the vocabulary which precisely emphasizes the element of commercial transaction that distinguished the diabolical pact. One "treats" or is pleased to "make a deal with the devil"; one "sells pacts" for several écus or for substantial amounts. One makes "appointments," concludes "contracts," and receives "receipts" to obtain a treasure protected by a spirit.[40] Nothing more than illusions? The lieutenant general spoke out vociferously, but in vain, against these "illusions." The authorities' scorn, if we believe Saint-Simon, seemed to dissipate on other occasions, especially when financial support was missing, which, after numerous years of war, was particularly felt towards the end of Louis XIV's reign. In 1703 it would be the king himself, writes this savvy observer of the court, for whom "the need for money…made him pay attention to an invalid who claimed to have worked formerly to make in Meudon a hiding place for a large treasure, at the time of M. de Louvois," minister and secretary of state, dead in 1691. The man in question then began to excavate "for a long time and in many places, always maintaining that he would find it. We had the expense of making up for what he wasted and the shame of having seriously believed in that."[41] D'Argenson himself, doubtless acting quite seriously, told in a report to the controller general Desmarets in 1713 about the treasure hunts which he himself had undertaken in the company of several people in a

38. Letter by d'Argenson, in Mandrou, *Possession*, 279.

39. Which will elsewhere become more and more explicit during the eighteenth century: see Michel Porret, "Magiciens, devineresses ou imposteurs? La répression des 'superstitions' au XVIIIe siècle: L'exemple genevois," in *Pré-actes du Colloque international: La Petite délinquance du Moyen Age à l'époque contemporaine, Dijon, 9–10 octobre 1997*, 191–95.

40. In order to "faire son marché avec le diable," AB 11780, 1749; "assignation" and the "récipissé": AB 10545, 1703; "débiter des pactes," AB 10590, 1708.

41. Louis de Rouvroy, duke of Saint-Simon, *Mémoires*, ed. A. M. de Boislisle, vol. 11 (Paris, 1895), 169.

lightless cave.[42] They learned this secret about hidden riches through a person who, just before dying, told it to one of the participants. Someone had recently buried a certain amount of money in the underground location in question. Far from being unusual, these accounts clearly show the ambiguity that these concepts likely revealed, even more as the legal situation concerning the ownership of valuable found goods was hardly regulated.[43]

All the troublemakers were not subject to the same coercive attention. In effect, embarrassment about the implication of highly placed persons made itself felt as much in the cases examined as in the directives of the magistrate. Those who, d'Argenson wrote, "have reason to believe that they have been consulted by people of a distinguished rank of whom it will perhaps be a service for the king to know [their] visions and follies" should merit "very particular attention."[44] Some of the criminals, once torn from the secrecy of the cabal, no longer hesitated to brag about their illustrious clientele. Thus, the field of activity of the woman Chabry, arrested in 1725 for telling fortunes, extended to the highest *noblesse de sang*, according to the report of an advisor to Inspector De la Jannière:

> "I see everyday," she declared, "all of the people of quality, who confide in me. Her Highness Madame the Princess of Conty who is at Port Royal, wanted me to assist her at various times. Yesterday that Princess sent to find my daughter, who still surpasses me in this knowledge, and She kept her in Her parlor for more than an hour, although this Princess has a footache, and She had told to His Highness Monseigneur the Duke of Orléans that She could not have the honor of receiving him that day. Madame the Duchess of Noailles, whose trust I have, also definitely wants sometimes to refer herself to me and to a number of others that I do not name."[45]

The claim to unite lines of confidence, an indispensable quality for all social and economic operations, across the hierarchy of estates quickly met up with the disorganized indignation of the police. Would a woman living in very modest conditions, who "although she is old...uses make-up, skin whiteners,

42. A. M. de Boislisle, ed., *Correspondance des contrôleurs généraux des finances avec les intendants des provinces*, 3 vols. (Paris, 1874–1897), vol. 3 *(1708–1715)*, no. 1531, report of 23 Dec. 1713.

43. Boislisle, *Correspondance*, vol. 3, no. 1298, letter of 15 June 1712, by M. Nouet, *avocat des finances*, at Paris, to the controller general.

44. Letter by d'Argenson, in Mandrou, *Possession*, 281.

45. AB 10873, 1725, dossier of the woman Chabry, fol. 6.

and ribbons"—in short a woman who literally seeks to disguise her true nature—have the "trust" of all these people of the "first rank"? How could Chabry not be perceived as "dangerous" by the police?[46] If one can trust the report from the inspector, who had not hesitated in 1702 to send his own wife to a woman named Fleury to lay a trap for this "devineresse" who had a large book in parchment on chiromancy to tell the horoscope of the men and women who asked it of her. Above all, Fleury would have noticed "that it is only by the means of the talisman that Madame de Maintenon arrived where she is and that she had predicted for Monsieur de Chamillart everything which has happened to him."[47] More than trust, it was to direct influence over the men and women guiding the monarch—in this case the mistress of the king and the controller general and minister of state—that Fleury dared to claim. Despite two years in the Bastille followed by being banished to thirty leagues from Paris, Fleury did not stop pursuing these activities. More than twenty years later, Fleury entered the police's purview for divination; as always "she deceives and seduces…people of either sex," but this time she was content with predicting for a young woman that she would have a child with a man of such a rank that she would "restore her honor by marrying him."[48] Persuasive strategy? Probably. Nevertheless, it seems that only evoking the names of highly ranked people sufficed to give credit to legal procedures against a false witch (sorcière), as much in the eyes of potential "dupes" as in the eyes of the police. The latter showed itself quite attentive to the techniques of false witches (sorciers and sorcières) used to "corrupt the youth" and "weak spirits."[49] The expression of such an ambition seemed a gesture to touch sensitive points while articulating, notably, past disquiets with a new social vision manifested in the insistence on the equation of ignorance and crédulité among other things.[50]

In the cases cited, women acted alone, at once secretly and publicly but especially to their profit—which the widow Fleury, like many others who were sharply aware of the illegality that this represented, denied firmly. When men acted alone it was through their knowledge of chemistry, which made

46. Disguise, at once social and moral, was a powerful theme among the moralists at the end of the seventeenth century who particularly make a connection with diabolical falsehood.

47. AB 10530, 1702, dossier femme Fleury, fol. 87.

48. AB 10826, 1724, dossier femme Fleury, fol. 210.

49. AB 10873, 1725, dossier femme Chabry, fol. 7.

50. See Wirth, "La naissance du concept," for the slide towards a negative connotation of the word crédule since the Middle Ages.

them both suspect and interesting, seeing that they could possess the highly coveted secret of making gold.[51] The false witch (*sorcier*), fortune-teller Jacques Vigoureux, lived entrenched in modest lodgings surrounded by numerous books which had the signs of the zodiac, planets, and dreams and by papers filled with figures and crosses. Having a taste for drink and "frightening demonstrations," he seems to have built for himself a solid knowledge of the cabala and of good angels which he invoked, according to the denunciation, to find lost objects, purses, and rings.[52]

Often, however, men and women acted together, and from there, in the language of the police, it was a matter of "cabals" or of "sects." Thus, this "cabal of several people who abuse the public, [included] among others a quality of young people from good families, and even ... officers in the royal troops."[53] To these young people they are said to have sold talismans, particularly to "be invincible, to be lucky in gambling, to be loved by Woman and Finally ... to give the hope of succeeding in everything that they could undertake." But who would be able to know the aspirations of the common "people," who the police feared and in whom they were condescendingly disappointed at the same time?[54] This situation was made more complex because it was extremely difficult to "penetrate" these (supposed) associations and, especially, to find proof of the illicit nature of their transactions. Were the demonologists not confronted with a comparable problem, when they openly recommended the recourse to sordid testimony and denunciation to ease the verification of the "deeds" of witchcraft? In his missive, d'Argenson estimated that "in ordinary tribunals it is quite difficult to convict these crimes."[55] Only the use of informers (*mouches*), often themselves being suspect, would be capable of curing it. He recommended police action in this new sense, of which he made himself the promoter, rather than the instruction of legal cases which, he feared, would cause too much commotion in the public. It was not only on this occasion that he expressed such a preoccupation, because this method concerned many

---

51. For example, the Neapolitan Vinache or Vinaccio, AB 10548, 1704; the Swiss Chevalier, BnF MS Clairambault 983, 1706; the famous Delisle, AB 10598, 1711, who very much intrigued the court; Diesbach, AB 10620, 1715; the so-called baron of Serlach, German, AB 10804, 1723; or again another Italian called Forassassy, AB 11186, 1732.

52. AB 10861, 1724, fol. 119.

53. AB 10555, 1704, fol. 14.

54. Arlette Farge, *Dire et mal dire: L'opinion publique au XVIIIe siècle* (Paris: Sevil, 1992), insists on the inseparable line between the authorities' distrust and contempt of popular speech and the determination to take control of it.

55. Letter by d'Argenson, in Mandrou, *Possession*, 282.

other fields of police interest and justified secret intrusions into the most secluded zones of the city.

Now, covered in the polished façade of the social body, lay the danger of *crédulité*, of this belief called easy and so easy to exploit. It was a threat which disturbed as much as it claimed to be able to bring to life again the memory of the uncontrollable meanderings of the "*spectacle des poisons*." Indeed, as soon as the police managed to seize powders and elixirs, they were carefully examined to know if they were good or bad, dangerous or inoffensive. At times even the overt suspicion of poison emerges in the investigations. When the room of the widow Gaillard was searched, the commissioner Cailly found there "a great chest full of powders, herbs, liqueurs, and papers" serving to heal even "the most infamous sicknesses," that is to say, venereal diseases.[56] Not without pride, the defendant acknowledged that she used these substances in the fabrication of medicinal secrets whose effectiveness would be highly appreciated by people of different quality—among those whom she did not hesitate to name were priests and nobles. In the 1670s and 1680s, the traffic in noxious substances knew how to reach both the physical body of court members and that of the entire community. This clearly shows the divide which had occurred since the Religious Wars through the seventeenth century between the unobserved and tolerated *private* and the *public* which monarchical visibility sanctioned. In this private sphere, where "personal interest" reigned, sometimes contractual and horizontal lines were made which formed societies, as opposed to the organic model of the state.[57]

The importance given to the figures, otherwise distinct, of libertine atheism, mysticism, and witchcraft at the beginning of the seventeenth century concerned this disarticulation in reference to the unified faith.[58] The police at the beginning of the eighteenth century took this attitude towards sodomites and libertines, often workers and shop boys, who they feared were capable of opening the path to an unheard-of social mixture. The danger of the libertine consisted precisely in his talent to corrupt and to "seduce" others and to incite them to make ties between themselves.[59] In a similar fashion, the police's

---

56. AB 10590, 1709.

57. Hélène Merlin, "Représentation du sabbat et représentation du politique au XVIIe siècle: Du *sabbat* au *cabinet*," in Jacques-Chaquin et Préaud, *Le sabbat des sorcières*, 111–26, esp. 122–23; eadem, "Figures du public au 18e siècle: Le travail du passé," *Dix-huitième Siècle* 23 (1991): 345–56.

58. Certeau, "La formalité des pratiques," 160 ff.

59. Piasenza, *Polizia e città*, 134; Michel Rey, "Police et sodomie à Paris au XVIIIe siècle: Du péché au désordre," *Revue d'histoire moderne et contemporaine* 29:1 (1982): 113–24; Angela Taeger,

focus could assimilate magic to the practice of alchemy, the art of transmutation so appreciated by the prince as long as it did not escape his sphere of influence.[60]

Could one also be seeing in miniature the troubling idea of a countersociety founded on contractual exchanges at once out of the ruler's field of vision and advancing by disrespect of the social hierarchy, which took such an important place, under differently accentuated forms, in the demonological writings? Jean Bodin considered witchcraft, that evil imported to France from Italy, as rebellion—an idea repeated by Pierre de Lancre, among others—"which tries to divert divine power to its profit" and thus to overturn the natural order of religion.[61] Voluntary association, the "faire société"—here around a common belief shared differently—worked not only to disincorporate individuals but to create a detached margin for maneuvering.[62] If, in certain seventeenth-century texts, the sabbat figured as a comparative term in relation to sociopolitical disorder, the false witches (*sorciers*) seemed to incorporate, in a totally known fashion, the most unsuspected disorders in a space which was in the process of reorganization, because of their ability to establish social links through the manipulation of belief.[63] The sects—no longer nocturnal but clandestine—which met outside monarchical purview to conclude their business acted for their own benefit, that is against the benefit of the state. The juridical text notes a motif that only recurs outside of the norm—these people sell to the *foreigner,* a political metaphor stressing their illegitimacy.[64] If the majority of the arrested chemists were effectively foreigners in French territory, the false witches as a whole threatened even more the functioning of the realm as a union of natu-

---

"Die Karrieren von Sodomiten in Paris während des 18. Jahrhunderts," in *MannBilder: Ein Lese- und Quellenbuch zur historischen Männerforschung,* ed. Wolfgang Schmale (Berlin: German Spitz, 1998), 113–29.

60. See Joël Cornette, "L'alchimiste, le Prince et le géomètre," *Revue de synthèse,* 4th ser., 3–4 (1991): 475–505.

61. Nicole Jacques-Chaquin, "La *Démonomanie des sorciers:* Une lecture philosophique et politique de la sorcellerie," in *Jean Bodin: Nature, histoire, droit et politique* (Paris: PUF, 1996), 43–70, esp. 64.

62. Merlin, "Représentation du sabbat," 118.

63. See Alain Boureau, "La croyance comme compétence: Une nouvelle histoire des mentalités," *Critique* 529–30 (1991): 512–26; indeed the author refers to the acceptance of this concept, elaborated by Luc Boltanski, *L'Amour et la justice comme compétences: Trois essais de sociologie de l'action* (Paris: Editions Métailié, 1990).

64. On the connection between witchcraft and xenophilia in the metaphor of the leech, see Charlotte Wells, "Leeches on the Body Politic: Xenophobia and Witchcraft in Early Modern French Political Thought," *French Historical Studies* 22:3 (1999): 351–77.

union of naturally hierarchical bodies.[65] The public face of this field was given to it by the staging of the monarchy which looked to enclose narrowly the appearances and movement of knowledge.[66] Foreigners to this space which finally, among other things, defined itself by the exclusive withholding of all kinds of "secrets," the false witches (*sorciers* and *sorcières*) were introduced here "imperceptibly," almost as regulars.[67] Thanks to their affinity with the world of secrets, their wandering outside of the frameworks of monarchical symbols and control could only appear as an illicit obstacle.[68]

The stakes were serious, and this "public crime" risked shaking the foundations of order in the city. From whence came the police insistence on extricating the camouflaged existence of this particular talent? Without the concurrence of the elites, at once detached from all magical practices and attached to the services of "specialists" in that area, however, would the "affaires" of the witches (*sorciers*) have flourished in the same manner? And wasn't it also the new disposition of even the means of investigation which gives the *faux sorciers* this remarkable power of seduction which, nevertheless, was not meant to belong to them? In placing them in the role of seductive demon, the police gave them a power to act beyond the nighttime universe of this culture of the people which would be theirs.[69] It was as if these characters encroached in an unforeseen way onto a scene which was in the process of

65. It is doubtless not accidental that the chemists held by the Paris police come from abroad, first from Italy, but also from Germany and Switzerland, which not only follows the trajectory of Niccolo Exili in the 1660s, advertising the *Affaire des poisons* to some extent, but also the multiple facets of the figure of the foreigner, notably Italian, that was so largely employed in political discourse since the end of the sixteenth century, producing an ambiguous amalgam of economic interest, scientific knowledge, artistic talent, and political ambitions; see Jean-François Dubost, *La France italienne* (Paris: Aubier, 1997).

66. See Farge, *Dire et mal dire*, 203–12; Michèle Fogel, *Les cérémonies de l'information dans la France du XVIe au milieu du XVIIIe siècle* (Paris: Fayard, 1989).

67. The concept of secrecy indeed covers a whole range of significations from simple medical recipes to alchemical and magical compositions and the principle of absolutist government, which is the *secret du roi*, passing through artisanal know-how; see Georg Simmel, "Das Geheimnis: Eine sozialpsychologische Skizze," in *Aufsätze und Abhandlungen 1901–1908*, 2 vols., ed. Georg Simmel et al., Bd. 8, *Oeuvres complètes* (Frankfurt am Main: Suhrkamp, 1993–95), 317–23. Since the seventeenth century, there has been a certain impoverishment of this plurality; see for example William Eamon, introduction to *Science and the Secrets of Nature: Books of Secrets in Medieval and Early Modern Culture* (Princeton: Princeton University Press, 1994).

68. Merlin, "Représentation du sabbat."

69. The association of *vox populi* with the *vox diaboli* is made for the first time at the end of the Middle Ages; see Vauchez, "La nascita del sospetto," 49.

forming itself, feeding from deeds and words which, through their rooting even in old traditions, appeared maybe less anachronistic than one might think at first. By making the figure of *séducteur-crédule* play on the ordered terrain of the city, there emerge the striking echoes of a reasoned universe in movement, animated by simple people who, at the threshold of the century of Enlightenment, always have the "weakness" of believing in magic.

God Killed Saul

Heinrich Bullinger and Jacob Ruef on the Power of the Devil

Bruce Gordon

The power of the devil greatly occupied the mind of Heinrich Bullinger during his last ten years as chief minister of the Zurich church. He had buried many of the colleagues with whom he had labored over four decades, men such as Konrad Pellikan, Theodor Bibliander, Peter Martyr Vermigli, and Konrad Gesner. Most had been taken by plague, a scourge which Bullinger, along with his contemporaries, interpreted as divine punishment for human wickedness.[1] God, as Bullinger frequently noted in his diary, was angry. The winter of 1570/71 was especially brutal in Zurich: the Zürchersee froze over, causing widespread hunger and social unrest.[2] Severe weather, poor crops, and price inflation had brought unprecedented hardships upon the people, in particular those in the rural areas, and many perished through hunger and

The author is grateful to Peter Maxwell-Stuart, Fiona Campbell, Peter Marshall, and Rainer Henrich for their suggestions and comments.

1. As succinctly put by Heinrich Bullinger, *A hundred sermons upon the Apocalips of Jesus Christ*, trans. John Daws (London, 1561), 481–82, in his sermons on the book of Revelation, "Men for the most part ascribe the causes of plagues to the starres, and to other matters: and therefore do not tourne to the Lord strikyng them, in amendement of life most evill, but we are taught by the treatise of Moses, which we alledged out of Exodus and by this present disputation of S. John, that God himselfe punisheth the sinnes and wickednes of men, although he use the service of menne and elementes unto whom as to the nexte causes men impute the evils received, which they suffer iustely of God for their sinnes."

2. See Hans Ulrich Bächtold, "Gegen den Hunger beten: Heinrich Bullinger, Zürich und die Einführung des Gemeinen Gebetes im Jahre 1571," in *Vom Beten, vom Verketzern, vom Predigen: Beiträge zum Zeitalter Heinrich Bullingers und Rudolf Gwalthers: Prof. Dr. Alfred Schindler zum 65. Geburtstag*, ed. Hans Ulrich Bächtold, Rainer Henrich, and Kurt Jakob Rüetschi (Zug: Achius, 1999), 9–44. I am grateful to the author for allowing me to read the article in manuscript.

exposure.[3] Johann Jakob Wick chronicled the portentous events of that harsh winter, including in his tales a report of a strange bird which had appeared in Swiss lands, a harbinger of God's wrath.[4] Ludwig Lavater, Bullinger's colleague and later head of the Zurich church, had his plague sermons printed by Christoph Froschauer in 1571 in which he left no doubt that the terrible weather, starvation, and economic crisis of the early 1570s was a form of divine flagellation.[5]

The Reformation in Zurich had not failed, nor had it entirely triumphed. Long years of hard work and delicate leadership had secured the place of the Reformed church in the Swiss confederation: Anabaptism was defeated and the Catholics were more or less at bay. Yet there was a pronounced sense of gloom hanging over the Zurich church by the middle of the sixteenth century. Take as an example Konrad Gesner's great bibliographical work, his *Bibliotheca universalis* of 1545, which had been produced in the expectation that western Europe was soon to be overrun by the Turks and that all learning would perish.[6] Through his bibliography, Gesner believed he could at least bequeath to posterity a list of what had been destroyed. What we now hail as a triumph of humanist scholarship was grimly prepared as an obituary.

Bullinger's interest in the devil arose first from his concern with understanding the historical context of the struggle between good and evil. Through his studies of history and biblical exegesis, Bullinger, following a long exegetical tradition, saw his own age as standing between the loosing of Satan and the Second Coming. Antichrist was in the church, and the gravest threat to the faithful was internal, false religion masquerading as obedience to the true God. In his commentaries Bullinger struggled to divine the prophecies of Daniel and John of Patmos as texts for reading the realities of his day. This aspect of Bullinger's work has received a considerable amount of scholarly attention.[7] My intention in this short essay is to look at a less well known

3. Bullinger wrote in his diary, "Die armen leelüt lidtend groß angst und not." *Heinrich Bullingers Diarium (Annales vitae) der Jahre 1540–1574*, ed. Emil Egli (Basel, 1904), 107.

4. Mathias Senn, ed., *Die Wickiana: Johann Jakob Wicks Nachrichtensammlung aus dem 16. Jahrhundert: Texte und Bilder zu den Jahren 1560 bis 1571* (Zurich: Raggi, 1975), 187. See Bächtold, "Gegen den Hunger beten."

5. Ludwig Lavater, *Von thüwre un\l\ hunger dry Predigen/ uf\l\ dem 6: cap deß anderen buchs Para=lipom oder der Chronick gepradiget* (Zurich, 1571).

6. Urs B. Leu, *Conrad Gesner als Theologe: Ein Beitrag zur Zürcher Geistesgeschichte des 16. Jahrhunderts* (Bern: Lang, 1990), 105–6.

7. Most notably the uneven work of Aurelio A. Garcia Archilla, *The Theology of History and Apologetic Historiography in Heinrich Bullinger* (San Francisco: Mellen Research University Press, 1992), esp. 117–65.

work written by Bullinger in his last five years, a text in which he turned from historical considerations of Satan to more pastoral ruminations on the real presence of the devil in the world. This late piece, entitled *Wider der schwartze Kunst*, is anything but original.[8] It is a composite text full of familiar arguments in which the author reveals his indebtedness to traditional (primarily scholastic) lines of argument, as well as to the work of colleagues in his city.

What makes *Wider der schwartze Kunst* worthy of attention, however, is the insight it offers on the mind of Bullinger the pastor. It is a vernacular text, clearly designated a short tract, not a sermon, and although it does not name its intended audience, the historical context and the tone of Bullinger's approach suggest that it was written to be circulated among ministers.[9] It is a didactic writing, derived from Bullinger's work on Acts of the Apostles, the book on which he was preaching in 1571. The tract is a fairly breezy exegesis of Acts 19, Paul's preaching in Ephesus, but the more important underlying biblical texts are Lev. 20 and Deut. 18, where the conjuring of sorcerers and witches is proscribed by God. Formal theological arguments in *Wider der schwartze Kunst* are not prominent; rather, the reader is offered a forensic analysis of the nature of the black arts in terms of their pastoral implications. In a manner similar to the pastoral writings of reformers such as Ambrosius Blarer, Bullinger made frequent use of questions as posed by the people in the parishes.[10] The tract has the flavor of a dialogue between a pastor and his people, and although our perspective on this conversation is shaped by the intentions of the author, these pastoral dialogues offer us a window on the nature of belief and practice in the lands of the Swiss Reformed churches. Unlike Blarer, however, Bullinger's writing does not really offer pastoral advice which

---

8. Joachim Staedtke, *Heinrich Bullinger Bibliographie*, 2 vols. (Zurich: Theologischer Verlag, 1972), 1:305.

9. The original text is preserved in Zentralbibliothek Zurich (hereafter ZBZ) MS B285, 360–75. There is a copy from 1574 by Johann Jakob Wick in Zurich ZBZ MS F63, 356v–63v. A seventeenth-century copy exists in the Hottinger Collection Zurich ZBZ MS F36, 488–98. The work was printed in *Theatrum de veneficis: Das ist: Von Teufelsgespenst, Zauberern und Gifftbereitern, Schwartzkünstlern, Hexen und Unholden, vieler fürnemmen Historien und Exempel...* (Frankfurt am Main, 1586).

10. The text of Ambrosius Blarer, *Der geistlich Schatz Christenlicher vorbereitung und gloubigs trosts wider Tod und Sterben... gepredigt druch Ambrosius Blarer* (Zurich, 1566), would certainly have been known to Bullinger. Blarer's work is essentially a Protestant *ars moriendi* in which he often uses the device of answering questions and objections made by parishioners. See Bruce Gordon, "Malevolent Ghosts and Ministering Angels: Apparitions and Pastoral Care in the Swiss Reformation," in *The Place of the Dead: Death and Remembrance in Late Medieval and Early Modern Europe*, ed. Bruce Gordon and Peter Marshall (Cambridge and New York: Cambridge University Press, 2000), 102–3.

would have suited people in the parish churches, and this suggests the conclusion that the work was intended for clerical instruction, possibly for circulation at the synodal meeting in the city.[11] Whatever its provenance, *Wider der schwartze Kunst* reflects the mind of a man who understood all too well, if somewhat wearily, why the people remained syncreticistic in their religious lives. The power of the devil lay not in dramatic acts of temptation, but rather in immediate and psychologically appealing solutions to prosaic matters of daily existence. In truth, the devil appeared the better bishop.

To understand the provenance of *Wider der schwartze Kunst* it is important to bear in mind the collective nature of scholarship in Zurich. The spiritual and intellectual center of the church was rooted in daily preaching in the three main churches (Grossmünster, Fraumünster, and Saint Peter's) and the lectures of the theological school, the *Schola Tigurina*. For example, between 1532 and 1560 Theodor Bibliander, a specialist in oriental languages, gave three cycles of lectures on the whole of the Old Testament. In addition, he also lectured on Revelation between 1543 and 1544. Almost all of these lectures have been preserved in the handwriting of Heinrich Bullinger and Rudolf Gwalther, who, between them, attended the daily sessions. The sodality of churchmen in Zurich bore fruit of many varieties: editions of scripture, biblical commentaries, Latinate works of theology, and increasingly during the sixteenth century, a corpus of pastoral literature.[12] The high degree of theological consistency among these works must be attributed to the watchful eye of Bullinger, who along with men like Johannes Wolf and Rudolf Gwalther, was responsible for ensuring conformity of thought.[13] Such regulation, however, does not suffice to explain why the Zurich church was able to speak with one voice: the striking parallels in exegesis and mode of argument to be found across a range of authors and texts points to a collaborative effort in biblical interpretation and theological formulation unmatched in the Reformation period. The very arguments about demons and ghosts which Bullinger rehearsed in his sermons on Acts and in the *Wider der schwartze Kunst* are to be found in detail in Ludwig Lavater's *Das Gespensterbuch* of 1569. Similarly,

11. On the meetings of the synod and Bullinger's role in supervising the clergy of Zurich, see Bruce Gordon, *Clerical Discipline and the Rural Reformation: The Synod in Zurich 1532–1580* (Bern: Lang, 1992).

12. The best resource for Zurich printing in the sixteenth century is Manfred Vischer, *Bibliographie der Zürcher Druckschriften* (Baden-Baden: Koerner, 1991).

13. The best study of this subject is Mark Taplin, "The Italian Reformers and the Zurich Church, c. 1540–1620" (Ph.D. thesis, University of Saint Andrews, 1999).

the medical and physical arguments employed by Bullinger were drawn from the work of the prominent Zurich doctor Jacob Ruef, whose 1554 text we shall consider below.

We know that from 1554 to 1556 Bullinger preached on the book of Revelation at the Tuesday morning sermons in the Grossmünster, having worked his way through the book of Daniel ten years earlier.[14] The sermons on the Apocalypse were printed in 1558 (first translated into English in 1561), a year after Bullinger's commentary on Revelation, and they are suffused with the reformer's attempt to arrive at a historical account of the place of the devil in creation. In his discussion of Rev. 20:2 Bullinger sought to make sense of the binding of the devil for a thousand years. The 1561 English translation reads:

> I know that the opinions of the expositours, touchyng these thousande yeres, be diverse.... And I understande playnely and simply, that S. John speaketh of a thousande yeres, whiche ranne on by continuall course from the time of Christ, untill the laste corrupting of the Evangelical preachyng and church of Christ.[15]

Bullinger calculated when this period of a thousand years should commence, concluding that counting should start from Christ's thirty-fourth year, which represented the year of his ascension, the year of Paul's calling to the ministry, and the year in which Gentiles were drawn into the church through preaching.[16] It was the preaching of the Word which bound the devil. Bullinger suggested several starting points for the reckoning of a thousand years and each, he believed, had sufficient warrant in scripture:

> Or beginne the supputation of the thousande yeres from that time, wherein Paule beying bounde for the Gospell at home, terrified that the gospell was preached through out the worlde. That was aboute the yere of our Lorde 60. frome thence accompiyng a thousande yeres, thou shalte come to the yere of our Lorde 1060. when Nicholas the seconde was pope, under whom it is written that the veritie was

14. Bullinger preached on Revelation from 21 August 1554 until 29 December 1556 and on Daniel from 27 July 1546 until 19 July 1547. For both books he preached once a week, on Tuesday mornings. See Fritz Büsser, "Bullinger—Der Prediger," in *Wurzeln der Reformation in Zürich* (Leiden: Brill, 1985), 143–58. The Latin outlines of Bullinger's sermons survive in ZBZ Car III 206c.

15. Bullinger, *Hundred Sermons*, 593. I have used the English translations, as I did not have access to the German.

16. Bullinger, *Hundred Sermons*, 593.

diversely tempted and corrupted, and that Gregory the seventh dyd than also by his craftes and enterprises trouble the whole world. Or beginne the supputation from the destruction of hierusalem, what time the Jewes cast of, the Gentiles in great numbre entred and were receyved into the place of the Jewes reiected, whiche was the yere of our Lorde. 73. Even to Pope Gregory the seventh: in the whiche time not a fewe historiographers wryte that the Devill him selfe raygned. Doubtless never manne hurte godlines, or more stoutely avannced impietie than dyd this Gregory, otherwyse called Hildebrande.[17]

Bullinger was satisfied, due to the richness of the historical evidence, that from some point during the age of the Apostles until the middle of the eleventh century—he commented "1073 or there aboute"—the Gospel prospered in the church because the devil was restrained by the faithful preaching of the word of God. With the fulfillment of this period, however, all had changed: the devil was loosed and the church had fallen into ruin. Bullinger interpreted the idolatry and superstition of his day as evidence for the seductive powers of the devil and his minions, now free to wreak havoc upon the faithful with the connivance of the papacy. The contrast between his own time and the thousand years following the apostolic age was not brought about, according to Bullinger, by the end of a fall from grace. The thousand years during which the devil was bound was a period of mixed fortunes as the forces of evil had still been able to infect the church.[18]

Some man wil say, I cannot see that the preaching of the Gospel hath continued in the worlde so long tyme, to witte a thousande yeares, for it appeareth by histories, that the doctrine of merites, satisfactions, and iustificatione of works, did incontinently after the Apostles time, lay their first foundations. We knowe that the intercessions of Sainctes, and the worshipping of relicques, were defended of Saincte Hierome, which departed out of this world the yeare of our Lordes incarnation. 422. We knowe that the Bishop of Rome did immediately after the death of Gregory the firste, take upon him to be head and catholique pastor of the church universall. We knowe that about the same time, to

17. Bullinger, *Hundred Sermons*, 594.
18. On the binding and loosing of the devil in eschatology, see Stuart Clark, *Thinking with Demons: The Idea of Witchcraft in Early Modern Europe* (New York: Oxford University Press, 1997), 347–49.

160 KATHRYN A. EDWARDS, ED.

wit, about the yeare of our Lordes incarnation: 630 Mahomet seduced a great parte of the world. We knowe that shortely after, arose that detestable contention about the having of images in the churches of Christians. We have heard that S. Jhon hath assigned to Antichriste yeares 666. Fynally, it is manifeste that the Devyll hath by murther, parricidie, and all kynd of mischief raigned in the children of misbelefe. Wherfore thou sayeste, "I see not how the Devyll hath ben bounden a thousand yeares: and locked in chaynes."[19]

The array of heresy and misdeeds which plagued the church during its first thousand years had to be explained. Bullinger asserted that the devil had been driven from the church, but not the world, and that it was from his perch in the world that he continued to harass the faithful: "He is cast out of the church, and of the faithful, not that he cometh not againe, and tempteth, for alwayes he returneth, and seketh to plucke backe the redemed (but for that he possesseth no more the ful empire). For Christ now liveth, and raineth in the church and sainctes."[20] The victory of Christ had denied the devil his old empire. In a favorite phrase of Bullinger's (drawn from Zwingli), the faithful have been translated out of the kingdom of darkness to the kingdom of light.[21] During this first thousand years the devil "possessed not the faythfull of Christe through out the worlde, nor ruled them at his pleasure, and after his malice, although he hath tempted and vered them."[22] The devil, once almighty on earth, had been humiliated by Christ and was reduced to grasping attempts to seduce believers, against whom he remained impotent on account of their faith. Although the faithful were protected, the devil's sovereignty over the unfaithful was hardly diminished. He could still peddle his wares of unbelief and heresy, and the historical evidence demonstrated, Bullinger argued, that the devil had more than a few customers. Now that he was unleashed, however, the faithful were in the greatest peril, the walls were breached, and the final battle which precipitated the return of Christ had begun.

19. Bullinger, *Hundred Sermons*, 595.

20. Bullinger, *Hundred Sermons*, 595.

21. Bullinger, *Hundred Sermons*, 592, wrote "S Paule sheweth that Christ hath overcome Sathan, an that the same Christ hath redeemed us, and brought us out of the kingdome of darkness into the kingdome and light of the sonne of God. Therefore where the Apostles and ministers are here saide to binde and shute up Sathan, it is by the waye of their ministerie to be understande."

22. Bullinger, *Hundred Sermons*, 592.

But in whome the Devill possesseth his kindome, in the same also he uttereth his mallice against the elect, and that his great mallice. For he rageth most cruelly against the godly, and against godlines. He rageth also most extremely against those his worshippers, whom he polluteth with all kinde of filthiness, and with al shame and reproche defileth.[23]

As Howard Hotson has pointed out, the problem with sixteenth-century attempts to construct a historical framework for the thousand years when the devil was bound is that pieces do not quite fit together.[24] If during the period of a thousand years Satan could not damage the faithful, although as Bullinger freely admitted he could do a great deal of harm, then what could the devil achieve once he had been loosed? Did it mean that the age of faith had come to an end in the eleventh century? Or that Satan could now steal back God's elect? No Protestant theologian could admit any of these points. What of the age between the thousand years and the Second Advent of Christ? A period in which Rev. 20:3 states "he must be set free for a short time." It was during this time that the devil's black arts were spread among the faithful by his legion of spiritual and human agents destroying the church, and it was from the perspective of the pastoral implications of this warfare that Bullinger wrote his *Wider der schwartze Kunst*.

Bullinger was not an enthusiastic demonologist, the subject occupying only a small part of his corpus of writings, and for the most part his thoughts were compiled from the work of others. Within the walls of Zurich, however, there were figures who made the work of the devil very much their business. Jacob Ruef, the distinguished medical doctor and dramatist, provided Bullinger with access to scientific thinking about the devil; the interest of the medical profession in the demonic was as great, if not greater, than among theologians.[25] In 1554, the year in which Bullinger began his sermons on Revelation, Jacob Ruef published a work in which he considered in six chapters

23. Bullinger, *Hundred Sermons*, 362.

24. Howard Hotson, "The Historiographical Origins of Calvinist Millenarianism," in *Protestant History and Identity in Sixteenth-Century Europe: The Later Reformation*, ed. Bruce Gordon (Aldershot: Scolar Press, 1996), 159–81.

25. Jacob Ruef (family name is variously spelt Ryef, Ruf) was born in Constance before coming to Zurich to serve as city doctor. Between 1543 and 1546 he published a series of medical and astronomical works: Jacob Ruef, *Historisches-biographisches Lexikon der Schweiz*, 7 vols. (Neuenburg, 1926) 5:752. See also Elke Ukena Best, "Jacob Ruef," in *Literaturlexikon: Autoren und Werke deutscher Sprache*, ed. Walther Killy (Gütersloh: Bertelsmann, 1991), 10:79.

all aspects of conception, pregnancy, and birth.[26] The work is a compendium of medical advice and spiritual comfort, drawn from Ruef's personal observations and the experience of midwives. Most of the *Trostbuch* has little to say about God and the devil, confining its interests to the natural processes of conception and childbirth and the practical steps to be taken to facilitate them. In the fifth book, however, where Ruef treated the subject of monstrous births, the tone changed markedly. Here, consistent with the whole genre of literature on prodigies which flowed from Protestant presses in the second half of the sixteenth century, Ruef turned to the confluence of scientific and theological themes.[27] Drawing upon traditional medical (especially Galen) and scholastic arguments, Ruef considered the question of whether monstrous children were evidence that the devil could produce offspring.

> No one should doubt that the devil may assume human form and appearance and move about and speak with men. It is also possible for the devil to take on the likeness of an angel (as Paul says), as well as the appearance of a man, and this has often happened. Whether, however, the devil is able to sleep with humans and have sexual intercourse to the end that children are implanted must be decided.[28]

In virtually all Zurich literature about the devil, Antichrist, ghosts, and the revenant, the primary authority remained Augustine. Ruef cited the bishop of Hippo in support of the fact that the devil takes on various guises, particularly as Sylvani, to have sexual intercourse with humans.[29] Augustine had been a great believer in the power of the devil, arguing that the omnipotence of God was never so clearly manifested as in his restraining of Satan.[30]

Ruef wrote that the activities of spirits were not limited to the pages of ancient texts, for they were still active in his time, and in the tradition of writers such as Caesarius of Heisterbach he offered a collection of exempla in the

---

26. Joacob Ruef, *Ein Schon lustig Trost‖buchle von der empfengknussen und ‖ geburten der menschen/ vnd jren vilfaltigen zu=‖ falen vnd verhindernussen…* (Zurich, 1554). The book was originally printed in Latin as *De conceptu et generatione hominis, et iis quae circa haec potissimum consyderantur* (Zurich, 1554). It was translated into English as *The Expert Midwife, or an Excellent and Most Necessary Treatise of the Generation and Birth of Man* (London, 1637). The English edition is a truncated version of the Latin and German editions.

27. On the subject of monstrous births, see Philip M. Soergel, "The Afterlives of Monstrous Infants in Reformation Germany," in Gordon and Marshall, *Place of the Dead*, 288–309.

28. Ruef, sig. xcii recto.

29. Augustine *De Civitate Dei*, 20 8:41.

30. Peter Brown, *Augustine of Hippo* (Berkeley: University of California Press, 1969), 367.

form of stories to illustrate his argument.[31] We can look at two examples. The first concerns a harlot who after being seduced into physical relations with a demon was tormented with the most hideous pain: "Then she began to burn in her private parts with gangrene (*kalten brand*), and no operation could avail her anything and by the next day she was dead. She was so wretched and her suffering so great that all her intestines fell out (*ir all ir yngeweid uffiel*)."[32]

The physically specific nature of the affliction visited upon the women featured is a recurring theme. Another story tells of a butcher who went out into the street at night looking for satisfaction and was rewarded by an encounter with a beautiful woman, who was a demon. His lust satisfied, he too was rapidly struck down by excruciating pain, and like the harlot, his sexual organs burned [*im seine gemaecht mit aller zuogehoerd erbrunnen und erfulet*].[33] In both stories, the deception worked because the victims found precisely what they sought: sex. The consequences, Ruef insisted, were entirely due to the desires and actions of the man and the women. Devils cannot be blamed for being devils.

Indeed, there is a certain integrity to the devil and his demons. Ruef's work stood in a tradition, dating back to the thirteenth century, which reflected a fascination for the idea of supernatural creatures' having sexual intercourse with humans. Consonant with scholastic writers, Ruef asserted that demons derived no pleasure from sexual encounters; they did not experience physical stimulation and they certainly did not lust after men and women. Their sole intention was to tempt the faithful away from God; that was their nature and they behaved consistently in their pursuit of the art of seduction. In the moral universe demons existed because men and women sought their services; they were external manifestations of inner struggles between good and evil fired by the human need for gratification. As Augustine had written, "the devil is not to be blamed for everything; there are times when man is his own devil."[34] Relations between humans and demons were, according to Ruef, a false form of friendship grounded in the inability of men and women to discern true good and evil from the appearance of good and

31. On Caesarius, see Jacques Le Goff, *The Birth of Purgatory*, trans. Arthur Goldhammer (Chicago: University of Chicago Press, 1981), 300–310. Written in the same manner, as a compendium of stories and tales: Ludwig Lavater, *Von Gespänstern unghüren…* (hereafter *Das Gespensterbuch*) (Zurich, 1569).

32. Ruef, Historisches-biographisches, sig. xcii verso.

33. Ruef, Historisches-biographisches, sig. xcii verso.

34. Quoted in Brown, *Augustine of Hippo*, 245.

evil. The genital punishment is described with the verb *erfullen* (*verfaulen*) to convey a vivid sense of suppuration and putrefaction. The dreadful burning which both endured before their deaths was understood by Ruef as divine punishment. God made examples of these two in order to warn men and women of high and low estate to avoid such forbidden intercourse.

In his book on pregnancy and childbirth Ruef wanted to assert that although there was more than sufficient evidence for carnal relations between the devil and humans, such relationships had never resulted in progeny: "Therefore, concerning the truth of the matter, these things are to be accounted for by the subtlety and deceit of the devil, and the wicked persuasion of men, so that we do not believe that devils can cause women to be with child, nor, on the other side, that devils taking the form of women may conceive a child with men."[35] There is not one person in this world who was not born of human parents by natural means, and no one, with the exception of Jesus Christ, has been conceived by a spirit.

Ruef then recounted several tales that seemed to lend credence to the notion that the devil produces offspring in the world. His purpose was to demonstrate that these were misunderstandings of what had occurred. The first came from Ruef's native city of Constance, where a beautiful maiden had had carnal relations with the devil.[36] The ministers and other godly people endeavored to have her forswear Satan, but he would not leave her alone, and day and night she was tormented. Many believed that she would bear a child and the midwife was sent for, but the whole thing was a delusion (*Trug*), for instead of a child, out of her body came nails, hair, bones, glass, and other things, leaving the spectators in no doubt that the devil dwelt in her. Ruef was referring to a witchcraft trial from 1546, of which he had personal knowledge, concerning a young maidservant known as Magdalena who had mysteriously become ill and was taken to the civic hospital.[37] It was believed that she was connected to Margreth Scholl, who was executed as a witch, but in the end the sufferings and death of the girl were interpreted by the Protestant authorities of Constance as divine judgment upon both her and the city for their faithlessness.[38]

---

35. Ruef, Historisches-biographisches, sig. xcii verso.

36. Ruef, Historisches-biographisches, sig. xxciiii recto.

37. On this case, see Wolfgang Zimmermann, "Teufelsglaube und Hexenverfolgung in Konstanz, 1546–1549," *Schriften des Vereins für Geschichte des Bodensees und seiner Umgebung* 106 (1988): 29–57.

38. Ruef was informed of the case by Ambrosius Blarer, who had written to both him and Bullinger: Zimmermann, "Teufelsglaube," 44.

The second story came from Vicentius and told the tale which came from the time of Roger of Sicily.[39] A young man who liked to swim in the ocean came upon a mermaid, and grabbing her by the hair he pulled her out of the water. He dressed the mermaid in his coat and took her to his home, where they married. She was good to him but never spoke. Many around him suspected, quite reasonably, that she was no ordinary wife but a delusion or ghost, and they attempted to persuade the man to find the reason for her silence. Soon the mermaid became pregnant and bore the man a son. Frustrated and angry, and desiring to kill their child on account of its accursed parentage, the man forced her to speak, to say who she was, and to explain why she remained silent. The mermaid answered: "O unholy man, do you know that you have lost a good wife, because you force me to speak. I would have always remained with you and you would have been happy with me if you had allowed me to remain silent. Now you shall never see me again." With those words she vanished. The son, like the father, loved to swim in the ocean, and one day as he was in the water his mother appeared to him. Taking hold of him she dragged him below the surface, and he was never seen again. Many believed that had the son been a natural human, his body would have washed up on the shore. Ruef's interpretation of the story accepted that he was no regular child. "To discern whether this son was a naturally conceived child or a ghost, you should pay heed to the following matters: although he ate and drank, and had a natural upbringing, he was no natural human, but a devil who had the appearance of a child."[40] What of the mermaid? She too, according to Ruef, was a devil but of a particular type. She was a succubus, who was known for taking female form in order to entrap men.

Ruef stressed the fundamental difference between sexual intercourse and impregnation under the laws of nature. The power of the devil lay in deception, not in an ability to transgress the laws of nature. The devil was constrained by the order of creation, and while intercourse may take place, it was against God's ordinance for the devil to produce children:

> Many people believe or understand that the devil succubus can take female form and live with a man and also receive from him his nature or seed, and retain the same. Also that he can change his form to that

39. Ruef is referring to the *Speculum naturale* of the Dominican Vincent of Beauvais (c. 1190–1264). See W. J. Aerts, E. R. Smits, and J. B. Voorbeg, eds., *Vincent of Beauvais and Alexander the Great: Studies in the Speculum Maius and Its Translation into Medieval Vernaculars* (Groningen: Forsten, 1986).

40. Ruef, Historisches-biographisches, sigs. xciv verso, xcv recto.

of the man incubus and go to evil women or witches, who have been promised to him, and impregnate them with his nature or seed and make them pregnant. From this children are born. All of this is contrary to Christian belief, natural laws and all likelihood. Whether or not the devil is able or wishes to receive human seed, as soon as it is mixed up nothing living, good or natural is born. Although he might have come to a woman and had intercourse with her that which results is cold and without force. Even if it were possible for the devil to mess with the seeds of men and animals and defy the powers of nature, what would men make of this with their reason? What would be seen is how the natural laws were breached by the devil leading to the misbirths among men and animals, as well as to other terrible and senseless things about which it is not proper for Christians to write or speak.

In advancing this argument Ruef was relying upon traditional medical and scholastic lines of thought. Ruef cited Galen:

Therefore from this I conclude that the devil cannot use human seed with fertility, because the seed comes from the heart and is warm. And although the devil, with the aid of evil and desperate women, and with the permission of God, may engage in sexual acts, without power and virtue nothing, as we have said already, nothing living, good or energetic can be born.[41]

The scholastic basis for incubus and succubus was well established. William Auvergne and Albertus Magnus had considered the matter, declaring that incubi and succubi could take the form of handsome men and women who seduce gullible or lustful victims.[42] These demons were projections of prevalent sexual attitudes: women were seen as having an enormous sexual appetite which threatened to destroy men by undermining the rational faculties of the soul. As the *Malleus Maleficarum* made clear, women were susceptible to the devil and this dependence was realized in sexual intercourse, which sealed the pact between the two.[43] The underlying theory was that the devil, although not in need of sex, required an embodied person to make himself real in the world. The particular danger posed by succubi and incubi lay in their constant ability to

41. Ruef, Historisches-biographisches, sigs. xcv recto, xcvi recto.
42. Jeffrey Burton Russell, *Lucifer: The Devil in the Middle Ages* (Ithaca: Cornell University Press, 1984), 183.
43. Dyan Elliot, *Fallen Bodies: Pollution, Sexuality, and Demonology in the Middle Ages* (Philadephia: University of Pennsylvania Press, 1999), 155.

change forms, a fear evident in Ruef's stories. The ability to move between male and female forms struck at the external structures of society whose culture was deeply gendered at all levels, in particular the family, with its ordered notion of sexual activity for procreation.[44]

The question of whether demons could produce children had a long lineage in scholastic thought. The Aristotelian understanding of natural laws was employed by Ruef to argue for the physical impossibility of demonic impregnation. This was not new, but the scholastics had found a way around this objection: Thomas Aquinas wrote that demons gathered male seed produced in nocturnal emissions and used it to impregnate women.[45] This they achieved by taking the forms of succubi and incubi, so that although they were unable to produce the necessary seed for procreation, they were still active agents in the process. Thus the offspring could still be thought of as progeny of the devil. Ruef eschewed this aspect of the scholastic argument, preferring to remain with a discussion of what was physically possible. Monstrous births may be signs of God's disfavor, but they were not offspring of the devil. Sexual relations between humans and demons, though frequent, were not fecund; ultimately they were about physical gratification and were, therefore, sinful acts for which the individuals involved would be held to account.

As city doctor, Ruef belonged to the sodality of learned men in Zurich surrounding Heinrich Bullinger. The harmony of medical and theological interests was well represented in the city, as Konrad Gesner had also studied medicine in Basle. Ruef's book was printed by Christoph Froschauer, likewise a contemporary and intimate member of the Zurich circle. But we have further reason to ponder the importance of Jacob Ruef for the development of the religious culture, for he was one of the leading biblical dramatists of his period. Many of the religious themes which dominated the homiletic, theological, and pastoral literature printed in Zurich was vivified on the stage in Ruef's productions. Among his many works were *Die Geschichte Hiobs* (1535), *Die Geschichte Abrahams* (1535), and *Geschichte des Lazarus* (1552). In his passion play, *Das lyden unsers Herren Jesu Christi*, Ruef, in his treatment of the suffering of Christ, gave dramatic expression to the Zwinglian distinction between the symbol and the thing symbolized, crucial to the eucharistic theology of Zurich.[46]

44. Elliot, *Fallen Bodies*, 60.

45. Elliot, *Fallen Bodies*, 25.

46. On Ruef's dramatical work, see Wolfgang F. Michael, *Das deutche Drama der Reformationszeit* (Bern: Lang, 1984), 149–61.

As noted, Bullinger wrote his treatise *Wider der schwartze Kunst* during 1571,[47] while engaged in his Sunday sermons on Acts, which he held from 1568 until 1573.[48] The story of Paul's arrival in Ephesus and his confrontation with those who were practicing sorcery provided Bullinger with the opportunity for some mature reflections on the nature of evil in the world. The miracles performed by Paul, such as the healing of the sick and the driving out of evil spirits, brought about a sense of *wunder* among the people.[49] These were signs of God's authority made evident in Paul's ministry, but they were also dangerous. For in performing miracles Paul had entered into the world of visible demonstrations of God's power, a world in which people valued their deities according to their ability to act in nature. This is the plane upon which the devil operates with his *schwartze Kunst*, where the appearances of things can deceive men and women. The devil could take on Paul on this level and by performing his own tricks seek to make the Apostle appear foolish. But it cannot work. The devil ultimately recognizes the truth, even if he seeks to undermine it. The story of the Jewish chief priest in Acts 20:14–16, for Bullinger, is instructive. The priest is envious of Paul's powers of exorcism and seeks to demonstrate his own talents, but upon his approach the evil spirit calls out, "Jesus I know, and I know about Paul, but who are you?" This humiliation at the hands of the evil spirit is derived from the final humiliation that God has inflicted upon the devil: despite his machinations, he and his minions must always bear witness to the truth.[50] The devil has no loyalty to his followers, abandoning them at the crucial moment and making them look ludicrous as they flail about in their impotence.

Bullinger felt no need to justify his assertion that God had proscribed the black arts; he cited a few key scriptural texts to demonstrate that not only were such acts contrary to divine will, they were to be punished. What the reformer really wanted to explore were the real effects of the devil and his work upon the people. In scripture God has clearly proscribed commerce with magicians, witches, and practitioners of the black arts (Bullinger frequently alighted upon familiar biblical passages), but the more serious issue is the broader (*weittlauffiger*) pastoral issue posed by continued adherence to the black arts on account of popular belief in the efficacy of these customs

---

47. Bullinger, *Diarium*, 105. Bullinger wrote "Item 2 tractetli von dem gloggenlüten und verbotnen künsten. Und sind die viere nit truckt."

48. Büsser, "Bullinger—Der Prediger," 155.

49. Bullinger, *Wider der schwartze Kunst*, 298.

50. Bullinger, *Wider der schwartze Kunst*, 299.

(*gebrauchen*). Bullinger had no illusions that the reasons for which people consulted such men and women were entirely practical and probably innocent: they needed help and they had gone to those who they thought could provide it. Yet it was these forms of magic which drew the most intense fire from Bullinger; he was much more damning of those popular practices which appeared harmless, and he devoted far more of his text to explaining how they were at the root of the threat to true faith. For Bullinger, common sense and practicality were the devil's sharpest knives.

Bullinger was a well-informed pastor, versed in the mentality of the people. Although God had forbidden the black arts and had instituted medicine for the repair of the body, the tendency to seek alternative forms of assistance came with the awareness of the limitations of doctors. In this discourse, framed in dialogue, Bullinger posed the dilemma: when one is sick one naturally seeks to become healthy again. If the devil can help, then why should I speak against this? This for Bullinger was the ultimate strength of the devil and his arts: the readiness to offer immediate comfort or psychological relief when neither the church nor medical doctors would do anything. Yet Bullinger's God could seem hard, and the counsel to patience in the face of adversity was cold consolation: "One should seek the advice of doctors or other learned men for comfort, but where no help is to be found or expected, one must patiently bear the hand of God, never abandoning the cross, believing that God has replaced it with the help of the devil and the forbidden arts, as the godless never cease to declare."[51]

Bullinger stated that the forms of the black arts were a pendant of blasphemy.[52] They are tricks (*Teuffels kunst*) behind which lay a malign spirit whose greatest talent was the art of dissembling. Deception was the devil's game, but his purpose was by no means harmless or unreal, for it played upon human desires for spiritual and material comfort. For Bullinger, the devil and his agents formed a counterchurch ministering to the needs of the people. In a sense, the devil had stolen a march on the true church precisely because he was such an effective purveyor of pastoral care. He tended to the sensual, physical, emotional, and spiritual desires of the people in a most effective way; so much so that they clamored for his return, even if they thought they were followers of the true religion. The devil dressed his deceits in the sanctity

51. Bullinger, *Wider der schwartze Kunst*, 299.
52. Bullinger, *Wider der schwartze Kunst*, 299, lists the proscribed arts as "Magia, Mathematica, & Venefica, Divinatio, Incantatio, Augurium, Auspicia, Geomantia, Necromantia, Hydromantia, Pyromantia."

of the church just as he took human form to seduce men and women as succubi and incubi.

The most prominent form of magic, according to Bullinger, were blessings (*segnen*).[53] Here the devil's ability to play with the ambiguities of human existence was brought into stark relief, for not all blessings were forbidden. They were the common coinage of human discourse, conveying a range of quasi-religious meanings from familial affection to a sense of belonging to the community. Bullinger cited Num. 6:23, where God says to Moses, "Tell Aaron and his sons, 'This is how you are to bless the Israelites.'" The Aaronic blessing is the model for the work of the church: the words given by God to the priests have only the function to proclaim (*verkunden*). They are to be pronounced openly and audibly that no one might think there is any sense of mystery to them. The Aaronic blessing indicated God's will that the words be understood as tools of God's power, and not, as in magic, as having any forensic authority. Scripture provides the only legitimate form of blessing:

> In the New Testament the holy Apostles clearly (*heiter*) with their words and expressions declared that God alone bestows and gives [the power], and this they have written and spoken of: Grace, peace and mercy from God our Father and the Lord Jesus Christ be with you. This blessing is still given rightly and fruitfully in all our churches at the start of the preaching service by the clergy. This indicates that which the preacher says from God works upon the faithful not by the power of the words, but by the power of God (*Gottes kraft*).[54]

Bullinger attempted to sort out the difference between this form of blessing, which clearly had its place in the worship of the community, and those forms of blessings which were part of the everyday commerce of the people. It was a wonderful practice of old, he wrote, that parents should bless their children. Indeed, it is part of God's will that parents tend and protect their families, and the offering of a blessing upon children or fellow Christians when one takes one's leave is a charitable act. To say "God and the Holy Cross," or, "God and the Holy Mother bless you," as was common among the people, was, however, to fall into error. Bullinger's objection, predictably, was that these seemingly inoffensive formulations, no doubt mere commonplaces

---

53. On this point, see Euan Cameron, "For Reasoned Faith or Embattled Creed? Religion for the People in Early Modern Europe," *Transactions of the Royal Historical Society* 8 (1998): 170–71.

54. Bullinger, *Wider der schwartze Kunst*, 300.

among the people, signaled false religion in that they deprived God of his place as the source of all power and grace.

The discussion turned on the relationship between symbols and reality. These popular forms of blessings attributed magical powers to the cross through the implied understanding that the material substance of the cross conveyed God's sanctifying power, a misunderstanding, according to Bullinger, of the biblical intention. Paul in 1 Cor. 1 refers to the cross as the foolishness of Christ, and it was this foolishness which was a stumbling block to those Jews and Greeks who sought signs and wisdom. Bullinger's discussion of magic, in all its forms, is reduced to a debate about the nature of signs, that the significance of an object lay in that which it signified, not in its outward appearance. The nature of signification was a well-established subject in Zurich as it stood at the root of the eucharistic controversies which had dogged the Swiss Reformed churches from the mid-1520s.

Bullinger moved on to those forms of blessings associated with healing and the enhancement of animal fertility. Once more evil is found lurking under the guise of goodness and common sense. Although they appear to effect good in the cure of wounds and the fertility of animals, incantations associated with popular medicine are signs of *Teuffelswerck* on account of the false conjunction of words and deeds. Bullinger commented that he was not referring to the medicinal powers of herbs and roots, which he calls *naturlicher artzeney*, but rather those forms of healing which required particular incantation, the making of the sign of the cross, or use of a crucifix. This dependence of the act upon these words makes them full of *abgoetterey* (superstition). Such minor infractions could not simply be dismissed as *adiaphora* as they pointed to a more fundamental issue relating to popular understanding of the relationship between the divine and the human. If such incantations were permitted, Bullinger ruminated, one should not be surprised when the people demanded to know how when they prayed to God in churches or in the home their prayers could possibly be efficacious without any accompanying act or blessing (*braeuch und segen*). Bullinger argued that conjurers would reply that prayer without such rituals was of no use, with the consequence that those who performed magic and those who sought the benefits of such acts were bound in a pact of sin. The innocence or naiveté which led the faithful to such extraecclesiastical sources of access to the supernatural was no defense in God's eyes.

The attitudes displayed by Bullinger towards popular medicine reflected what Lawrence Brockliss and Colin Jones have referred to as the "cult of the secret" which surrounded the vast number of local, part-time healers who rarely possessed a license and who, consequently, suffered the endless oppro-brium of elite culture.[55] Brockliss and Jones argue that although the surviving literature successfully distanced elite culture from popular medicine, the two worlds were hardly far removed from one another, as both belonged to the "same world of discourse."[56] Their shared ideas of diagnosis and treatment evolved from the popularization of medical knowledge, referred to by the authors as "popular Galenism," through vernacular books (such as that by Ruef) and through access to elite medical knowledge in cities with medical fac-ulties. The lines between formal and informal medicine were highly porous.

Bullinger then turned his attention to the subject of exorcism. Succinctly put, Christ drove out devils and the Apostles did likewise in his name, but the church was left with no mechanism to perform *exorcismos* because it had been a special gift limited to the early years. The ritual of exorcism was mocked by Bullinger for all its solemn nonsense: forcing some poor soul to stand in a bath of cold water, sprinkling him with holy water, and beating his naked body with branches. Bullinger deliberately conjured up this comical scene because of the seriousness of the matter he wished to address. His reply to exorcism concentrated not on what the church should do—he had denied that it had any power to drive out demons—but on how the individual pos-sessed by a dark force should respond. The biblical evidence was clear for Bul-linger, namely that men and women plagued by demons should go straight to Christ. Bullinger's response to the question: "Yes, but he is no longer on earth, how can I go to him?" repeated the statement of Ludwig Lavater in his *Gespensterbuch* of 1569: "Christ is in his church, and one should go there and beseech the community to pray, seek medicine whereby the ill are made well so that neither the individual nor the community are led into error. Further, he should wait upon the mercy of God."[57]

The deception of the devil was revealed in his mendacious handling of those conjurers (*beschwerer*) who used his name. The devil makes it appear as though he can be summoned as supplicant by certain formulations of words, thereby deceiving the conjurer into thinking he is in control. The deceit depends on human pride, a need to have a sense of power, which enables the devil to perform his tricks. It is the disposition of the person which is critical; the devil appears to those who are vulnerable to temptation. Bullinger spoke

55. Lawrence Brockliss and Colin Jones, *The Medical World of Early Modern France* (Oxford: Clar-endon, 1997), 273–74.

56. Brockliss and Jones, *Medical World*, 276.

57. Bullinger, *Wider der schwartze Kunst*, 301.

of the different types of spirits which appear in this context: *paredros, familia-res spiritus,* and *Pythonem*. Not only was contact forbidden with these spirits which predicted the future, but was to be punished.[58]

Bullinger's concern to locate responsibility with the individual and not with a supernatural power led to his next assault on astrology as a black art which led men and women into superstition. The argument is not developed in any detail, being confined to the assertion that God had not given the power of the planets to humans; no knowledge of the future can be derived from reading the heavens.[59] Bullinger's objections lay mostly in the observation that many people born under the same sign have turned out completely different from one another; the biblical example is of Jacob and Esau, one of whom was loved by God, the other hated. Astrology places signs above God's revealed will, and these signs cannot be read by humans with accuracy. Bullinger concluded with a brief remark that astrology was not to be confused with the respectable science of astronomy.

Bullinger returned to the subject of apparitions. First he addressed the question of whether the living can consult the dead, a subject always treated by the Zurich divines through an exegesis of the story of the witch of Endor (1 Sam. 28).[60] The crucial matter, according to Bullinger, was expressed by Paul in 2 Cor. 11:14: "And no wonder, for Satan himself masquerades as an angel of light." Neither the saved nor the damned can return to the living, but the devil can make it appear as though they do. This has fooled the Catholics into believing that ghosts (*apparitionibus* and *revelationibus*) are the souls of the dead, bringing information from the beyond and seeking intercession. Bullinger, following the work of Ludwig Lavater, did not deny the existence of ghosts, but forbade any communication with them.[61]

Bullinger's brief rehearsal of his views on ghosts is followed by a lengthier assessment of the related matter of fortune-telling (*warsagen*). Whereas the attraction of commerce with ghosts resided in their ability to speak of the next world, the fortune-tellers draw people to them on account of more immediate interests: they can identify a thief or tell where stolen goods are to

58. Bullinger, *Wider der schwartze Kunst*, 301.

59. The value of astrology was disputed by the Protestant reformers. Philip Melanchthon's interest in astrology, for example, was not shared by Luther, who was deeply suspicious of the subject. See Charlotte Methuen, *Kepler's Tübingen: Stimulus to a Theological Mathematics* (Brookfield, Vt.: Ashgate, 1998), 80–82.

60. The classic Zurich treatment of the passage in 1 Samuel is found in Lavater, *Das Gespensterbuch,* fol. 68v. See Gordon, "Malevolent Ghosts," 87–109.

61. Gordon, "Malevolent Ghosts," 100.

be found.[62] Bullinger conceded the attractiveness of such talent; the people were desperate for such knowledge. His objection, now quite familiar, was that God had not permitted such power and it must, therefore, come from the devil. The devil had no interest in truth or justice, so the information divined by the fortune-tellers can only serve to undermine the community, such as through accusations against innocent people. Divination and fortune-telling turned people against one another by emphasizing their rival interests.

Prognosticators and fortune-tellers were a lesser form of the great evil perpetrated by magicians and witches. Essentially, Bullinger commented, these latter two were the same: they are bound to the devil by a pact and serve his purposes of undermining the Christian faith. This they do by performing wonders. Bullinger's account of witches is entirely conventional: they sleep with the devil, dance with him, and with his help damage crops and farm animals. The devil appears to them as a handsome man (Incubus) who promises to preserve them from all harm if they serve him faithfully; his words beguile them as the serpent tricked Eve. In the end, naturally, he betrays them and they find themselves in wretched poverty. What the devil gives with one hand, he removes with the other.[63]

Bullinger paused to consider a crucial question of "whether the magicians, those who practice the black arts, and witches are actually able to do that which they appear able to do?" In other words, is it all really a deception? Although Bullinger first cited the objection held by many that it is all done by sleight of hand, he accepted that this was not enough. The Bible provides plenty of evidence for the real work done by magicians opposed to God: the magicians of Pharaoh who could also produce a serpent, or Simon the sorcerer in Samaria. The explanation would have to rise above mere dismissal, and Bullinger wished to reveal a deeper purpose. Yes, it is the hand of the devil which makes such magic possible, but this magic does not entirely serve his ends. The sting in the tail is that the black magic is ultimately from God; the devil is an agent of God, making use of his own servants (witches, magicians, and sorcerers) as part of God's judgment upon the earth.

The biblical basis for this, Bullinger argued, is found in the story of Job.[64] God allows the devil to punish Job, to destroy his home and children, but not

---

62. Bullinger, *Wider der schwartze Kunst*, 302.

63. Bullinger, *Wider der schwartze Kunst*, 303.

64. Ludwig Lavater was to write a vernacular commentary on Job 19 in which the suffering man offers up his plaintive cry, asking how long he will be punished for his sins. *Des gedultigen Jobem Glauben vnnd Bekanntnß von todten/ vom jüngsten tag* (Zurich, 1577).

to kill him. Job is blameless, a godly man. "You will ask," Bullinger wrote, "why God permitted the devil and evil people to do such things?" The answer is simple and direct: God's judgment is always right, even when it remains beyond human comprehension (*unerforschlich*). God does whatever he deems just, and the only human response is to cling to his Word. The logic is brutal and unequivocal. God is testing humanity: he allows humans to suffer in order to see whether they will remain faithful or turn away (*abwenden*) from truth. The parable for Bullinger's understanding of divine testing is to be found in Deut. 13, where the performance of signs and wonders leads the people of Israel to seek another god. Bullinger cast the whole discussion of the supernatural in terms of idolatry: will the people remain faithful to true religion or be seduced into apostasy by outward forms? The question of idolatry stood at the root of the Zurich Reformation, and Bullinger's connection of popular belief with false religion enabled him to bring down the weight of more than a half century of Reformed writing. Zwingli had framed his argument against the mass in terms of Old Testament concepts of impurity and idolatry; Bullinger was building upon this connection.

The sum of Bullinger's argument is that, like the Israelites, Christians are required to serve one God, who will protect his faithful. Bullinger, following Zwingli, held that unbelief was the unforgivable sin.[65] It is the lack of faith which is being punished and the devil is God's servant in this respect. Those who do not love the truth will fall for his signs and tricks. What condemns the ungodly, however, is their failure to discern the true signs God has placed in the world. Bullinger used the same word (*Zeichen*) in arguing that God has provided sufficient signs of his will, but these are to be found in scripture. The faithless seek signs in the natural world, rejecting God's revealed will in the written Word.[66] But by no means was this intended to suggest that the magic of the devil was not real: "If you say, pious, god-fearing people also encounter magical spells (*verzauberung*), I would reply that it happens to them as it did to Job."

What might appear to be the arbitrary cruelty of God can only, Bullinger insisted, be understood as his pronouncement upon the sins of the people. The most dramatic and painful example of this was Job's loss of his children. The question is asked in *Wider der schwartze Kunst* as to whether children

---

65. See Huldrych Zwingli, *A Commentary of 1525*, where Zwingli wrote that the sin against the Holy Spirit which is never forgiven is unbelief. Cf. W. P. Stephens, *The Theology of Huldrych Zwingli* (Oxford: Clarendon, 1986), 148–49.

66. Bullinger, *Wider der schwartze Kunst*, 304.

could be held responsible for the actions of their parents. God is all-powerful, responded Bullinger; what he gives he can also remove, not only with regard to the children of Job, but "to all the children of the world." When parents see terrible things happen to their children they must take this as God's judgment upon their own lives. Yet, the tragedy of the loss of a child as a consequence of human sin should, in Bullinger's mind, make God's gracious gift of redemption seem all the more wondrous.

Bullinger's summation of his argument returned to his principal point regarding the relationship of God to the devil:

> God, our God and father is the lord, holder of power and ruler of all creation, visible and invisible. He leads and maintains humanity in his almighty governance, providence and order, and the devil has no power over humanity, can do no harm to either the soul, honour, body and good of [men and women] without the permission of God.

Further:

> When God allows the devil to do something it is for a particular purpose and for a particular reason. It is for the good of the faithful and to punish the wicked. [God] does not allow the devil and his minions to do whatever they wish. God rules over the demons and restrains them with his bridle (*Zaum*), as one sees in Job.[67]

Bullinger then concluded the *Wider der schwartze Kunst* with an enumeration of biblical texts, including Deut. 18 and Lev. 20, in which God's declaration that those who practiced the black arts be put to death is clearly pronounced.[68] The Mosaic law provided the framework for Bullinger's treatment of the devil and his arts; the work of conjurers and magicians was located in the proscription of other moral offenses such as blasphemy and adultery.[69] To these biblical texts Bullinger appended the decree in Imperial law mandating capital punishment for those who offend against the natural

---

67. Bullinger, *Wider der schwartze Kunst*, 304.

68. Deut. 18:9–13 reads "Let no-one be found among you who sacrifices his son or daughter in the fire, who practices divination or sorcery, interprets omens, engages in witchcraft, or casts spells, or who is a medium or spiritist or who consults the dead. Anyone who does these things is detestable to the Lord, and because of these detestable practices the Lord your God will drive out those nations before you. You must be blameless before the Lord your God."

69. Clark, *Thinking with Demons*, 462–63, has demonstrated the centrality of these biblical texts to the large number of demonologies produced in the second half of the sixteenth century.

order. In the end, Bullinger concluded, Saul died because he consulted a witch and not God, and for this God killed him.[70]

The power of the devil occupied the mind of the aging Bullinger for various reasons. The destitution and suffering of the people was more than sufficient evidence for the reality of the demonic in the world. The devil was no mere metaphor for sin and temptation, no hapless straw man to be knocked down by moral preaching, but a dark force which twisted the lives of men and women. Bullinger's historical understanding of the eschatological import of the devil was interwoven with his daily pastoral concern for the irregularity of most people's beliefs. The theological and pastoral were closely linked in Bullinger's conception of the devil because the whole matter turned on the issue of idolatry. The confusion of the external with the internal, which characterized popular piety in villages and towns, mirrored the repeated attempts of the Zurich reformers to articulate their view of the Eucharist in which the difference between the sign and the thing signified was clearly delineated. Just as the Zurich reformers were frustrated in their attempts to persuade Lutherans, and later Calvinists, of their understanding of the relationship between the spiritual and material, *Wider der schwartze Kunst* reflected a gloomy anxiety about the failure of the Reformed church to win over the people. Bullinger's discussion of the devil and of satanic powers in the world, while certainly grounded in a firm belief in the reality of dark forces, was also a means of explaining why the Reformed churches had not succeeded in rooting out Catholic practices and beliefs. The association of demonic practices with papistry bespoke the vexation of Protestants, particularly of the second generation of the Reformation, who lived in a period of religious syncretism in which older medieval beliefs and rituals were accommodated by the people to the new learning. The apparent willingness of the people to work out for themselves a relationship between what they were taught from the pulpit and in the catechism with ingrained beliefs and practices forced Protestant writers like Bullinger into an increasingly dualistic view of the universe, in which the struggle between idolatry and true religion could be variously portrayed as the Evangelical church against the Roman, and God against Satan.

Bullinger shared with his Protestant contemporaries the conviction that the work of the devil had to be understood within the bounds of God's sovereignty and the laws of nature, and his work on the demonic served as an important touchstone for Reformed spirituality in the second half of the sixteenth century. Yet he was aware that this protean opponent, with his ability

70. Clark, *Thinking with Demons*, 506.

to change forms to suit the needs of the people, offered something more to men and women than the church's counsel to faith and patience. Bullinger faced the limitations of sixteenth-century Protestant church writers who had to comfort their people with counseling to patience and trust in God's inscrutable judgments. The devil, in contrast, as the peddler of idolatry, knitted together the material and spiritual in a manner that was anathema to Protestants. In the end, however, the devil did render the reformers a great service. He forced them, in order to offer the people the care they craved, to consider how men and women could embrace their God in ways meaningful to them. The devil challenged the church to be more pastoral than he was.

Such an Impure, Cruel, and Savage Beast…

Images of the Werewolf in Demonological Works

Nicole Jacques-Lefèvre

The werewolf has been defined as a "kind of imp or witch changed into a wolf which, for a long time, made country folk afraid and is still used to frighten children." In this definition, a werewolf is thus a belief from a rustic past become a means of scaring the young. Chronological and ideological distance between a credulous past and insightful present is established at the outset. The entry next refers to classical authors: "Werewolves, or lycanthropes, are not caused by the overexcited imagination of the Middle Ages, as one would likely believe; Virgil, Solon, Strabonius, Pomponius Mela, Dionysius Afer, Varron, Saint Augustine, and Saint Jerome allege their existence." Nevertheless the definition returns at the end to werewolves' being "a very fine invention" from the domain of "medieval superstitions" as if the werewolf could not be imagined outside the supposed obscurantism of a caricatural Middle Ages. This Middle Ages is credited with a doctrinal unanimity that greatly simplifies an extremely complex problem: "All of the theologians and jurisconsuls of that time are unanimous in recognizing their existence."[1]

If in the medieval period unanimity about the nature and even the existence of the werewolf was far from evident, learned theorizing about this hybrid of humanity and animality continued into the early modern period. The theological and philosophical implications of Renaissance debates over lycanthropy are manifest most clearly in the greater framework of theorizing about witchcraft. The best known demonologists—all learned men, lawyers, theologians, and medical doctors, such as Henri Boguet, Jean Bodin, Pierre de Lancre, Martin Del Rio, or Johannes Weyer—devoted at least some pages,

Translated from the French by Kathryn A. Edwards.
    1. *Le Grand Larousse du XIXe siècle* (1873), s.v. "Loup-garou."

indeed some chapters, to werewolves. Three texts, written during the same twenty years, are particularly focused on this question, even at the dawn of the "rational" age: the *Dialogue de la lycanthropie* of Claude Prieur (1596), the *Discours de la lycanthropie* of Beauvois de Chauvincourt (1599), and *De la lycanthropie, transformation et extase des sorciers* by Jean de Nynauld (1615).[2]

THE HORROR OF THE LYCANTHROPE

In 1599, Lord Beauvois de Chauvincourt, a gentleman of Anjou, wrote the *Discours de la lycanthropie ou de la transformation des hommes en loups*. After having there recalled the evils of the French Wars of Religion, especially in the Anjou countryside, he evokes an additional scourge, "the bloody incursion of wolves maddened with hunger," and adds:

> But alas! when I myself came to ponder this said emergency, not a hair on my head stood upright, a fearful cold froze my heart, seized all of my limbs, not knowing if these are true and natural wolves or if, following common accounts, they are men so denatured, that they have made bastards of their first origin, leaving this divine form, and transforming themselves into such an impure, cruel, and savage beast![3]

The horror expressed here at the opening of Beauvois de Chauvincourt's *Discours de la lycanthropie*, a horror with no correspondence to a simple fear of wolves, is emblematic of the figure of the lycanthrope in the majority of the texts discussed here. This horror is born of distinctive symbolism associated with the lycanthrope, and it doubtless conditions the conjuration strategies which accompany its evocation by figures such as Beauvois de Chauvincourt. A clear example appears in the *Discours*: "Naturally a learned 'gentleman' should not totally take into account 'common allegations,' to which hypotheses about lycanthropy refer."

Certain traditions, which are not the subject of this essay, accept the figure of the werewolf without any problems. For example, northern and Germanic traditions express a conception of being quite different from that of the

---

2. See the critical edition which I have prepared, with my research team, of this last text: Jean de Nynauld, *De la lycanthropie, transformation et extase des sorciers (1615)*, édition critique augmentée d'études sur les lycanthropes et les loups-garous, ed. Nicole Jacques-Chaquin and Maxime Préaud (Paris : Frénésie, 1990).

3. Beauvois de Chauvincourt, *Discours de la lycanthropie ou de la transformation des hommes en loups* (Paris, 1599), 2.

Aristotelian Christianity which became the church's official position.[4] In these two traditions, he "becoming-animal" (*devenir-animal*), to take up an expression of Giles Deleuze and Felix Guattari, does not seem to cause any difficulty.[5] It is a part of existence (*l'être*) which does not exactly correspond with the Christian soul, but which does have something in common with the *spiritus phantasticus* mentioned by Saint Augustine in book 18 of the *City of God*. It is sometimes designated, perhaps a bit simplistically, as a "double," which can, in moments of sleep or trance, abandon the body, appear in animal form, and can initiate experiences. The memory of these experiences continues after reunification of the individual. Here there are two essential characteristics: the wounds eventually carried on this double will be found on the body of the person, and this person must stay intact while being a werewolf under penalty of seeing the double incapable of reintegrating with the first form.

This particular conception of existence, and especially of certain beings, has shamanistic characteristics, studied by Carlo Ginzburg in *Night Battles*, and is found in other parts of Europe.[6] Like Ginzburg's *benandanti*, Lithuanian werewolves are seen to fight on the side of good against witches.[7] The writings of Herodotus, Olaus Magnus, and Gaspard Peucer, among others, had restored these familiar beliefs to Renaissance men, and the same stories about troops of wolf-men crossing certain very precise epochs and, for a limited time, city limits are suggested in the Renaissance texts mentioned above, like those of the ancient literary witnesses. But these narrations are then themselves doubled by a theorizing which tends, not without difficulties, to mitigate disturbing effects.

There definitely is a disturbing effect in the figure of the werewolf, which gives him a specific status in demonological texts. These texts, as Michel de Certeau has written, had an undeniable function of cultural homogenization, because they integrated quite readily an entire body of pagan cultural elements, from the Sibyls to Melusine or to the *chevalier au cygne*, from Merlin to the Wild Hunt, into a Christian symbolic framework. It should then suffice to interpret this figure according to demonological tests, without denying the

4.   Studied today, aside from the research in Scandinavian universities, by Claude Lecouteux. See esp. Claude Lecouteux, *Fées, sorcières et loups-garous au Moyen Age: Histoire du double* (Paris: Imago, 1992).

5.   Gilles Deleuze and Felix Guattari, *Capitalisme et schizophrénie: Mille plateaux* (Paris: Editions du Minuit, 1980), 284 ff.

6.   Carlo Ginzburg, *The Night Battles: Witchcraft and Agrarian Cults in the Sixteenth and Seventeenth Centuries* (Baltimore: Johns Hopkins University Press, 1983), trans. of idem, *I Benandanti: Stregonevia e culti agrari tra Cinquecento e Seicento* (Turin: Einaudi, 1966).

7.   See Mircea Eliade, *Occultisme, sorcellerie et modes culturelles* (Paris: Gallimard, 1976).

reality of the object of belief. In a sense, this task is a simple problem of herme-neutics. The physical and theological justification of the witches' flight, the existence of the sabbat or diabolical copulation, would not pose much more of a problem, at least at the level of theoretical possibilities. On the other hand, metamorphosis in general, and lycanthropy in particular—except for the case of lycanthropy as an illness more or less likened to an extreme form of melancholy—has appeared as a stumbling block in these writings. Not only do disagreements arise among theoreticians, but very odd textual strategies are used where one can find an echo of that "horror" evoked by Beauvois de Chauvincourt.

There is definite agreement in the demonological texts that the werewolf is a diabolical figure and is associated with witchcraft. There is also agree-ment that certain witches really do practice acts of cannibalism and that chil-dren are their favorite food. Opinions diverge when it is a question of knowing if these sorcerers—who have confessed to the metamorphoses and have been seen in the form of a werewolf, recognizable by a somewhat special morphology in comparison to true wolves—have undergone a true meta-morphosis or if there is only a semblance, an effect of the skill of Satan, that great master of illusion.

THE THEOLOGICAL DEBATE

"There is much disputing," as the great judge of Dole, Henri Boguet, wrote in 1606 in his *Discours exécrable des sorciers*, "as to whether it is possible for men to be changed into beasts, some affirming the possibility, whilst others deny it; and there are ample grounds for both views."[8] With the notable exception of Jean Bodin and several other, less celebrated authors like Jean de Sponde, Cas-par Peucer, and Joachim Camerarius, most demonologists nevertheless worked to demonstrate the illusory character of such physical transformations.[9] At the heart of the debate was a theological quarrel, which is summarized here, about the powers of demons.[10] For the majority of authors, a demon should

8. Henri Boguet, *Discours exécrable des sorciers: Ensemble leur procez faicts depuis 2 ans en çà en divers endroicts de la France...* (Rouen, 1606; repr. with preface by Maxime Préaud, Marseille: Laffitte Reprints, 1979), 262. All translations of Boguet, *Discours*, are from *An Examen of Witches ...* trans. E. Allen Ashwin, ed. Montague Summers (1929; repr., New York: Barnes & Noble, 1971), here 138.

9. For a more general discussion of the problems posed by diabolical illusions, see Nicole Jacques-Chaquin, "Lumière noire et anamorphoses: Pour une optique diabolique," in *Le siècle de la lumière, 1600–1715*, ed. Christian Biet and Vincent Jullien (Fontenay-aux-Roses: ENS Editions, 1997).

10. This quarrel has been analyzed in depth in other studies; see, for example, Nicole Jacques-Chaquin, "Jean Bodin: Une lecture politique et philosophique de la sorcellerie," in *Jean Bodin: Nature,*

not know how to modify the universal order established by God, to act against essences, or to produce natural forms unless these forms are of imperfect animals born by corruption or putrefaction.[11] The demon cannot then change a human body into an animal's body. This first controversy is reflected in a second, both metaphysical and religious, on the nature of man and, particularly, on the relation between the soul and the body. The demonstration used by demonologists is based on the neo-Aristotelian conception of the nonseparability of the body and soul, the body constituting the form of the soul. As the Jesuit Martin Del Rio writes, "It is impossible that the human soul should be able to give form to the body of a brute beast. No more could the body of a horse contain the soul of a lion or the body of a man the soul of a horse. Every substantial form requires inclinations specific and suitable to itself in order to communicate with its being."[12] The most common conclusion to this discussion is well summarized by Pierre de Lancre in his *Tableau de l'inconstance des mauvais anges et démons*: "the transmutations, which one reads that magicians and witches do, do not truly and essentially happen, but only in appearance and with diabolical prestige and illusion."[13]

In relation to this common demonology, the position of Bodin is original and of interest; it enters into the great philosophical debate about nature as well as into the political issues of the author.[14] Bodin accuses his adversaries of thoughtlessly mixing together books on the metaphysical and the material and referring unduly to nature because:

---

histoire, droit et politique, ed. Charles Yves Zarka (Paris: PUF, 1996); idem, "Nynauld, Bodin et let autres: Les enjeux d'une métamorphose textuelle," in Jean de Nynauld, *De la lycanthropie, transformation et extase des sorciers ou les astuces du Diable sont mises en évidence…; avec la réfutation des argumens contraires que Bodin allègue* (Paris, 1615); and idem, "Le théosophe et la sorcière: Deux imaginaires du monde des signes: Études sur l'imaginaire saint-martinien et sur la démonologie," 4 vols. (thesis, Université de Lille, n.d.), esp. vol. 4, "Structure et enjeux de quelques grands textes démonologiques."

11. See esp. Boguet, *Discours exécrable des sorciers*, 277.

12. Martin Antoine Del Rio, 3 vols., *Disqvisitionvm magicarvm libri sex, in tres tomos partiti* (Louvain, 1599–1601); idem, *Les controuerses et recherches magiques de Martin Delrio…: Diuisees en six liures, ausquels sont exactement & doctement confutees les sciences curieuses, les vanitez & superstitions de toute la magie: Auecques la maniere de proceder en iustice contre les magiciens & sorciers, accommodee à l'instruction des confesseurs…*, trans. André du Chesne (Paris, 1611), 208.

13. Pierre de Lancre, *Tableav de l'inconstance des mavvais anges et demons, ov il est amplement traicté des sorciers, & de la sorcelerie* (Paris, 1612), 244; repr. with notes and introduction by Nicole Jacques-Chaquin, *Tableau de l'inconstance des mauvais anges et démons: Où il est amplement traité des sorciers et de la sorcellerie* (Paris: Auber, 1982).

14. See Jacques-Chaquin, "Jean Bodin: Une lecture politique."

the great works and wonders of God are impossible by nature, and in all cases true: and the actions of the intelligences, and all that is metaphysics, are impossible by nature, which is the reason why metaphysics is wholly distinct and different from the physics, which touches only nature. One thus should not measure the actions of the spirits and demons on the effects of nature.[15]

Lycanthropy is thus situated in a vision of the whole. God, the "first eternal cause," can at the level of second causes, grant great power to one of His creatures. Like the ruler in Plato's *Republic,* nothing restrains God, not even respect for natural laws. He can change universal laws or delegate His powers. But Bodin also redefines the concept of the human form: the "essential form" of the being from which the soul is effectively inseparable is not body, which is only a "figure," but reason. In the case of lycanthropy, "if the human figure changes, the spirit and reason remain in their entirety." Then reason, the essential characteristic of man, stays untouched by the metamorphosis; on the other hand, reason is in an untenable, scandalous promiscuity with the animal body. Bodin was judged by his colleagues to be the worst of the sorcerers for having dared to make that connection.[16]

The figure of the lycanthrope is thus at heart a reflection on the definition of nature, being, and man. For the majority of these authors, the theoretical discussion put at a distance an anxiety, an uneasiness about the possible source of an intact unity for this personage, who is not himself content with juxtaposing—like some costumer for a seventeenth-century court ballet—the figure of the wolf and the man, but who mixes them intimately. It was a scandalous, inadmissible, indeed unrepresentable figure to which the rhetorical texts juxtapose, in order to conjure it better, an entire series of hypotheses and explanations destined to explain that certain individuals might have been able to believe themselves transformed and that the spectators might have been able to believe that they saw werewolves. At the price of often extreme subtleties, these explanations want to substitute for an unthinkable apparition a rational justification that included the powers granted to the devil by Christian tradition. The devil—great physician, doctor, manipulator, even artist, creator of games of water and mirrors, of anamorphosis, of true theatrical staging—acts on the interior as on the exterior of the actors and spectators of

15. Jean Bodin, *De la démonomanie des sorciers* (Paris, 1580; repr. s.l.: Gutenberg Reprint, 1979), 204v–205.

16. For a more complete discussion of the problems of lycanthropy from a metaphysical perspective, see Jacques-Chaquin, "Nynauld, Bodin et les autres."

the drama, on the humors and the imagination, but also on the surrounding air, objects, and bodies. To evoke the werewolf, writes Claude Prieur, one must speak about simulacras and images, of "magic, evil deeds, enchantment, witchcraft, charms, phantasms, dazzlement, sensory deception, illusion, or mockery," of "prestige."[17]

One discourse alone integrates the figure of the man-animal without too much problem. It is moral philosophy, of which one of the most cited representatives is Boethius and his *Consolation of Philosophy*. The relations between man and beast are codified as a metaphor for, to cite Beauvois de Chauvincourt again, "the sensual appetite after which the soul lets itself move too easily."[18] But this is quite far from the monstrous reality of the Renaissance man-wolf.

THE SYMBOLISM OF THE WOLF

Other arguments further repudiate this figure of the werewolf. For Boguet, for example, "it would be a shameful thing for man, to whom all the beasts of the earth are subject, to be clothed in the form of a beast. For the Law has so much respect for the human face, since it was formed in the likeness of celestial beauty, that it has not permitted it to be disfigured... for any crime."[19] The same reaffirmation of an unbreakable divide between animal and man, image of God and master of animals from the beginning, appears in the text of Beauvois de Chauvincourt, who refuses to think about the possibility that man, "abandoning this beautiful human representation, can so shred his humanity that, being stripped, he redresses himself in the form of unreasoning beasts."[20]

The symbolism proper to the wolf came gradually to accentuate the "repugnancy," in the philosophical sense of the term, in just conceiving of a possible mixture of the two natures. Even after the Fall, which deprived man of his privilege of absolute mastery over the animal world, a part of his original prerogatives remains. For example, Beauvois de Chauvincourt argues that "although wild beasts by their nature are enemies of mankind, nevertheless they revere man as their master and lord, and, from being untamable, change their savage and solitary style into a companionable one."[21] But the wolf is not susceptible to being tamed, as treatises on hunting, among others,

17. Claude Prieur, *Dialogue de la lycanthropie ou transformation des hommes en loups, vulgairement dits loups-garous, et si telle se peut faire* (Louvain, 1596), 92, 101.
18. Chauvincourt, *Discours de la lycanthropie*, 3–4.
19. Boguet, *Discours exécrable des sorciers*, 275; Summers, ed., *An Examen of Witches*, 145.
20. Chauvincourt, *Discours de la lycanthropie*, 3–4.
21. Chauvincourt, *Discours de la lycanthropie*, 3–4.

recall. The wolf has, writes Gaston Phoebus, a "bad nature," from which Robert de Salnove deduces the necessity of a wild hunt, "the most animated and heated, by the aversion which one naturally has against this animal."[22] At the same time, the wolf is, as another text calls it, a "beast made mundane" which lives in society, in the immediate margins of human territory.[23]

NARRATION

What is the importance of the numerous accounts, which nineteenth- and twentieth-century collections of popular legends recovered?[24] If Bodin is one of the rare demonologists to affirm the reality of the metamorphosis, recollections of metamorphosed men and women are not, however, missing from demonological texts. All these authors admit that the devil, this manipulator of images, works hard to maintain a belief in which he has great interest so as to "diffuse," as the authors of the *Malleus Maleficarum* had already written, "the error of pagans" and to exploit the insatiable taste of men for "stories" that appeal to their curiosity and their gullibility, and turn them away from the true faith.[25] The demonologists, however, did not deprive themselves of the right to hold opinions based on these accounts and, in order to produce a more effective narrative, they quite often forgot their theoretical convictions for an instant. Thus Boguet recounts in detail and affirms, according to "one who may be believed, who went that way fifteen days after this thing had happened,"[26] the classic story of a hunter attacked by a monstrous wolf from which he succeeds in cutting off one of the paws, which has a golden ring on it. Staying that same evening in a castle, the hunter ascertains that the lady of the castle, whose husband has recognized his ring, has a bloody bandage on her arm. During the course of the narration no sign reveals the critical position of the narrator, who only becomes a theoretician again after having transcribed a

22. Gaston Phoebus, *La chasse de Gaston Phoebus, comte de Foixe* (Paris, 1897), 70; Robert de Salnove, *La Vénerie royale* (Paris, 1655), 213. See Sophie Houdard, ""Le loup-garou ou les limites de l'animalité," in Nynauld, *De la lycanthropie* (1990). Houdard notes that the wolf is "the animal which, at both the zoological and symbolic level, plays most on the limits which separate it from man: its extreme wildness and its proximity to man make it the animal most likely to question ... the coherence of humanity."

23. Commentary of d'Auge on the arrest of Gilles Grenier. See Aristide Dey, Michel Collée, and Jules Finot, *Histoire de la sorcellerie au Comté de Bourgogne* (1861; repr., Marseille: Laffitte reprints, 1983).

24. See Lise Andries, "Contes du loup," in Nynauld, *De la lycanthropie* (1990).

25. Henric Institoris and Jakob Sprenger, *Le marteau des sorcières*, trans. and ed. Amand Danet (Paris: Plon, 1973), 241, 472.

26. Boguet, *Discours exécrable des sorciers*, 266–68; Summers, ed., *An Examen of Witches*, 141.

certain number of these extraordinary stories. Then he recalls pedantically, "Nevertheless it has always been my opinion that lycanthropy is an illusion, and that the metamorphosis of man into a beast is impossible."[27]

Beauvois de Chauvincourt also does not escape the rule that denies the reality of the metamorphosis, but he does not question himself less about "these strange cases that we see with our own eyes" and, before telling a werewolf story, gives, for example, the testimony of a "certain person, not a liar, and whose life and morals have been sufficiently approved."[28] As another sign of the disquiet provoked by the figure of the werewolf, the texts waver between theory and fiction, the first taking sometimes the form of fantasy when the authors describe the satanic manipulations against the supposed lycanthrope and his spectators, while the fiction gives all the proofs of truthfulness. It is not by chance that Nicholas Malebranche, in the *Recherche de la vérité*, takes the werewolf as the starting point to meditate on the imagination and the means of transmitting belief.[29]

The attempts to portray the werewolf, such as they appear in the accounts of witnesses, are much more interesting to the extent that they mark the location of the untenable. In this way Montaigne evokes the werewolf in the *Apology of Raymond de Sebond*: "half-breed and ambiguous form(s) between human and brutish nature." The form of the werewolf is never stable. Neither wolf nor man, he is at the same time both the one and the other in a continuous mutation: "the said beast being bigger and shorter than a wolf, with a reddish coat, a short tail; which beast withdrew from her around ten or twelve paces, sat on his hindquarters, as a dog does, considering with a furious expression what was the reason that she fled; that this beast has a head smaller than a wolf." Again, more precisely, the absence of a tail is cited: "the two forefeet like a man's hands covered on the top with hair," the "hands resembling paws," or again "a wolf…which had toes on the hindfeet like those of a person."[30] The tales push these descriptions to the limit, at the same time stating the failure of differentiating between man and animal and playing with the "character at once the antithesis and fusion of the two kingdoms." The story

---

27. Boguet, *Discours exécrable des sorciers*, 272; Summers, ed., *An Examen of Witches*, 143.

28. Chauvincourt, *Discours de la lycanthropie*, 29.

29. See Nicole Jacques-Chaquin, "La passion des sciences interdites: Curiosité et démonologie (XVème–XVIIIème siècles)," in *Curiosité et Libido sciendi, de la Renaissance aux Lumières*, 2 vols., ed. Nicole Jacques-Chaquin and Sophie Houdard (Fontenay-aux-Roses: ENS Éditions, 1999).

30. See Michel Meurger, "L'homme-loup et son témoin: Construction d'une factualité lycanthropique," in Nynauld, *De la lycanthropie* (1990); de Lancre, *Tableau* (1982), 257; Boguet, *Discours exécrable des sorciers*, 284; Summers, ed., *An Examen of Witches*, 149.

of Bretagne thus mentions "this wolf which rolled on the ground, mixed with the father, to the point of seeming to believe, [because of] clothes on its fur, that one thing alone made the two."[31] On the other hand, just as one could remark that medieval literary texts, like the *Lai du Bisclavret*, carefully avoided describing the metamorphosis scene, the demonologists insist on the manifestly human comportment of werewolves in order to show better that it is only a matter of a disguise. Thus de Lancre writes:

> It is also necessary to notice, to show that it was not truly and really transformed into a werewolf, neither in body nor in heart, because, as the witnesses said, or when he took these girls by their dress or other clothing to eat them, he did not tear their dress at all. With the assistance of the devil, the victims were rather stripped of their coats or garderobes, while no animal nor true wolf would be able to strip them clearly without tearing them. Moreover, it took them by the throat with its teeth, as a natural man would, and not by its legs, which is normal for wolves.[32]

If there is a resemblance in figure and behavior, it is explained by the lifestyles of those men who, half sick and half witches, think themselves wolves and, living like that, commit "brutal and bestial" actions; we are then in some sort of realist continuation of Boethius's moral philosophy. The metaphor takes form and deforms the body even of man, as in the illustrations of physiognomy treatises, but without ever going to the point where doubt could be resolved. De Lancre still makes the comparison but not with the ambiguity about nature; men have then, he writes: "frightening, gleaming eyes like wolves, ravage and are cruel like wolves,...have a taste for human flesh like wolves. Their teeth and nails are strong and sharpened like those of wolves,...they run on four paws;...when they run together they are used to leave from their hunt, some with the others, and if they are alone they howl to call the others." More precisely, he describes in these terms the young Jean Grenier, a wild child who was sentenced to spend his life in a convent: "He had very bright teeth, larger than normal...broken and half-black from gnawing animals and people; his nails also [were] long and entirely black from the root to the end."[33]

Another werewolf mentioned by Beauvois de Chauvincourt, Jacques Rollet, who was captured near Nantes, is described as:

31. Andries, "Contes du loup," in Nynauld, *De la lycanthropie*.
32. De Lancre, *Tableau* (1982), 320.
33. De Lancre, *Tableau* (1982), 293, 315.

so stinking and revolting that no one in the world can approach him; [he is] covered with grease as thick as two fingers' all over his body, his gaze is extremely misleading, his eyebrows frowning, his eyes set deeply in his head, which are indices and relevant suggestions, in addition to his confessions, that having lived this miserable life for so long, it seemed to have already removed all of his humanity, and [he] did not seem, nor represent himself anymore as man except in his physical features, having been bastardized and subjected by his master, Satan, to brutality....[34]

The explanation for Rollet's appearance and behavior wavers between diabolical intervention, sensual appetite, and "the bad habits and food of this poor Rollet before today," which were responsible for the impurity that makes "a vital spirit equally impure and morose." We should add here a zoophilic phantasm, the werewolf, which is a part of two kingdoms, appears then as "the incarnation of the most monstrous and intolerable erotic partner—and also the most fascinating," to use the words of Lise Andries.[35] Certain demonologists even go so far as to mention that lycanthropes take their pleasure with real female wolves.

THE WEREWOLF AND POLITICS

A figure of disorder, of trouble which must absolutely be warded off, the lycanthrope also tells something about politics. Witchcraft often appears in the texts already mentioned as a representation of social or political degeneration. In Plato's *Republic* (565d) it is the king's metamorphosis into a tyrant that gives birth to the emergence of the werewolf figure. In certain traditions, still alive in fourteenth-century Normandy, for example, the *varouage* designates a nighttime journey that an excommunicated individual accomplished on generally set dates, from Christmas to Candlemas or during Advent, and for a set length of time, most often four or seven years. These journeys were linked to the practice of monitories in which the threat of excommunication was seen as compelling the author of a crime to denounce himself or witnesses to reveal themselves. According to a Norman folklorist of the nineteenth century, Louis Dubois, "the peasants were persuaded that if, despite the different publications of the monitories at the sermon of the mass, the

---

34. Chauvincourt, *Discours de la lycanthropie*, 34.
35. Andries, "Contes du loup," in Nynauld, *De la lycanthropie*.

criminal remained unknown and let the third publication pass, he belonged to the devil and was obliged to run as a werewolf."[36]

According to informers, there was a question of either a true metamorphosis or the use of a wolf skin, but whether real or symbolic, in these accounts the metamorphosis symbolizes the placement of society's ban through solemn expulsion outside of the church's heart. The expulsion was generally only for a limited period, and we find a curious echo in two of the most celebrated legal cases brought against lycanthropes: that of Jacques Roulet, where the confession mentions among the causes of his metamorphosis his having been "excommunicated by a sentence of excommunication," and the case told by de Lancre about Jean Grenier, who calls himself the "son of a priest."[37] In this way sometimes the excluded person, who is not himself guilty, takes collective guilt onto himself. Thus, in the example given by Girard de Barri, some couples take turns every seven years living in the forest in the form of wolves to expiate the curse which a saint placed on their village.[38] Other mythical accounts from southern and northern Europe alike—found in the works of Pliny the Elder, Herodotus, and Olaus Magnus—evoke calendrical rituals. In some accounts, the transformation of some of the city's members occurs on precise and significant dates. In others, the "heroes" cross a river, a symbolic limit of the civilized domain into which they will only be reintegrated after a variable time during which they return to "savagery."

Sometimes the entire group is struck. Nynauld cites, after many others, the cases of Lycaon and the Arcades, who "lived like a wolf" and "fed themselves on raw meat."[39] We find another moral reinterpretation of the metamorphosis, but it is characteristic that here a grave symbolic transgression may be alluded to. The importance of cannibalism in the figure of the witch-werewolf is well known.

Moreover, the figure of the wolf appears frequently in the reports of banishment in the Germano-Scandinavian realms. It is not accidental that

36. Louis Dubois, *Recherches archéologiques, historiques, biographiques et littéraires sur la Normandie* (Paris: Dumolin, 1843), 301.

37. Thus he was subject to excommunication because of the original curse; see Jules Baissac, *Les Grands jours de la sorcellerie* (1890; Marseille: Laffittee Reprints 1982), 369.

38. See Laurence Harf-Lancner, "La métamorphose illusoire; des théories chrétiennes de la métamorphose aux images médiévales du loup-garou," *Annales ESC* (1985); and idem, *Métamorphose et bestiaire fantastique au Moyen Age*, ed. Laurence Harf-Lancner (Paris: Ecole Normale Supérieure de Jeunes Filles, 1985), no. 28.

39. Nynauld, *De la lycanthropie* (1990), 104.

Giorgio Agamben took, in his translation of *Homo sacer*, the werewolf as one of the examples of this figure, where the sacred and the impure are in essence indistinguishable, at the same time liable to great shame and unable to be sacrificed.[40] He recalls that the werewolf is "from the beginning he who had been banished from the community" and who, incarnating the "threshold of indifference and of passage between animal and man," can symbolize all "exceptional states through which...the city is dissolved and men enter a zone of indifference with the deer." Did Bodin have in mind the text of the *Republic* (565d), also cited by Agamben, where Plato brings together the transformation of the protector into a tyrant and the arcadian myth of Zeus, when he makes the bad king a powerful sorcerer? One could cite also the passage from the *Tragedies* entitled "The Gilded Chamber," in which the judges of this judicial chamber are explicitly described by Agrippa d'Aubigné as lycanthropes.[41]

In Renaissance demonological texts, the werewolf—while participating in this symbolism of a monstrous political evolution—appears more specifically linked to one of the most grave aspects of political and religious degeneration, a situation which pushed the social body to the side of a particularly monstrous extraordinary event, that is, civil war. The text of Beauvois de Chauvincourt is explicitly situated in the framework of civil war, and this treatise is one of those that guides my study. It is into this same framework that Franciscan Claude Prieur places himself in *Dialogue de la lycanthropie ou transformation des hommes en loups, vulgairement dits loups-garous, et si telle se peut faire* (1596). It opens with a nostalgic evocation of platonic banquets in which the "sociable friendship (through which man lets himself know that he is a man)" participates in the definition of a "natural and essential distinction of humanity." Prieur there opposes the situation of the "[present] times and sufferings as much in general as in particular"; the evocation of the "sad and melancholic company" which he stages in his text reflects the "common sufferings" of the "same disaster" that affects all of a social body at war with itself where "men waging war against each other are maddened against the blood of their true neighbors," and where we see "one province against another, city against city, father against son, son against father." When the unity of the

---

40. *Homo sacer: Le pouvoir souverain et la vie nue*, trans. Giorgio Agamben (Paris: Seuil, 1997), 116ff. Agamben's words from a definition by Jean-Luc Nancy of the "ban" as "constrained to appear absolutely under the law as such and in totality," the banished "is delivered complete to the law," being "also abandoned beyond all of its jurisdiction," in *L'impératif catégorique* (Paris: n.p., 1983), 149–50.

41. Agrippa d'Aubigné, *Les Tragiques*, in *Les Oeuvres Complètes* (Paris: Pleiade, 1969), 95.

realm and religious unity are jointly broken, one runs afoul of an almost inexpressible reality: the same becomes the Other all the while remaining the same. Then "ravishing wolves," the natural and thinkable effects of divine wrath after Adam's fall, no longer appear. Now they are werewolves, whose position is radically anomalous in relation both to the social fabric of the community and to all of the animal species and those who symbolize the "vicious and enormous excesses" of the time.[42]

Thus violence, an irrecoverable, intransformable violence—contrary to the violence of the warrior who can, after a ritual bath, reintegrate into the community that they have saved by delivering their being temporarily to bloody savagery—is linked to the figure of the werewolf. First there is the violence of cannibalism; all the authors accentuate the horror of this transgression, which does not even spare the children of witches, and bring out scenes of bloody carnage, mutilated bodies, and scattered limbs. There is also the violence of physical marks, which for the community, distinguish the werewolf in human form: "clothes torn apart, bodies soiled and torn by brambles, almost flayed alive...."

Yet violence is also found at the level of medical representation; one type of text which, since antiquity, has been concerned with the lycanthrope is the medical corpus. Lycanthropy is in effect considered as one of the extreme forms of melancholy, and the demonologists invoke willingly this "wolf folly" to distinguish it more clearly from witch lycanthropy. These medical texts developed a portrait of a melancholic lycanthrope, which reappears everywhere, even in the *Encyclopedia* of Diderot in an article which mentions:

> [T]his type of melancholy in which men believe themselves transformed into wolves; and in consequence, they imitate all of their actions; following their example, they leave their house at night, they roam around graves, they take refuge there, mix and fight with ferocious beasts, and often risk their life, their health in these kinds of combat.... They have a pale face, sunken eyes, bewildered expression, dry tongue and mouth, an immoderate thirst, sometimes also bruised, torn legs, fruits of their nocturnal debates....

Among the cures, the *Encyclopedia* finally notes that one must "pay attention to chain them up to keep them from going out at night and from going to risk

---

42. Prieur, *Dialogue de la lycanthropie*, 17.

their life among the most ferocious animals, if one has no other means to contain them."[43]

The violence appears at the level of even the sick person's body, the internal body, prey to the violence of the humors which fight among themselves, because of the effects of excessive black bile, to express the same thing. The impulse to autodestruct is here carried to its highest point. It is this same violence, carried this time to an unthinkable level, that expresses itself in the theoretical reflections which our authors summarize when questioning the possibility of human forms' slipping into an animal body.

It is all a problem of the relationship between being and appearance which is here posed by those who, according to Claude Prieur "seem to be what they are not," who "carry more than truth lets us believe," and of whom, in a significant question, the author asks himself "how one must name such an appearance or such a body."[44] The interrogation about naming is a new expression of the issue of self-identity which makes the disquieting figure of the werewolf ambiguous.

CONCLUSION

The werewolf is an overdetermined figure, seeing that it inherits all of the attitudes underlying the real wolf, but also the tradition which metaphorically situates the relations between man and animal in terms of individual or social morality. The werewolf is also condemned, because it makes itself guilty of cannibalism. Sometimes it has been suggested that the possible influence of a famine, or simply a very peculiar case of dementia, would have led certain individuals actually to attack children in order to eat them. It is more likely that in the accusers' unconscious the ancient hatred of this absolute crime rose up and that the accusers then transformed the accused into a kind of expiatory victim. In this respect, the story of Lycaon as it is recounted by Ovid is quite interesting; Lycaon is turned into a wolf after having made Jupiter eat human flesh. One cannot help but mention here another sort of inaugural meal and one which precisely defines humanity in relation to divinity and animality: that which Prometheus offers to Jupiter.[45] It can then be suggested that the werewolf functions symbolically as an "anti-Prometheus"; it constantly threatens the ontological status of being human.

43. *Encyclopedie, ou Dictionnaire raisonée des sciences, des arts et des métiers* (1751–72), s.v. "Lycanthropie."

44. Prieur, *Dialogue de la lycanthropie,* 100.

45. See Jean-Pierre Vernant and Marcel Détienne, *La cuisine du sacrifice en pays grec* (Paris: Gallimard, 1979), 33.

The werewolf also links some of the ambiguous figures cited by Pierre Vernant which in the mind belong to a "zone of the supernatural," characterized by nonconformity, to the principle of contradiction.[46] Not only is the werewolf neither man nor beast, considering that the metamorphosis is reversible, but it keeps, as a wolf, certain traits of its humanity: its reason and sometimes a part of the human body. On the other hand, the werewolf rarely kills like a wolf; according to Boguet, it strangles, drags its victims across rocks, or even uses a knife and, respecting certain taboos, does not eat the head nor the right side of its victim. At the limit of savagery, it is neither found in the city nor in an "other" territory; it is on the margins (pasture lands, for example). The extreme figure of the *versipelles* of Padua is significant: having affirmed that his fur was "within," he was burned alive by his executioners, who miserably tried to gauge the symbolic system with the measurement of reality, as do the majority of our authors, who quote this history like proof of the illusory character of the metamorphosis.[47]

The werewolf is fantastically doubled: not successively man and wolf but both at the same time, it is a manifestation of the Other, where "wild and civilized exist side by side certainly in opposition, but also thoroughly interpenetrated."[48] Carrier of sacred characteristics, of which the relation to the diabolical (with which the demonologists invest it) is only an avatar, the werewolf is ambivalent. Even if texts tend to reduce it into only its evil aspect, however, de Lancre echoes other traditions, referred to at the beginning of this study.[49] "Many good authors," wrote Caspar Peucer as quoted by de Lancre in the *Traité des mauvais anges*, "do not put the lycanthropes at the level of sorcerers where their judicial enemies place them... the lycanthropes boast of being deputed to hunt witches."[50] Here again, to the extent it is an instrument symbolic of expulsions and reintegrations, the werewolf seems to work with symbolic cohesions *at the same time* that it incarnates the permanent risk of disintegration.

It is not surprising that the symbolism of the werewolf knew a reactivation in a period of civil war. While respect for agonistic ritual allows the differentiation of adversaries, the civil war is "chaos, pure violence, as with

46. Jean-Pierre Vernant, *La mort dans les yeux* (Paris: Hachette, 1985).

47. Jacob Fincel, *Wunderzeichen: Warhafftige Beschreibung und gründlich Verzeichnis schrecklicher Wunderzeichen und Geschichten* (Frankfurt am Main, 1556–57).

48. Vernant, *La mort dans les yeux*, 17.

49. Eliade, *Occultisme*.

50. De Lancre, *Traité des mauvais anges* (1982), 313.

savage beasts who know neither rule nor justice."[51] For the city, it is the absolute risk of autodestruction. With Beauvois de Chauvincourt and Prieur, the community sees clearly how the specificity of the werewolf (even better than a wild beast) makes it an apt metaphor for social ills, the loss of values, the individual and collective depravation and degeneration. Because, writes Prieur, "there is no savage beast wilder than man if he is left to himself."[52] More than animality, human impulses lead to fear when pushed to their limits, outside of the norms and habitual controls of socialization.

As can be maintained for all cases of strongly symbolic figures, that of the werewolf always exceeds all the functions that we can assign to it, as well as the schemas to which the demonologists attempted to reduce it. Held as a type of diabolical "representation," the werewolf is rather an irrepresentable figure. Having paid attention to the importance of myth, we possess elsewhere few images of the werewolf. It is, as Claude Prieur writes, that werewolves "seem to be always what they are not."[53] To put it another way, they can only define themselves in the absence of being.

51. Vernant, *La mort dans les yeux*, 24.
52. Prieur, *Dialogue de la lycanthropie*, 100.
53. Prieur, *Dialogue de la lycanthropie*, 18.

CHARCOT, FREUD, AND THE DEMONS

H. C. Erik Midelfort

While many branches of history have registered the impact of psychohistory, one of the more fruitful has been the study of European witchcraft. This is perhaps understandable because psychological experts are often called in when people confront weird behavior, actions that appear irrational and hard to understand. If witchcraft seemed no more irrational than embezzlement, and if witchcraft trials were no more unusual than cases of petty theft, people would probably be less inclined to think of calling in the shrinks. In recent years a number of stimulating histories have developed that claim the support or even the inspiration of psychology. Three of the more successful works in English include John Demos's effort to employ the psychoanalytic theories of Heinz Kohut to explain the narcissist tensions within the witchcraft suspicions and trials of early New England; Lyndal Roper's application of the theories of Melanie Klein in order to explain the fantasies of witches and witchhunters in certain south German witchcraft trials; and Robin Briggs's use of evolutionary psychology to illumine the archetypal images of the witch, the witches' sabbat, and the devil in the general history of mankind.[1] One could easily extend this list, but these three works suffice to illustrate an important and little-discussed problem:[2] How is it that such diverse psychological approaches can all claim to explain, clarify, or illuminate the history of witchcraft? Is it true that almost any psychological method, if applied intelligently,

1. John Demos, *Entertaining Satan: Witchcraft and the Culture of Early New England* (New York: Oxford University Press, 1982); Lyndal Roper, *Oedipus and the Devil: Witchcraft, Sexuality, and Religion in Early Modern Europe* (New York: Routledge, 1994); Robin Briggs, *Witches and Neighbours: The Social and Cultural Context of European Witchcraft* (London: HarperCollins, 1996).

2. For an earlier example, see Ralph Linton, *Culture and Mental Disorders*, ed. George Devereux (Springfield, Ill.: Thomas, 1956), 109–11, 118, for reflections on "adolescent hysteria," the witchcraft trials at Salem, hysterical seizures, and spirit possession.

will yield explanatory force or heuristic value? These three psychohistorical examples also illustrate the continuing lack of agreement among psychohistorians about which facts concerning human nature and psychic functioning and which psychological frameworks are adequate to the task of understanding weird thought and behavior in the past. This dilemma may be characteristic of the field of psychology or psychiatry in general, but for nonexpert historians the resulting temptation to opportunistic eclecticism is great. It remains a continuing weakness of this kind of history that there are rarely any discussions of why one approach or model is deemed better, richer, more productive, than others. If it is true that one needs epistemological eyeglasses, would it not be reasonable to try on several before adopting one as the most effective or the best fit? But most psychohistorians seem to believe that the glasses they happen to wear, the ones they use and advertise, are the only possible, the only reasonable, or the only valuable glasses. It's a sorry spectacle.

This lack of discussion, this relative silence especially among Freudian and neo-Freudian psychoanalytic historians, would be worth a separate discussion in its own right. Such a conversation, however valuable, will be all the more difficult, of course, if Stephen Jay Greenblatt is right that the "modern self" and the psychoanalytic views that inform us as modern subjects are themselves more the result of an early modern literary and legal discourse concerning the self than constituting an independent procedure that could yield independent results. Greenblatt concluded in a famous essay that psychoanalytic literary studies and histories present the "curious effect of a discourse that functions *as if* the psychological categories it invokes were not only simultaneous with but even prior to and themselves causes of the very phenomena of which in actual fact they were the results."[3] To avoid these difficulties, Greenblatt recommended that the procedures and characteristic assumptions of psychoanalysis themselves should be historicized. Without here agreeing or disagreeing with Greenblatt's larger project, this essay suggests that putting psychoanalysis into its historical context may help us to understand why psychoanalytic efforts so often seem to provide an uncanny understanding of demonology and witchcraft.

3. Stephen Jay Greenblatt, *Learning to Curse: Essays in Early Modern Culture* (New York: Routledge, 1990), 142. See also David W. Sabean, "Production of the Self during the Age of Confessionalism," in *Central European History* 29 (1996): 1–18; Ann Goldberg, *Sex, Religion, and the Making of Modern Madness: The Eberbach Asylum and German Society, 1815–1849* (New York: Oxford University Press, 1998).

As a result of these theoretical considerations, it seems useful momentarily to turn the question around, and instead of asking how psychoanalysis can be used to investigate the history of witchcraft, to ask rather how the history of witchcraft can illuminate the origins of psychoanalysis. This essay does not examine the psychological tools with which one might try to "open" the mystery of witchcraft, the psychoanalytic glasses through which one might decipher witchcraft trials and fears of the devil, but actually how the late-nineteenth-century understanding of witchcraft and demonology influenced the new art and science of psychoanalysis.

Our starting point is the curious fact that Sigmund Freud and other founders of psychoanalysis spoke often of the devil and of subterranean forces. We will recall that Freud's defiant epigraph to *The Interpretation of Dreams* was a quotation from Virgil's *Aeneid*, the goddess Juno's furious threat, prompted by her desire to prevent Aeneas from founding Rome: "If I cannot move the higher powers [the gods], I will churn up hell [the river Acheron]" (*Flectere si nequeo superos Acheronta movebo*). These much-quoted words obviously resonated with Freud and have been subjected to a variety of biographical and psychological interpretations, but at the very least they point to the way that Freud here employed a notion of the "underworld," literally of Acheron or of hell, to describe the demonic forces of the unconscious.[4] Where did this fascination with demons and the demonic come from?

This story begins in France, where Alexander Axenfeld inaugurated, in 1865, an informal series of lectures on the history of medicine for doctors. Axenfeld had been born in Russia but had taken his medical training in France.[5] A professional neurologist, he nonetheless delivered his lectures in such an elevated and rhetorically effective manner that they attracted a wide following well beyond the expected groups of medical students. A journalist present noted: "Never had [the public] been more numerous or more tightly

4. See Carl Schorske, *Fin-de-siècle Vienna: Politics and Culture* (New York: Knopf, 1980), 200; John Farrell, *Freud's Paranoid Quest: Psychoanalysis and Modern Suspicion* (New York: New York University Press, 1996), 50–51, 137–38; Peter Swales, "Freud, Minna Bernays, and the Conquest of Rome," in *The New American Review* (spring–summer 1982): 1–23, esp. 5, 15, 19.

5. Axenfeld took his degree in 1857 with a thesis entitled *Des influences nosocomiales*. In 1864 he edited a large work entitled "Des névroses," in A. P. Requin, *Éléments de pathologie médicale* (Paris, 1864), 4:125–692. A second edition, edited by Henri Huchard, bore the title *Traité des névroses* (Paris, 1883), and ran to 1195 pages. In 1867 Axenfeld copublished a 96-page pamphlet history: Alexander Axenfeld and Jules Auguste Béclard, *Rapport sur les progrès de la médecine en France* (Paris, 1867).

squeezed together on the steps of the amphitheatre."[6] Axenfeld's topic concerned Johann Weyer, the well-known Rhineland doctor of the sixteenth century, who had fought against the then-rising tide of witch trials. In Axenfeld's view, Weyer was not just a courageous doctor, who had declared that the witches were not guilty but rather mentally ill.[7] Instead, despite the elements of superstition that one could not overlook, Weyer represented an important example for Axenfeld of the eternal struggle between the humane and enlightened spirit of medicine on the one hand and the brutal and punitive fanaticism of religion, on the other. He conceded that there had of course been progress since those dark days: "People are no longer killed for a fantastic crime like magic," and he noted that the diminished legal liability of the mentally ill was now of course recognized generally by the law. But the process of moral reform had not yet gone far enough, and so Axenfeld expatiated upon the political and legal relevance of his history of witchcraft. "We continue to kill, with perfect tranquillity, criminals who are not insane because, apart from insanity, moral liberty seems indisputable.... The will is free, that is the dogma."[8] Thus, with the unlikely example of Johann Weyer, Dr. Axenfeld questioned contemporary Catholic ideas of personal culpability and freedom in an effort to annex a whole new territory for forensic psychiatry. But with what success? The Bonapartist regime reacted neuralgically in 1865 and canceled the rest of his lecture series. This psychiatric assault (in the name of what Axenfeld saw as physiology) upon central doctrines of the Roman Catholic Church was repulsed and officially forbidden. Three years later the medical degree of a student was even annulled and his doctoral adviser, again Alexander Axenfeld, held up to ridicule. Both of them had tried to apply the latest research on the physiology of the brain in order to attack orthodox teachings on the freedom of the will.

Somewhat surprisingly, Johann Weyer and the history of witchcraft were hot topics among French physicians of the Second Empire. The clerical party identified itself with idealist psychology while the medical faculty increasingly identified itself with a physiological (sometimes frankly materialist) understanding of the brain and nervous system.

After the Franco-Prussian War of 1870–71 and the establishment of the Third Republic, this situation shifted dramatically. Jan Goldstein has discovered

---

6. Jan Ellen Goldstein, *Console and Classify: The French Psychiatric Profession in the Nineteenth Century* (New York: Cambridge University Press, 1987), 356.

7. *Jean Wier et la sorcellerie* (Paris, 1866), a work of 95 pages.

8. Goldstein, *Console and Classify*, 356.

the reports of police spies in Paris of those years, men who attended the lectures given by the medical faculty at the University of Paris and reportedly detected in the lectures of the famous neurologist Jean-Martin Charcot signs of an "entirely pure materialism, not that gross, brutish and bestial materialism, but that studied scientific materialism that seduces you."[9] Anticlerical jokes flowed forth all too easily from his disrespectful lips. In the year 1875 one spy reported on a scene he had witnessed in the mental hospital called La Salpêtrière: "To a perfectly natural question of the professor [Charcot], the patient replied, 'I saw the devil with two parish priests at the Botanical Gardens [*Jardin des Plantes*]!' The entire audience burst out laughing. The professor added, 'That is a very characteristic group,' [and] a new smile underscored these words of Monsieur Charcot."[10] By the late 1870s in France a fully anticlerical psychiatry was reaching ascendancy. Jean-Martin Charcot was now close friends with Léon Gambetta and other Republicans. So too was the neurologist Désiré-Magloire Bourneville, who had been a student of Charcot and was now the chief of psychiatry at the hospital of Bicêtre as well as a city councilor of Paris (1876–83) and a representative in the Chamber of Deputies (1883–87). These psychiatrists began immediately to implement their anticlerical views. Hospitals were secularized, and in 1882 a new academic chair was established on positivist foundations for diseases of the nervous system (with Charcot as the first professor). Moreover, as Goldstein argues, the diagnosis of hysteria was now fundamentally politicized. Charcot had earlier described the four great phases of a hysterical attack:

1. The "Période épileptique," the convulsive or epileptoid phase.
2. The "Période de clownisme," the phase of contortions and body dislocations, of gymnastic postures.
3. The "Période des attitudes passionelles," the phase of passionate agitation and attitudes, a stage of performed hallucinations.
4. The "Période de délire," a slow regaining of consciousness accompanied by a state of melancholy, crying, sobbing, laughter, and dazed confusion.[11]

Since sometimes only one phase of hysterical attack appeared, Charcot suggested that there were actually four kinds or species of hysteria, corresponding to the four phases of the full-fledged attack. He generally associated the second

9. Goldstein, *Console and Classify*, 360.
10. Goldstein, *Console and Classify*, 360.
11. For discussion of these phases, see for example, Georges Didi-Huberman, *Invention de l'hystérie: Charcot et l'iconographie de la Salpêtrière* (Paris: Macula, 1982); Martha Noel Evans, *Fits and*

phase, characterized by large gestures and wild movements, with demonic possession: the wild, twirling arms and legs, the open mouth with outstretched
tongue, the bulging eyes, the patient's ripping of her or his clothes and pulling
out hair by the roots. Such persons were just like "wild beasts" and "demoniacs." The third phase of "passionate attitudes" and postures, in contrast, was
equated with the religious ecstasies of well-known mystics. In this way he was
also able to explain religious visions as hallucinations and the hearing of
angelic or divine voices as other hysterical conditions. Using a method of
"*médecine rétrospective*" or historical diagnosis, Charcot and his student Paul
Richer appropriated the whole history of demonic possession for modern psychiatry. In an interesting book, *Les démoniaques dans l'art* (Paris, 1887), these
two positivist physicians attempted to prove that the seizures and bodily gestures of those thought possessed from the fifth until the eighteenth century
could all be confidently unmasked as cases of hysteria.[12] Concerning the paint-
ings of Peter Paul Rubens, for example, Charcot and Richer declared: "This
artist painted demoniacs with such terrifying and realistic expression that we
could hardly imagine more perfect pictorial representations of just those
attacks which we have described fully in recent textbooks but which we also
have daily before our eyes in our work at the Salpêtrière."[13] Concerning a
fresco of Andrea del Sarto (showing Saint Philip Neri freeing a possessed
woman, in the Florentine cloister of SS. Annunziata), these two psychiatrists
even remarked that "in the composition of this painting we note such
undoubted signs and symptoms that the artist could only have painted directly

---

Starts: A Genealogy of Hysteria in Modern France (Ithaca, N.Y.: Cornell University Press, 1991); Elisabeth Bronfen, *The Knotted Subject: Hysteria and Its Discontents* (Princeton: Princeton University Press,
1998), 176–205; and Malcolm Macmillan, *Freud Evaluated: The Completed Arc* (Amsterdam: Elsevier
Science, 1991), 55–67. The latest twist in the modern reinterpretation of the history of hysteria sees
the "hysterical paroxysm" as a medical term for what was actually the female orgasm. See Rachel P.
Maines, *The Technology of Orgasm: "Hysteria," the Vibrator, and Women's Sexual Satisfaction* (Baltimore: Johns Hopkins University Press, 1999). Recent research has illuminated the rise and fall of the
hysterical epidemic; see Elaine Showalter, *Hystories: Hysterical Epidemics and Modern Culture* (London: Picador, 1997); Edward Shorter, *From Paralysis to Fatigue: A History of Psychosomatic Illness in
the Modern Era* (New York: Free Press, 1992), 166–200; and Mark S. Micale, "On the 'Disappearance'
of Hysteria: A Study in the Clinical Deconstruction of a Diagnosis," in *Isis* 84 (1993): 496–526, an article with excellent bibliographical notes.

    12. Goldstein, *Console and Classify*, 370–71; Jean-Martin Charcot and Paul Richer, *Die Besessenen
in der Kunst*, ed. Manfred Schneider, trans. Willi Hendricks (1887; repr., Göttingen: Steidl, 1988). This
German edition is valuable because of the commentary by Schneider.

    13. Charcot and Richer, *Die Besessenen in der Kunst*, 77.

from nature. It's possible that he even had a possessed woman before him during one of her attacks, which at that time must not have been a rare occurrence."[14] Other artists, such as Raphael for example, painted demoniacs with such an unexpected or unusual appearance that their convulsions "do not reflect any true-to-life features or even any recognizable traits."[15] In other words, Charcot and Richer were willing to regard only those cases as true cases of possession that they could interpret as cases of hysteria.

It is therefore no wonder that Bourneville undertook to republish a whole series of old books, in which one could find the same lesson. Between 1882 and 1897 he brought out eight volumes that mainly dealt with demonic possession or witchcraft trials, with the purpose of underlining the sharp difference between the superstitious practices of the church and more humane scientific methods.[16] According to this political program the supernatural was translated into secular terms. It is understandable, given this context, that we once again encounter the work of Johann Weyer, which Bourneville published as part of his *Bibliothèque Diabolique* in 1885. Once again the zealous but credulous Renaissance physician from Graves and Düsseldorf was deployed, despite his profound belief in the devil, on the side of the positivist anticlerical party, as if one merely had to read Weyer in order to draw the correct political and scientific conclusions.[17]

The physiologist Charles-Robert Richet read through a variety of such pictures and books so quickly and superficially that he drew the following common but unjustified conclusion: "Among the patients imprisoned in the Salpêtrière there are many who would have been burned to death in times past and whose diseases would have been interpreted as a crime."[18] He jumped to this thesis by reading modern clinical evidence back into historical materials, saying confidently, "Logical order is not the same as chronological

14. Charcot and Richer, *Die Besessenen in der Kunst*, 39.

15. Charcot and Richer, *Die Besessenen in der Kunst*, 11.

16. A. R. G. Owen, *Hysteria, Hypnosis and Healing: The Work of J.-M. Charcot* (London: Dobson, 1971), 71–72, 247.

17. This attitude survives in George Mora's introduction to *Witches, Devils, and Doctors in the Renaissance: Johann Weyer: De Praestigiis Daemonum*, ed. George Mora et al. (Binghamton, N.Y.: Medieval & Renaissance Texts & Studies, 1991); for an attempt to correct this approach, see the introduction to *On Witchcraft: An Abridged Translation of Johann Weyer's De praestigiis daemonum*, ed. Benjamin G. Kohl and H. C. Erik Midelfort (Asheville, N.C.: Pegasus, 1998), xv–xxxiii.

18. Goldstein, *Console and Classify*, 372; Charles-Robert Richet, "Les démoniaques d'aujourd 'hui," and "Les démoniques d'autrefois," in *Revue des deux mondes*, n.s. 9, 37 (1880): 340–72; 552–83;

order. In order to judge correctly of error, it is necessary first to know the truth."[19] Thus the truths of modern medical investigation could unmask the "errors" of a superstitious age. This hasty amalgamation and confusion of demonic possession with witchcraft was so compelling, so clear, that from that time to our own day one can read that most witches (and of course most demoniacs) were obviously mentally ill.[20] As recently as 1988 Manfred Schneider could blandly adopt Richet's thesis, writing, "There have been cases of possession in almost all cultures, but the Christian innovation was to think that demonically possessed women must be killed."[21] These days this misleading conclusion is no longer used only as a weapon against the church, but as one against a kind of psychiatry, a literature and culture that understand women "less as succubi of the devil than as succubi of a sexually specific semiotic," subordinating women to a "semiotics of the feminine."[22] The feminist psychoanalyst Monique Schneider has pushed this conclusion even further in her book *From Exorcism to Psychoanalysis (De l'exorcisme à la psychanalyse: Le Féminin expurgé)*, in which there is no fundamental distinction between the modern doctor (Charcot or Freud) and the old exorcist.[23]

Goldstein remarks, correctly, that such a connection between supposed ecstasy or demonic possession and hysteria had been asserted or posited as early as the eighteenth century. But the years after 1880 made this Enlightened

---

828–63, at 340. Richet asserted that "la relation qui existe entre l'hystérie et la sorcellerie apparaîtra en pleine évidence" (828); and concerning Louise Cadière, a possessed nun from the eighteenth century, he affirmed that she was obviously "folle, démoniaque et hystéro-épileptique,... ce qui nous paraît aujourd'hui si simple" (859). He concluded, "Au lieu de guérir ces malheureux, on s'acharna contre eux.... Ils furent, par milliers, condamnés à la torture et jetés aux flammes" (863).

19. Richet, "Les démoniaques d'aujourd 'hui," 341.

20. The most compelling reformulation and reconsideration of this thesis is Barbara Newman's careful article, "Possessed by the Spirit: Devout Woman, Demoniacs, and the Apostolic Life in the Thirteenth Century," *Speculum* 73 (1998): 733–70. See also H. C. Erik Midelfort, *A History of Madness in Sixteenth Century Germany* (Stanford: Stanford University Press, 1999), 49–78.

21. Charcot and Richer, *Die Besessenen in der Kunst*, 149.

22. Schneider's comments in Charcot and Richer, *Die Besessenen in der Kunst*, 149. Schneider continues (149–50): "The literature of the eighteenth and nineteenth centuries becomes the central place of formation for this feminine susceptibility to attack; a susceptibility that was administered in antiquity only by doctors, in the Middle Ages also by saints and bishops, and in the early modern period also by judges. The series of these relations of women to doctors, priests, judges, and to literary writers make up the cultural and historical matrices in which femininity was symbolically constituted."

23. Monique Schneider, *De l'exorcisme à la psychanalyse: Le Féminin expurgé* (Paris: Retz, 1979). See also the work of feminist literary criticism, based on the same assumption: Uta Treder, *Von der Hexe zur Hysterikerin: Zur Verfestigungsgeschichte des 'Ewig Weiblichen'* (Bonn: Bouvier, 1984), and

thesis into a medical program and it became part of the republican and positivist political position, whose impact we can still feel.

In October of 1885 the twenty-nine-year-old neurologist Sigmund Freud traveled to Paris to study with Charcot in his famous clinic for research into nervous disorders. From Freud himself we know that this visit represented a turning point. When he arrived he still wanted to investigate the anatomy of the nervous system, but when he returned to Vienna at the end of March 1886, he had left neurology behind. Now he wanted to study hypnosis and hysteria. With Charcot, however, he also experienced the typical interpretation of hysteria, with its "stigmata," according to which the disorder was seen as exactly the same condition that earlier centuries had adjudged with certainty as possession *or* witchcraft. Thus according to Freud, the female hysterics under Charcot's care were not malingerers or fakes, but examples of what science now understood as clear cases of a natural illness, despite earlier superstitious diagnoses. Freud was personally ready to concede that the Middle Ages had indeed recognized certain somatic signs of hysteria that his own time had almost completely ignored, suppressed, or forgotten.[24] Thus the young Freud clearly acknowledged the high empirical value of medieval demonological observations, even though he rejected the religious explanations of the church. Over the next ten years, as Freud developed the foundations of psychoanalysis, he never forgot this insight of Charcot's. Freud remained ready to interpret female hysterics not only as the modern form of

---

Maarten van Buuren, "Hystérie et littérature: La fissure par laquelle l'Esprit du Mal pénètre dans l'âme," in *Poétique* 25 (1994): 387–409. Cf. the remarks of Martha Noel Evans concerning the topic of so-called hysterical anesthesia: The needle probing practiced by Charcot in an effort to find stigmata "cannot but help recall the pricking technique used by the witch-hunters.... Thus the doctors of the new scientific age unwittingly[!] repeated actions they had described as barbarisms in their religious predecessors." Evans, *Fits and Starts*, 26n.

24. Sigmund Freud, "Report on My Studies in Paris and Berlin" (1886), in *The Standard Edition of the Complete Psychological Works of Sigmund Freud*, 24 vols., ed. and trans. James Strachey et al. (London: Hobarth, 1953–1974), 1:11 (hereafter SE). Cf. "Hysteria" in SE 1:41: "The poor hysterics who in earlier centuries had been burnt or exorcized, were only subjected in recent, enlightened times, to the curse of ridicule; their states were judged unworthy of clinical observation, as being simulation and exaggeration." Earlier in this essay he repeated the assertion of Charcot and Richer: "Documents from that period [the Middle Ages] prove that their [neuroses and especially hysteria] symptomatology has undergone no change up to the present day" (SE 1:41). "Disturbances of sensibility are the symptoms on which it is possible to base a diagnosis of hysteria, even in its most rudimentary forms. In the Middle Ages the discovery of anaesthetic and non-bleeding areas (stigmata Diaboli) was regarded as evidence of witchcraft" (SE 1:45).

witches and demoniacs, but also to see himself as physician as the modern form of the old inquisitor or confessor. Like Charles-Robert Richet before him, Freud regularly confused the fundamentally different images of the witch and the demoniac, as if these demonic forms disguised the same illnesses and the same unconscious impulses.

In 1892/93 Freud published an essay entitled "A Case of Hypnotic Healing," which told the story of his therapeutic success with a woman, who had twice been encouraged through the use of hypnosis to nurse her babies. He had told her, "Don't be afraid, you'll be an excellent wet-nurse."[25] In order to understand this curious cure, Freud developed an idiosyncratic theory of the unconscious, according to which contrasting ideas often led to the suppression of a *Gegenwille*, an opposing will.

> Everyone who knows hysteria will remark, however, that the psychic mechanism here described can explain… not just isolated hysterical attacks, but also great portions of the whole symptom-picture of hysteria. We maintain that there are painful contrasting ideas, which normal consciousness restricts and rejects, but which appear in moments of hysterical disposition and find their way into the nerves of the body…. [But here come the demoniacs again.] It is no accident that the hysterical madnesses of nuns in the epidemics of the Middle Ages consisted of terrible blasphemies and unrestrained eroticism.[26]

On this page Freud explicitly mentioned the diabolical or demonic as his metaphor for the unconscious: "On the whole, hysteria owes this appearance of the opposing will to that *demonic* tendency, which occurs so often, and which expresses itself in the fact that the patients are unable to do something at precisely that place and time where they most yearningly desire to do it."[27] From such expressions, Luisa de Urtubey has discovered that Freud used the

25. Sigmund Freud, "Ein Fall von hypnotischer Heilung," in *Gesammelte Werke, chronologisch geordnet* (hereafter GW), 18 vols., ed. Marie Bonaparte et al. (London: Imago, 1940–1952), 1:6.

26. GW 1:14. "Es ist nicht zufällig, daß die hysterischen Delirien der Nonnen in den Epidemien des Mittelalters aus schweren Gotteslästerungen und ungezügelter Erotik bestanden…."

27. GW 1:14. "Im ganzen verdankt die Hysterie diesem Hervortreten des Gegenwillens jenen dämonischen Zug, der ihr so häufig zukommt, der sich darin äußert, daß die Kranken gerade dann und dort etwas nicht können wo sie es am sehnlichsten wollen…." For other references from 1893 to hysterical (possessed) nuns during the Middle Ages (but also to the hysteria of well-brought-up boys), see "Preliminary Considerations" (SE 2:11); "Studies on Hysteria" (SE 2:249); "Early Lecture on Hysteria" (SE 3:38); and his note to his translation of Charcot's *Leçons du Mardi* (1892–1894) (SE 1:138, 153).

devil first as a metaphor for the unconscious. The opposing will appears evil and unpleasant, but also powerful. But soon she uncovers other motifs, which are also equated with the devil, for example the father as seducer, while Freud explicitly identified with Aeneas and with his journey down into hell, into the depths of the soul. "At every moment in the development of his thoughts, Freud uses the devil to express what he could least bring into harmony with his 'ego.'"[28]

In other words, with his ideas concerning the unconscious, Freud created an innerworldly, and even innerpersonal transcendental. It was not God or spirits who were the ruling spirits of a person anymore, but unconscious drives and anxieties.[29] In the historic witch trials Freud saw an exact parallel to the attacks of his anxious and depressed patients. On 17 January 1897 Freud wrote to his peculiar Berlin friend, Wilhelm Fließ:

> Now what would you say if I told you that my whole new primal history of hysteria was already known and published hundreds of times several centuries ago? Do you remember that I have always said that the theory of the Middle Ages and of the ecclesiastical courts concerning [demonic] possession was identical to our theory of the foreign body and the splitting of consciousness? But why did the devil who possessed these unfortunates usually fornicate with them in the most disgusting manner? Why were their confessions extracted under torture so similar to the statements of my patients under psychiatric care? Next I'll have to delve into the literature on this.

Notice that here as elsewhere, and like Charcot, Richer, and Richet, Freud confuses the conditions of the possessed with those of the witches. This is of importance because historically it was no crime to be possessed. In fact, some of the most revered saints were "obsessed" or even physically "possessed" by the devil. Witches, on the other hand, were thought to have renounced Christ and the saints and to have voluntarily given themselves to the Enemy of mankind. The possessed were victims, while witches were regarded as predators; ecclesiastical courts always recognized these basic differences. But the founders of psychoanalysis blended these two states together, based as they both were

---

28. Luisa de Urtubey, *Freud et le diable* (Paris: PUF, 1983), 21, 24–28, 29–54, 180.

29. Ernest Gellner, "Psychoanalysis as a Social Institution: An Anthropological Perspective," in *Freud in Exile: Psychoanalysis and Its Vicissitudes*, ed. Edward Timms and Naomi Segal (New Haven: Yale University Press, 1988), 223–29. See more generally Ernest Gellner, *The Psychoanalytic Movement, or the Coming of Unreason* (London: Paladin, 1985).

on what was for them the superstitious notion of the devil. Thinking of the anesthetic areas reported in hysterics, Freud continued:

These brutalities permit us moreover to understand several hitherto impenetrable symptoms of hysteria. The needles [previously used in the investigation of witches] come up in the strangest ways: the sewing needles that my unfortunate [patients] use to mutilate their breasts, which cannot be detected with X-rays, but which probably can be found in their stories of seduction.... So now the inquisitors are pricking again with needles in order to find the stigmata of the devil, and in a similar situation these victims fall into the old and gruesome fantasy (supported perhaps by images that disguise the seducers).[30]

This is a much-discussed letter, partly because Ernst Kris and others have used this passage to locate the "major turning point" in Freud's seduction theory, his abandonment of the view that hysterical patients had suffered real sexual abuse in childhood and his turn toward the theory that such stories were fantasies.[31] It is not a concern here to decide whether this was a heroic or tragic turn in the history of psychoanalysis. It is more to our purpose to remark in this context that it was the historical witchcraft trials and recorded cases of demonic possession that fundamentally impressed themselves onto Freud's own fantasies.[32] We can also notice that Freud, like many other non-historians of his (and our own) time, shared the view that the witchcraft trials

30. Sigmund Freud, *Briefe an Wilhelm Fliess, 1887–1904*, ed. Jeffrey Moussaieff Masson, Michael Schröter, and Gerhard Fichtner (Frankfurt am Main: Fischer, 1986), letter no. 118 (17 January 1897), 237–38. The editors of this edition conclude that in these sentences Freud expressed his opinion that "the supposed witches and also precisely the female hysterics were recounting their memories of real childhood experiences but in the form of fantasy" (238 n. 6).

31. Ernst Kris, introduction to Sigmund Freud, *Aus den Anfängen der Psychoanalyse: Briefe an Wilhelm Fließ* (London: Imago, 1950), 161; Max Schur, "Some Additional 'Day Residues' of the Specimen Dream of Psychoanalysis," in *Psychoanalysis: A General Psychology: Essays in Honor of Heinz Hartmann*, ed. Heinz Hartman and Rudolph M. Loewenstein et al. (New York: International Universities Press, 1966), 45–85, at 83; Jeffrey Moussaieff Masson, *The Assault on Truth: Freud's Suppression of the Seduction Theory* (New York: Farrar, Straus & Giroux, 1984), 103–6; cf. letter no. 126 in Masson et al., eds., Freud, *Briefe an Fließ*, 253–54, and n. 3 above. William J. McGrath, *Freud's Discovery of Psychoanalysis: The Politics of Hysteria* (Ithaca: Cornell University Press, 1986), 171–72, 197–98; Macmillan, *Freud Evaluated*, 208–31; Paul Vitz, *Sigmund Freud's Christian Unconscious* (New York: Guilford, 1988), 125.

32. Recent scholars have concluded that the key point may indeed be what Freud had in his mind, rather than what he heard in the supposedly spontaneous narratives of his patients. It seems likely that

were peculiarly *medieval* phenomena and also that ecclesiastical inquisitors were the driving force behind the witch-hunt.[33] As evidence of Freud's understanding of religion in general and of Roman Catholicism but also as proof of his self-understanding as a successor to and secularized replacement for clerical figures, these opinions are important. They are not just errors or pieces of trivial ignorance that one can easily ignore. Still more important was Freud's assumption that the witches' confessions, though mainly yielded up under torture, might have been nonetheless voluntary and thus formally comparable to the revelations of his patients. He did not seem to suspect that such tortured evidence was partly (or often totally) prescribed or dictated by magistrates, jurists, and torturers. In a similar manner Freud was brusquely unwilling to entertain the thought that his patients were reacting to his own suggestions or to his coercive efforts to break down what he saw as their unconscious resistance to unpleasant truths.[34] It has been one of the major advances in our understanding of witchcraft that we now regularly recognize how much of demonology was invented by learned theologians and jurists and then

---

he impressed certain notions upon his patients: Mikkel Borch-Jacobsen, "Neurotica: Freud and the Seduction Theory," in *October* 76 (1996): 15–43.

33. The best historians of Freud's own day knew very well that major European witchcraft trials occurred in the early modern period under secular (and not ecclesiastical) auspices. See Wilhelm Gottlieb Soldan, *Geschichte der Hexenprozesse*, 2 vols., ed. Max Bauer (Munich, 1912); Henry Charles Lea, *A History of the Inquisition of the Middle Ages*, 3 vols. (New York, 1888); Joseph Hansen, *Quellen und Untersuchungen zur Geschichte des Hexenwahns und der Hexenverfolgung im Mittelalter* (Bonn, 1901); and the first few essays in Sönke Lorenz, ed., *Hexen und Hexenverfolgung im deutschen Südwesten: Eine Ausstellung des Badischen Landesmuseum Karlsruhe im Schloß: Aufsatzband* (Ostfildern bei Stuttgart: Cantz, 1994).

34. For Freud's resistance to the claim that much of his clinical evidence was "epistemologically contaminated" by coercion and suggestion, see Frederick C. Crews, ed., *Unauthorized Freud: Doubters Confront a Legend* (New York: Viking, 1998), 7–9, 45–47, 51–52, 72, 76–84, 81–82; Borch-Jacobsen, "Neurotica"; Macmillan, *Freud Evaluated*, 208–11, 612; Stephen Collins, "Freud and 'The Riddle of Suggestion,'" in *International Review of Psycho-Analysis* 7 (1980): 429–37. These suspicions were earlier voiced by many others, including the head of the Nancy school, Hippolyte Bernheim, for whom the hypnotic trance was not a symptom of neurosis but merely a state of enhanced suggestibility to which most normal persons were susceptible. See Hippolyte Bernheim, *Suggestive Therapeutics: A Treatise on the Nature and Uses of Hypnotism*, trans. Christian Herter (New York, 1888). For a more general critique of Freud's procedures, see Adolf Grünbaum, *The Foundations of Psychoanalysis* (Berkeley: University of California Press, 1984); idem, *Validation in the Clinical Theory of Psychoanalysis: A Study in the Philosophy of Psychoanalysis* (Madison: University of Wisconsin Press, 1993); Hans J. Eysenck, *Decline and Fall of the Freudian Empire* (New York: Viking, 1985).

imposed upon folk testimony that often paid little attention to the devil, the pact, the sabbat, and the rest of learned demonology.[35]

The theme of demonology did not recede easily from Freud's thoughts. He wrote just one week later (24 January 1897) to Fließ again with an excited series of connections that he was now drawing between the fantasies of his patients and the history of witchcraft as he understood it.[36] He now emphasized that the witches' flight on a broom should be brought together with "Herr Penis"; that the secret gatherings of witches and their dance could be witnessed "every day" in the ritualized games and play of small children; that the money given by the devil to his latest recruits usually turned into dung, a fact that Freud compared to associations made by a patient concerning gold, money, and shit. "And so the stories of witchcraft are transformed back into the substance from which they originally arose." Here Freud was again doubtless speaking of the psychic origin of demonic fantasies, but nowhere did he utter even the suspicion that such modern clinical fantasies might rather have their basis in his own fantasies about witchcraft.

In this letter to Fließ of 24 January, Freud also wondered why the semen of the devil was always reported by confessing witches to be cold. Here, to be sure, Freud did not claim to know the answer, but he suspected where he needed to look: in the *Malleus Maleficarum*, the demonological treatise of 1487, which Freud had just ordered and which he intended to study energetically. In a flourish of spirited and ingenious excitement, Freud confessed: "The history of the devil, the lexicon of curses among ordinary people, children's songs and the habits of the nursery, all are gaining in significance for me."[37]

Now it was not only hysteria that stood out in profile. The perversions too (which Freud in this same letter to Fließ described as the opposite, the negative, of hysteria) now seemed to have a distinct and indeed unchangeable shape: "I dream thus of a primeval devil-religion, whose rituals are perpetuated in secret, and I now understand the harsh therapy of the witch judges. The relationships all go blurry."[38] To be sure they became so blurred that we can subject Freud's text to a variety of divergent interpretations. Was he speaking here of his sympathy for the witch judges or, by extension, for doctors

35. Richard Kieckhefer, *European Witch Trials: Their Foundations in Popular and Learned Culture, 1300–1500* (Berkeley: University of California Press, 1976); Norman Cohn, *Europe's Inner Demons: An Enquiry Inspired by the Great Witch-Hunt* (London: Chatto, 1975).

36. Letter no. 119 in Masson et al., eds., Freud, *Briefe an Fließ*, 239–41.

37. Letter no. 119 in Masson et al., eds., Freud, *Briefe an Fließ*, 239–41.

38. Letter no. 119 in Masson et al., eds., Freud, *Briefe an Fließ*, 240.

who had to deal with the disgusting thoughts and words of the witches (that is, the perverse)? Or was he speaking rather of the dreams and fantasies of the judges/doctors, who only fleetingly glimpse secret rites and a whole devil religion, that is, a suppressed, unconscious world of thought? It is possible that both interpretations are correct.

Demons and witches gave Freud no final relief, although for twenty years he did not discuss the topic with the same fascination he showed during his "pre-analytic" years. It is well known that he wrote on what he called a "neurosis of demoniacal possession" in 1923, providing a retrospective psychoanalytic interpretation of a seventeenth-century possession case.[39] Moreover, Freud's secularizing, reductionist writings on religion continued his general program from the 1890s forward to the 1930s.[40] This is not the place to pursue so general a topic,[41] but we may conclude by calling attention to a little-noticed passage in which Freud portrayed the magnitude of his revolution but revealed again his debt to demonology. In his *Introductory Lectures on Psychoanalysis*, published in 1916–17, he spoke proudly of the world-historical importance of his new science.[42] He claimed to have delivered the third and last decisive blow to grandiosity and narcissism of humankind. The first had been Copernicus, who had pushed the world away from the center of the universe; the second was Charles Darwin, who had proved that human beings were intimately related to other animals; and third was Freud himself, who proved (so he said) that human beings were not even "master in their own

39. SE 19:72–105. See Gaston Vandendriessche, *The Parapraxis in the Haizmann Case of Sigmund Freud* (Louvain: Publications Universitaires, 1965); H. C. Erik Midelfort, "Catholic and Lutheran Reactions to Demon Possession in the Late Seventeenth Century: Two Case Histories," in *Daphnis: Zeitschrift für Mittlere Deutsche Literatur* 15 (1986): 623–48.

40. James S. Preus, *Explaining Religion: Criticism and Theory from Bodin to Freud* (Atlanta, Ga.: Scholars Press, 1996); Karl Lüthi and Koloman N. Micskey, eds., *Theologie im Dialog mit Freud und seiner Wirkungsgeschichte* (Vienna: Böhlau, 1991); Hans Küng, *Freud and the Problem of God*, trans. Edward Quinn (New Haven: Yale University Press, 1990); Vitz, *Sigmund Freud's Christian Unconscious*.

41. A full consideration of this topic would require us also to investigate the full range of satirical or ironic references to the devil, demons, and even Satan among the early Freudians. The radical Freudian Georg Groddeck, for example, published a strange newsletter from his clinic in February–July 1918, under the distinctive title, *Satanarium*, a play on the word "sanatarium." See Georg Groddeck, *Werke*, ed. Otto Jägersberg, vol. 4 (Basel: Stroemfeld/Roter Stern, 1987–). Groddeck (15, 271) justified his title, however, with these words: "With the publication of these pages I intend to give people an opportunity to scream out their misery unimpeded by shame or shyness. The only place where one can scream this way seems to me to be hell; and therefore I am calling my journal *Satanarium*."

42. GW 11; SE 16:284–85.

house."[43] This opinion of Freud's is well known, but it reveals his curious "inability to mourn," in Peter Homans's memorable phrase. His triumphalist scientific joy was all too willing to throw ancient religious traditions, rituals, and values into the dustbin of history, and with all too little understanding and compassion.[44] Very few have noticed, however, that Freud only belatedly set himself into the triumvirate of modern scientific heroes. Ten years earlier, in 1907, as Peter Swales has pointed out, Freud responded to a questionnaire sent to him as part of a series published by the *Neue Blätter für Literatur und Kunst* in Vienna, a questionnaire that was also sent to such luminaries as Ernst Mach, Hermann Hesse, Thomas Masaryk, and Arthur Schnitzler. They were all asked to compile a list of "ten good books," the sort of well-intentioned reading list that modern intellectual celebrities are frequently asked for. In his answer Freud remarked that he had been asked to name "good" books, not the best in all of world literature, but also not the ten most important books. If one had asked about "important" books, one would have to list the achievements of natural science, with works by Copernicus, Charles Darwin (Freud mentions *The Descent of Man*), and the old physician Johann Weyer, whose relatively little known work on witchcraft Freud here elevated to a world-historical level. It is important that we find here again a scientific triumvirate, with Copernicus and Darwin, but with Johann Weyer in the very place that Freud later reserved for himself.[45] We won't go far wrong in concluding that by 1907 Freud had reached an intermediate stage between his young years with Charcot and Breuer, in which his new kind of psychiatry was seen as replacing the medieval doctrine of spirits and demonic possession, on the one hand, and the later years crowned with success, in which he claimed an equal and eternal place in world history with the other heroes of the modern disenchanted world, Copernicus and Darwin. For the argument of this essay, the form of this intermediate stage is of interest: Freud composed a little book list in which ten years later he replaced Weyer. The main thesis of this essay is, however, that Freud actually identified all his life with Johann Weyer and

43. SE 16:284–85.

44. Peter Homans, *The Ability to Mourn: Disillusionment and the Social Origins of Psychoanalysis* (Chicago: University of Chicago Press, 1989), esp. 75–81.

45. Peter Swales, "Freud, Johann Weier, and the Status of Seduction: The Role of the Witch in the Conception of Fantasy," in *Sigmund Freud: Critical Assessments*, 4 vols., ed. Laurence Spurling (London: Routledge, 1989), 1:331–58. See the excellent essay: Peter Swales, "A Fascination with Witches," *The Sciences* 27, no. 8 (1982): 221–25; and idem, "Freud, Krafft-Ebing, and the Witches: The Role of Krafft-Ebing in Freud's Flight into Fantasy" (privately printed, n.d.). See also McGrath, *Freud's Discovery of Psychoanalysis*, 79.

contended that psychoanalysis understood its role as the functional (but secular and natural) equivalent to exorcism and/or the interrogation of witches. The sharp opposition between religion and psychoanalysis in Freud's thinking rested in part on this basis.

In Freud's early understanding of psychoanalysis, however, it is important to note that by confusing the very different states of possession and witchcraft, Freud tellingly revealed his own conflicting versions of himself and his science. Was it mainly a "therapy of the word," a "talking cure," in which the skilled practitioner brought out into daylight the inner demons of a patient and in so doing expelled them? Or was it a process of guided interrogation, in which the patient was finally compelled to reveal her or his guilty secrets and forbidden fantasies? In either formulation it is evident that Freud saw less room for the supposedly free play of the dynamic unconscious of his patients and more scope for his own active intervention than he preached and pretended to practice. If we now return to the question with which I began, moreover, it will no longer surprise us that psychoanalysis gives the impression that it has the golden key with which to unlock the secrets of witchcraft and diabolical fantasies. Witchcraft (in the form of the Roman Catholic, ecclesiastical, and medieval doctrines of demonology) was built into psychoanalysis from the very beginning.

CONTRIBUTORS

DEAN PHILLIP BELL is associate dean and associate professor of Jewish Studies at the Spertus Institute of Jewish Studies in Chicago. His recent publications include *Sacred Communities: Jewish and Christian Identities in Fifteenth-Century Germany* and "Martin Luther and the Jews: The Reformation, Nazi Germany, and Today," in *The Solomon Goldman Lectures*. He is currently researching the confluence of memory, communal identity, and Jewish history in early modern Germany and on the history of anti-Semitism.

ROBIN BRIGGS is senior research fellow at All Souls' College, Oxford University. His recent publications include *Witches and Neighbours: The Social and Cultural Context of European Witchcraft* and *Communities of Belief: Cultural and Social Tensions in Early Modern France*. He is currently researching the witches of Lorraine.

KATHRYN A. EDWARDS is associate professor of history at the University of South Carolina. Her recent publications include *Families and Frontiers: Re-Creating Communities and Boundaries in the Early Modern Burgundies*; "Female Sociability, Physicality, and Authority in an Early Modern Haunting," in *Journal of Social History*; and *The History of the Apparition of a Spirit* (forthcoming). She is currently researching problems of confessionalization in frontier territories and the representation of the supernatural, such as ghosts and werewolves.

SARAH FERBER is lecturer in history at the University of Queensland. Her recent publications include "Charcot's Demons: Retrospective Medicine and Historical Diagnosis in the Writings of the Salpêtrière School," in *Illness and Healing Alternatives in Western Europe*; "Le Sabbath et son double," in *Le Sabbat des sorciers en Europe, XVe–XVIIIe siècle*; and *Demonic Possession and*

Exorcism in Early Modern France (Routledge, forthcoming). She is currently researching belief in demons and exorcism in early modern France.

BRUCE GORDON is lecturer in modern history and associate director of the Reformation Studies Institute at the University of Saint Andrews. He is the author of *Clerical Discipline and the Rural Reformation: The Synod in Zurich 1532–1580* and *The Swiss Reformation*. Gordon has edited *Protestant History and Identity*, and, with Peter Marshall, *The Place of the Dead: Death and Remembrance in Late Medieval and Early Modern Europe*. He is currently working on Heinrich Bullinger.

NICOLE JACQUES-LEFÉVRE is professor of literature at the University of Picardy, Jules Verne (Amiens), and a member of the Centre de recherches sur le romanesque (section–Littérature de l'Université). She is the author of *Le Théosophe et la sorcière, deux imaginaires du monde des signes: Études sur l'imaginaire saint-martinien et sur la démonologie, Les Sorciers du Carroi de Marlou: Un Procès de sorcellerie en Berry*, and, with Sophie Houdard, *Curiosité et Libido sciendi, de la Renaissance aux Lumières*. She is currently working on the intersection between learned and pious discourse in literature, particularly the philosophical, literary, judicial, ethnological, and medical treatment of witchcraft.

ULRIKE KRAMPL is lecturer at the University of Poitiers and University of Vienna and is finishing her dissertation, "Magic and Fraud in Eighteenth-Century Paris," at the University of Vienna and Ecole des Hautes Etudes en Sciences Sociales. She has several recent articles including "Le trésor d'Arcueil: Les chercheurs de trésor parisiens entre magie et escroquerie au début du XVIIIe siècle," in *Croyances et superstitions dans l'Europe des Lumières*, ed. Clothild Prunier. Her current research interests are on the intersection of magic, religion, and justice in Enlightenment France and Germany.

DAVID LEDERER is lecturer in history at the National University of Ireland, Maynooth. He is the author of *A Bavarian Beacon: Spiritual Physic and the Birth of the Asylum, 1495–1803* (forthcoming) and articles on witchcraft, penance, and exorcism. He is currently working on a history of suicide in the Holy Roman Empire, 1495–1806, under the auspices of the Alexander von Humboldt Foundation.

H. C. ERIK MIDELFORT is C. Julian Bishko professor of history at the University of Virginia. He is the author of *Witch-Hunting in Southwestern Germany, 1562–1684: The Social and Intellectual Foundations*; *Mad Princes of Renaissance Germany*, and *A History of Madness in Sixteenth-Century Germany*, as well as numerous articles. He is currently working on a study of the exorcist-healer, Johann Joseph Gassner (1727–1779).

SARA T. NALLE is professor of history at William Paterson University of New Jersey. She is the author of *"Mad for God": Bartolomé Sánchez, the Secret Messiah of Cardenete*; *God in La Mancha: Religious Reform and the People of Cuenca, 1500–1650*; and "Literacy and Culture in Early Modern Castile," in *Past and Present*. Her current research is on family and memory; anticlericalism, especially in early modern Spain; and on the fears that surround the year 1524 in general.

ANNE JACOBSON SCHUTTE is professor of history at the University of Virginia. She is the author of *Aspiring Saints: Pretense of Holiness, Inquisition, and Gender in the Republic of Venice, 1618–1750* and edited and translated *Cecilia Ferrazzi: The Autobiography of an Aspiring Saint*. She is currently investigating eighteenth-century monks, friars, and nuns who applied to the Congregation of the Council for release from their vows on the grounds that they had been forced to take them.

INDEX

possession. *See* demon possession
Prieur, Claude (Franciscan, demonologist), 186, 193, 195
Dialogue de la lycanthropie, 182, 197
psychiatry, as anticlerical, 203, 211
psychoanalytical theory
    and melancholic lycanthropy, 194-95
    and witchcraft beliefs, 22, 201-2, 211-15
psychohistory, and psychoanalytical theory, xxii, 199-215
purgatory, and cult of the dead/ghosts, 32-33, 43-47, 64, 66

R

Raphael (artist), 205
redemption of souls, by ghost exorcism, 44
Reformation, historiography of, viii
Reformed church, views of black arts, 158-79
religion. *See* belief
Rémy, Nicolas, *Demonolatry* (1595), xiv, 4, 21
Renaissance, and belief in supernatural, xix, xxi, 181-82, 187, 193
revolts, and religious extremism, 77-92
Richer, Paul (neurologist), 204
Richet, Charles-Robert (psysiologist), 205, 208
ritual. *See also* sacramental religion
    and magic, 114-15
    orthodox, against possession, 59
    and popular religion, 55-75
    for treasure-hunting, 49
Romeo, Giovanni, 119
Roper, Lyndal, 199
Rosina the Pious, 40-46
Rubens, Peter Paul (artist), 204
Ruef, Jacob, on power of the devil, 155-79

S

sabbat(h) (midnight assembly), 15, 20, 121, 124, 141
Saint-Jure, Jean-Baptiste, S.J., 69
Salnove, Robert de, 187
Sarto, Andrea del (artist), 204
Satan. *See* devil/Satan
Scaglia, Desiderio (cardinal), 119
    Prattica per procedere nelle cause del S. Offizio, 126
Schmidt, Willibald (folklorist), 26
Schmitt, Jean-Claude, 30
Schneider, Manfred, 206
Schneider, Monique, 206
Schöppner, Alexander (folklorist), 26
Schutte, Anne Jacobson, xvi, 119-35
séducteurs, 137-54, 137n1

seduction
    and exorcism, 71-72
    Freud's theories on, 210
self-fashioning, xvii
sexuality/eroticism, and witchcraft narratives, 22-23, 208
shapeshifting
    of incubi and succubi, 167-68
    relationship of belief to witchcraft, 23
    in trial records, 5, 8-13
skepticism
    and cult of the dead, 65
    about ghosts, by ecclesiastical authorities, 46-47
    about witchcraft trials, 1, 12
sleep paralysis, 15
social change, and reformulation of magical ideas, 146-47
societal behavior, tolerated/sanctioned, 143
Society of Jesus, and exorcisms, 31-33, 45, 52
socioeconomic conditions
    and black arts, 155-79
    and folklore, 52-53
    of Jews, 97-100
    and possession/exorcism beliefs, 58-64
    and supernatural treasure hunting, 48-49, 140-41
sociology, approach of to magic, 93-94
sorcery. *See* demonological theories; magic; witchcraft
spirits, evil, as angels, 16
spiritus phantasticus, and werewolves, 183
Sponde, Jean de (demonologist), 184
Sprenger, Jakob (inquisitor), *Malleus Maleficarum,* 141
suicides, superstitions about, 37-39
supernatural encounters, 16-17
    secularization of, 203-5, 213
superstition
    banned, without ecclesiastical authorization, 34-35
    contrasted with mental illness, 205-6
    and *crédulitie,* 144-45
    and exorcisms, 60
    mandate against, in Bavaria, 39-40
    and social behavior, 26-27
    and socioeconomic class, 74-75
    and theological evolution, 28-30
    treasure hunting condemned, 47-48
Swales, Peter, 214
Switzerland, Reformed views of black arts, 158-79